CIVIL SOCIETY IN CHINA

Studies on Contemporary China

THE POLITICAL ECONOMY OF CHINA'S SPECIAL ECONOMIC ZONES
George T. Crane

WORLDS APART
RECENT CHINESE WRITING AND ITS AUDIENCES
Howard Goldblatt, editor

CHINESE URBAN REFORM
WHAT MODEL NOW?
R. Yin-Wang Kwok, William L. Parish, and Anthony Gar-on Yeh with Xu Xuequang, editors

REBELLION AND FACTIONALISM IN A CHINESE PROVINCE
ZHEJIANG, 1966–1976
Keith Forster

POLITICS AT MAO'S COURT
GAO GANG AND PARTY FACTIONALISM IN THE EARLY 1950s
Frederick C. Teiwes

MOLDING THE MEDIUM
THE CHINESE COMMUNIST PARTY AND THE *LIBERATION DAILY*
Patricia Stranahan

THE MAKING OF A SINO-MARXIST WORLD VIEW
PERCEPTIONS AND INTERPRETATIONS OF WORLD HISTORY IN THE PEOPLE'S REPUBLIC OF CHINA
Dorothea A.L. Martin

POLITICS OF DISILLUSIONMENT
THE CHINESE COMMUNIST PARTY UNDER DENG XIAOPING, 1978–1989
Hsi-sheng Ch'i

CONQUERING RESOURCES
THE GROWTH AND DECLINE OF THE PLA'S SCIENCE AND TECHNOLOGY COMMISSION FOR NATIONAL DEFENSE
Benjamin C. Ostrov

THE PARADOX OF POWER IN A PEOPLE'S REPUBLIC OF CHINA MIDDLE SCHOOL
Martin Schoenhals

CHINA'S ECONOMIC DILEMMAS IN THE 1990s
THE PROBLEMS OF REFORMS, MODERNIZATION, AND INDEPENDENCE
Edited by the Joint Economic Committee, Congress of the United States

CHINA IN THE ERA OF DENG XIAOPING
A DECADE OF REFORM
Michael Ying-mao Kau and Susan H. Marsh, editors

DOMESTIC LAW REFORMS IN POST-MAO CHINA
Pitman B. Potter, editor

POLITICS AND PURGES IN CHINA
RECTIFICATION AND THE DECLINE OF PARTY NORMS, 1950–1965
Frederick C. Teiwes

MORNING SUN
INTERVIEWS WITH POST-MAO CHINESE WRITERS
Laifong Leung

CHINESE FIRMS AND THE STATE IN TRANSITION
PROPERTY RIGHTS AND AGENCY PROBLEMS IN THE REFORM ERA
Keun Lee

THE MARKET MECHANISM AND ECONOMIC REFORMS IN CHINA
William A. Byrd

CHINA, THE UNITED STATES, AND THE SOVIET UNION
TRIPOLARITY AND POLICY-MAKING IN THE COLD WAR
Robert S. Ross, editor

AMERICAN STUDIES OF CONTEMPORARY CHINA
David Shambaugh, editor

CHINA'S AUTOMOBILE INDUSTRY
POLICIES, PROBLEMS, AND PROSPECTS
Eric Harwit

DECISION-MAKING IN DENG'S CHINA
PERSPECTIVES FROM INSIDERS
Carol Lee Hamrin and Suisheng Zhao, editors

PRIVATE BUSINESS AND ECONOMIC REFORM IN CHINA
Susan Young

MAKING URBAN REVOLUTION IN CHINA
THE CCP-GMD STRUGGLE FOR BEIPING–TIANJIN, 1945–1949
Joseph K. S. Yick

CHINA'S ECONOMIC FUTURE
CHALLENGES TO U.S. POLICY
Joint Economic Committee, Congress of the United States

THE POLITICAL ECONOMY OF CORRUPTION IN CHINA
Julia Kwong

FAREWELL TO PEASANT CHINA
RURAL URBANIZATION AND SOCIAL CHANGES IN THE LATE TWENTIETH CENTURY
Gregory Eliyu Guldin, editor

PROVINCIAL STRATEGIES FOR ECONOMIC REFORM IN POST-MAO CHINA
Peter T.Y. Cheung, Jae Ho Chung, and Zhimin Lin, editors

CIVIL SOCIETY IN CHINA
Timothy Brook and B. Michael Frolic, editors

Studies on Contemporary China

CIVIL SOCIETY IN CHINA

Edited by

TIMOTHY BROOK

AND B. MICHAEL FROLIC

An East Gate Book

Routledge
Taylor & Francis Group
LONDON AND NEW YORK

An East Gate Book

First published 1997 by M.E. Sharpe

Published 2015 by Routledge
2 Park Square, Milton Park, Abingdon, Oxon OX14 4RN
711 Third Avenue, New York, NY 10017, USA

Routledge is an imprint of the Taylor & Francis Group, an informa business

Library of Congress Cataloging-in-Publication Data

Civil society in China / edited by Timothy Brook and B. Michael Frolic.
p. cm. — (Studies on contemporary China)
"An East gate book."
Includes bibliographical references (p.) and index.
ISBN 0-7656-0091-9 (alk. paper). — ISBN 0-7656-0092-7 (pbk. : alk. paper)
1. Civil society—China.
2. Democracy—China.
3. Associations, institutions, etc.—China.
4. China—Politics and government—1976–
I. Brook, Timothy, 1951–
II. Frolic, B. Michael, 1937–
III. Series.
JQ1516.C58 1997
301′.0951—dc21
97-16586 CIP

ISBN 13: 9780765600929 (pbk)
ISBN 13: 9780765600912 (hbk)

" 'Pon my word, Watson, you are coming along wonderfully. You have really done very well indeed. It is true that you have missed everything of importance, but you have hit upon the method."

—Arthur Conan Doyle, *A Case of Identity*

Contents

Epilogue

Acknowledgments

This volume grew out of a symposium convened in May 1995, by the University of Toronto–York University Joint Centre for Asia Pacific Studies. It was the second in what has become a series of annual research conferences to which the Joint Centre brings together specialists in Canada and beyond to ponder issues of current relevance to our understanding of Eastern Asia. Paul Evans, then director of the Joint Centre, suggested the theme of civil society in China in conjunction with a research project sponsored by the Canadian International Development Agency. Funding for the symposium was provided in part by a grant from the Vicbir Family Foundation.

In addition to the authors represented in this volume, Ping-chun Hsiung, Bernard Luk, Cynthia McLean, and Monica Wu made presentations at the symposium; and Heath Chamberlain, Diana Lary, Errol Mendes, and David Ownby contributed as discussants. We are grateful to them all for their collective contribution to our evolving understanding of the uses and abuses of civil society.

For their dedicated support in helping to make this volume possible, we wish to thank Carol Irving, the administrator of the Joint Centre who led in organizing the symposium, and Lynne Russell, who assisted inexhaustibly in editing the manuscript, compiling the bibliography and index, and otherwise keeping the project on track. We are also grateful to Douglas Merwin for encouraging us to publish with M. E. Sharpe, and to Angela Piliouras for managing the production of the manuscript.

Acknowledgments

List of Contributors

Timothy Brook is professor of Chinese history at the University of Toronto and associate director of the Joint Centre for Asia Pacific Studies. His books include *Quelling the People: The Military Suppression of the Beijing Democracy Movement* and *Praying for Power: Buddhism and the Formation of Gentry Society in Late-Ming China.*

Alfred L. Chan is assistant professor of political science at Huron College at the University of Western Ontario. He has published in *China Quarterly*, the *Canadian Journal of Political Science*, and *Journal of Contemporary China.*

Kenneth Dean is associate professor of East Asian studies at McGill University. He is the author of *First and Last Emperor: The Absolute State and the Body of the Despot* (with Brian Massumi) and *Taoist Ritual and Popular Cults of Southeast China.* He is currently engaged in long-term collaborative research on cults in Fujian.

Roger V. Des Forges is associate professor of Chinese history at the State University of New York at Buffalo. His books include *Hsi-liang and the Chinese National Revolution* and *Chinese Democracy and the Crisis of 1989: Chinese and American Reflections* (with Luo Ning and Wu Yenbo). *The Center Holds: Northeast Henan in the Ming-Qing Transition* is forthcoming.

B. Michael Frolic is professor of political science at York University and is currently the director of the Joint Centre for Asia Pacific Studies. His books include *Mao's People: Sixteen Portraits of Life in Revolutionary China* and *Reluctant Adversaries: Canada and the PRC, 1949–1970* (with P. Evans).

Ruth Hayhoe is professor of higher education at the Ontario Institute for Studies in Education of the University of Toronto, and is currently serving for two years as the director of the Hong Kong Institute of Education. In addition to editing three books on Chinese education, she is the author of *China's Universities and the Open Door* and *China's Universities 1895–1995: A Century of Cultural Conflict.*

Paul Nesbitt-Larking is assistant professor of political science at Huron College, at the University of Western Ontario. His work on political culture and on Chinese, Canadian, and comparative politics has been published in *Political Psychology*, the *Journal of Legislative Studies*, and the *Canadian Journal of Political Science.*

Yunqiu Zhang has a doctorate in Chinese history from the University of Toronto. His research on modern China has been published in *Issues and Studies* and the *Journal of Contemporary China.*

Ningsha Zhong is a doctoral candidate at the Ontario Institute for Studies in Education of the University of Toronto. She is a contributing editor and translator of *East-West Dialogue in Knowledge and Higher Education* (edited by Ruth Hayhoe and Julia Pan).

Introduction

The Ambiguous Challenge of Civil Society

Timothy Brook and B. Michael Frolic

The relationship between state and society in China has been a perennial topic in Western intellectual circles since Hegel theorized China as a state without a society. The relationship as it has unfolded since 1949 has posed challenges for Western scholars who view society as constituting a legitimate sphere apart from the state. It has also troubled Chinese intellectuals striving to find a position in Deng Xiaoping's reformed order from which to negotiate the power and duties of their state in its passage from socialism. The slow separation of government from the Party that occurred during the transition from Mao to Deng in the 1980s raised hopes at home and abroad that other norms besides hard authoritarianism might govern state-society relations. When, in 1989, students attempted to bring alternatives into being and assert a claim to the autonomy of society, the state moved decisively to block their path.

The uprush and suppression of the Democracy Movement renewed anxieties among Chinese and non-Chinese alike about how to understand the state-society relationship. The failure of student activists to secure a permanent foothold for autonomous organizing on the slopes of Chinese political life has set the subsequent agenda for thinking about Chinese political culture after Tiananmen. The first line of defense for those seeking to recuperate a legitimate space for public action was to argue prescriptively in favor of society as the force that created responsible government. The model was Western and historical: the model of civil society. China scholars in the West turned to it in the immediate aftermath of 1989 as a device to explain variously why the movement occurred and why it failed (e.g., Strand 1990; Sullivan 1990; Calhoun 1994); so too did Chinese intellectuals in exile (Ma 1994:187–92). Others rejected the application of the concept of civil society to a culture and history to which it is foreign (e.g., Huang 1993; Wakeman 1993). In the 1990s, civil society has been much discussed. The conceptual road we take in the future may not be marked with this ambiguous signpost for a variety of reasons (discourse has its fashions), yet the focus on civil society in the 1990s has provided an opportunity to confront our conceptual habits as well as to rethink the constraints and possibilities in the state-society relationship in China.

The Terms of This Inquiry

The purpose of this volume is to take stock of what boundaries and avenues the field of China studies has reached in thinking through the concept of civil society for China, and to reflect on the effects it has had on the study of contemporary China. The individual chapters were first presented at a symposium on civil society in China held in Toronto in 1995 under the sponsorship of the Joint Centre for Asia Pacific Studies of the University of Toronto and York University. We asked participants to apply the concept of civil society to China as they saw fit, and to draw their conclusions without being obliged to work with any particular model. We encouraged them, and ourselves as well, to approach the concept of civil society critically, to question our assumptions, and to assess the suitability of the concept in whatever form for understanding trends in contemporary Chinese politics and society. The authors represent four disciplinary approaches (education, history, political science, and religious studies), and their chapters express different theoretical stances and ideological positions. This multiplicity of perspectives proved to be an asset, for it cautioned us against either celebrating the Western narrative of democratic development or proclaiming Chinese exceptionality. The authors in this volume are not uniformly certain about what the manipulation of the concept of civil society can or should achieve. We recognize that the concept rarely answers a specifically Chinese question, but it does ask a few that might not have come up otherwise. In doing so, we believe, it has provided openings for creating new knowledge about the relationship between state and society in China.

We have grouped the chapters into two parts. The first provides general perspectives, whereas the second offers case studies. The three chapters in the first part distribute themselves across the current range of interpretation regarding the usefulness of what is fundamentally a Western concept. Timothy Brook's chapter on the sorts of autonomous organizations that can be discerned through Chinese history allows that the concept can be used to advantage in studying Chinese society, subject to adjustments to the circumstances of Chinese social institutions. B. Michael Frolic considers civil society as it is currently theorized to be culturally bound to popular Western narratives of democratic development and prefers to enlarge the category to include what he terms "state-led civil society." Roger Des Forges pursues the problem in a different direction by arguing that the Western-based concept of civil society cannot be substituted for an understanding of civility and society rooted more squarely in China's own historical experience. Only a concept of civil society constructed in relation to the Chinese context, he insists, can register the choices that Chinese people and Chinese states have made and continue to make.

The four case studies in the second part consider the concept of civil society in relation to particular sectors of Chinese society. Ruth Hayhoe and Ningsha Zhong look at expressions of group autonomy in the history of higher education and argue that the current resurgence of autonomous bodies similar to those in the Republican period is moving China toward becoming a more diversified society. The outcome of this movement will not necessarily look like society in the West, but it will display characteristics that we associate with civil society. Paul Nesbitt-Larking and Alfred Chan analyze attitudes among youth since the 1980s as sources of the kind of autonomous thinking that contributes to civil society. Yunqiu Zhang reviews the history of trade unions in the twentieth century and identifies the current expansion of union activity at the local level as evidence of growing civil society in terms that draw from both Frolic's and Brook's analyses.

The last case study breaks ranks with the other three. Focusing not on urban China but on rural society, Kenneth Dean objects to reading China in terms of civil society at all. He is deeply suspicious of the concept, not only for what it may misstate about China but for its complicity in the normalizing project of state building. In his analysis of ritual life in rural Fujian, Dean has been guided by the poststructural initiatives of Gils Deleuze and Félix Guattari. Their work has persuaded him to discover a process of simultaneous interruption and reconnection at the interface between the community and the state that he feels is beyond the concept of civil society even to begin to encompass. This process of interruption and reconnection is so powerful that it resists the nationalistic desires of the state to possess the local. It also confounds the conventional notions of state and society in the West which the idea of civil society unwittingly reproduces. From Dean's perspective, the concept of civil society in China not only fails to provide critical purchase on the smooth hegemony of the contemporary Chinese state, but conspires with that state against acknowledging the real forms of resistance and transformation that the disruptive communities of local culture are constantly reinventing.

Dean states the strongest refusal to think of China in terms of civil society, but he is not alone among the authors in expressing skepticism about the prospects for realizing civil society in China. Readers who pick up this volume expecting assurances that civil society is emerging in China, either as a prelude to democracy or as a sign that democratic structures and processes are growing, will be disappointed. That expectation was raised by the post-socialist transition in Eastern Europe and the former Soviet Union, when the concept of civil society came into prominence both to mobilize public action and to explain its results. However, it suggests outcomes that are unlikely in China in the near future. Thinking through the concept of civil society for China may help us to understand, among other things, why demands for democracy cannot be met quickly.

Readers expecting to find a unified model of civil society running through our analyses of Chinese society will also be disappointed. This lack of unity is not because we do not agree on a single lens through which to view China, but because we reject the simplification that a single-lens vision must impart to any analysis. Our goal is not to define or exalt any particular concept of civil society, but to think about China. The historians among us (Brook, Des Forges, Hayhoe, Zhong, and Zhang) feel uninhibited in using facets of the Western concept of civil society to read back from the present and find cognate strands—of auto-organization, moral community, and corporate life—at work in the past and woven in complex ways into the present, without necessarily finding what we consider to be civil society. The political scientists (Frolic, Nesbitt-Larking, and Chan) have tended to keep the concept closer to Western formulations, but do so to work toward new paradigms of state-society interaction that better accommodate the circumstances of Chinese life. The one specialist in religious studies (Dean) rejects civil society in favor of a locally based cultural model of "disruptive communities," doing so in the wake of the rejection of the civil society concept by French poststructuralism.

Where the contributors are in agreement is in recognizing the need to step back from many current Western assumptions that the concept of civil society invokes. We find, for instance, that greater attention must be paid to the state, and that the elements of civil society that may be discerned in China are the result as much of accommodations with the state as of resistance to it. And we see gradual change rather than sudden confrontation. None of the authors writes in terms of imminent regime collapse or of civil society rising up to chastise the Chinese state, which some might have done in the immediate wake of the Democracy Movement. Nor do we expect Chinese dissidents and intellectuals to act in ways that will allow them to emulate figures like Vaclav Havel and Adam Michnik in effecting regime change. As we approach the end of the decade following Tiananmen, Chinese intellectuals bear only a pale resemblance to their Polish, Czech, and Hungarian peers who were so successful in promoting what they saw as civil society against the state.

At the same time, while cautious about generalizing from Western models and experience, we have also been careful not to be seduced by arguments about an essential Chinese difference that must necessarily exclude China from all such expectations. Some observers of the Chinese state have found it tempting to resolve the contrast between China and Europe by appealing to Chinese exceptionalism, by discovering evidence of civil society in the Chinese past or by making a virtue of alleged communal values that contrast persuasively with the individualism conventionally ascribed to the West. The historical experiences of China and the West have indeed diverged, but we prefer to avoid resolving their differences either by essentializing them as culturally primordial (such as by asserting that the West "has" civil society and China "does not" or "cannot") or by dismissing them as extraneous to the underlying "laws" that are applicable to all societies at all times (by insisting that civil society in the West is something China should or will have). Sensitivity to difference does not negate the possibility that there may be some advantage in thinking in comparative terms. Something has happened in China, and is happening now, on which the historical experience of other societies may cast some light.

In the course of coming to terms with this issue, we appreciate Philip Kuhn's (1994) sensible observation that civil society is a model, not a reality. The ideal type of civil society, in which individuals make rational decisions about the common good as they link society and the state together through bonds of civility and public discourse, does not exist, either historically or in the current world of superstates and consumer-driven politics. In the realm of politics, it expresses a desire for the way in which societies, states, and citizens ought to interact, not how they do. Thus, civil society serves as a heuristic device for thinking through certain changes that China is currently undergoing, but neither reproduces nor fully explains that reality.

Further, our purpose in considering China in relation to this particular model is not to cast China in the role of a late developer struggling to catch up to an advanced West, which is how the concept of civil society is sometimes deployed variously for and against China. Rather, it is to seek new analytical openings for approaching the challenge of state-society integration, which all polities face, while remaining wary of the temptation to reduce China to a failed or infantile version of the West. Rapid globalization may well alter the terms within which any of us, Chinese included, think about China. For the moment, though, certain historically given understandings arising from state-society relations in the West can usefully be mobilized to provide ways of thinking about state power in whatever part of the globe it manifests itself.

Civil Society in History and Theory

The Western concept of civil society has its own precise history and intellectual context of formation. It emerged in the eighteenth century in Europe at a time when a new relationship between society and the state was evolving, as those who controlled capitalist production were seeking access to political power. Their demand for a voice in affairs of state constituted a space between the closed realms of business and family and the larger realm of the state. In that space, a public sphere took form in which members of the bourgeoisie and their allies negotiated a shared identity and common political purpose. As the urban public sphere became secure, the procedures of public representation and the associational forms of civic life that are referred to as civil society were gradually installed. These procedures and organizations emerged in opposition not to the state, but to the old regime's barriers to the entry of other political actors.

The close relationship of civil society to capitalism is both historical and theoretical. Just as the economic system of capitalism took shape in Europe above the realm of everyday barter and production in the eighteenth century, so too did civil society emerge above the social realm of personal interests and interactions. These were not simply parallel developments, but parts of the same process. Civil society was like capitalism in that its champions aspired to the ideal of self-regulation and sought to make the state the regulator. Capitalism obliged the state to keep its hands out of the till ; at the same time, though, it needed the state to act in ways that were supportive of investment and trade and nonexpropriative in its relations to property. The agitation of civil society worked to keep the state from meddling in the civil realm, while calling on the state to provide rules of procedure and civil codes that would guarantee freedom from arbitrary state actions. Capitalism and civil society joined hands to capture the state. No longer the embodiment of the king's desire, the state had become the captive arbiter of competing desires and interests within capitalism.

Most of the recent discussion of civil society has centered on the linking and mediating role that civil society is deemed to perform between state and society, primarily to control or provide a counterpoise to the state. This conception is rooted in the way in which Western thinking has come to characterize state and society. Following Raymond Williams (1983: 293), society distinguishes "that to which we belong" from the state as "the apparatus of power." The distinction implies a relationship of inequality, which developed historically in the eighteenth century when the state did in fact become more powerful, but did so in tandem with the growth of civil society. The concept of civil society was important to the process of drawing the distinction between society and the state: "The crucial notion of *civil society* was an alternative definition of social order, and it was in thinking through the general questions of this new order that *society* was confirmed in its more general and eventually abstract senses" (Williams 1983:57). The term "civil society" first appeared as early as the sixteenth century to designate the fellowship of the educated, in which context it was used without reference to any conflict between this elite, or society more generally, and the state. Individual members of the elite may have placed themselves in opposition to the monarch, but they did not think of themselves as counterpoised to the state in any structural sense. That meaning only took shape in the eighteenth century when the notion of bourgeois civil society against the state became established in European political rhetoric.

The theme of society against the state continues to dominate the discussion of civil society today, as the chapter by Frolic documents. It does so because of the international context of the late 1980s and early 1990s in which that discussion was revived, when authoritarian regimes of the left and right came under pressure to open up their political processes. Opposing or excluding the state is what gives civil society its critical force. But it also narrows the concept down from the original breadth of its historical meaning. We have found that to speak of civil society as a real social possibility, it is necessary to bring the state back into the discussion.

Civil Society and the State

The contributors to this volume recognize that civil society is a concept from which the state can never be far. To distinguish the two as poles in a confrontational relationship has not proved useful in our analysis and, what is worse, may mask other relationships. Indeed, in the Chinese context, we have found it necessary to view the state as an active factor, both in the contemporary Leninist setting and in the imperial period when, as Brook observes, the state was a "far more conspicuous element in constructions of the moral world than in the West." Chinese states may have been demonstrably authoritarian, but they also contributed much of "the moral terrain on which to stand."

Does our recovery of the state in state-society analysis mean that Chinese society plays only a weak role, and that China is, therefore, different in essence from its counterpart in the West? In his important contribution to the civil society discussion, Heath Chamberlain (1994: 117) reminds us that societies can be as tyrannical as states and warns against imagining idealized societies. This caution does not lead us to conclude that society has little role to play in shaping the Chinese world, but only alerts us to the danger of misrepresenting society in China on the basis of how society has come to be conceptualized in the West. The historians in this volume acknowledge that strong Chinese states have had powerful effects, yet they are unwilling to write off Chinese society as too weak to have significantly shaped the Chinese world. Brook argues strongly in this vein. Dean carries that argument still further to insist that no Chinese state, no matter how successful in enlarging its power, can ever overwhelm local culture. The local realm is where the real strength of Chinese society resides.

If the state-society relationship in China's past does not easily conform to the conventional model of civil society, neither does the contemporary Chinese state. This is a state in transition, modestly decentralizing itself and attempting to revise its Leninist principles. What is striking about the chapters dealing with contemporary state and society is the expression of a uniform willingness to bring the state back in, not just as a presence but as a leading player in promoting something analogous to civil society. Frolic focuses on "state-led civil society" in which the state sponsors or co-opts social organizations to help it administer society. Zhang finds a similar phenomenon among local-level trade unions, which the overloaded state recruits to act not as ideological watchdogs, but as mediators and purveyors of services the state cannot provide. Hayhoe and Zhong in their chapter show how the state is providing an opening for universities to acquire corporate autonomy in their affairs, which they do at the state's initiative and primarily for economic reasons rather than as a result of the stirrings of civil society, although the authors anticipate that greater autonomy will contribute to the growth of civil society in the future.

The state that some of the contributors to this volume are bringing back in appears more as a benign, if disciplinary, authoritarian than a tyrant. It mixes elements of the Confucian imperial state, the Leninist party-state, and what might be termed an early-capitalist state. In striving to find the right combination of elements from these models of popular mobilization, the state has been drawn to a blend of Confucianism and capitalism that elsewhere in Asia is being packaged as Asian communalism or soft authoritarianism. A distinctive pathway for Asian development is deemed to thrive on supposedly non-Western values, restricting civil society in favor of maintaining a strong state (see Brook and Luong 1997, and especially Woodside 1997). In the post-Mao Chinese state, this ideology is regarded as appropriate for directing the process of marketization and reform, not for promoting an open, democratic process. It has achieved a degree of persuasiveness among the people, as political training conditions Chinese to set a lower priority on demands for civil society in preference for letting the state fill in the space between itself and society. The future, therefore, is unlikely to be a series of Tiananmens at which people rise up to demand their rights, but rather a more nonconfrontational process of consumerist attachment to economic growth.

The presence of the state in society is not purely an element of Asian exceptionalism. Civil society emerged in the West in close relationship to the state, working with it more consistently than opposing it. At the level of practice, institutions of civil society are obliged to take account of the state's mechanisms of social control, and they frequently establish close relationships with government institutions and representatives. Indeed, the pressure to have the state register institutions of civil society comes more from society than the state, as a means of marking safe terrain on which to operate and to stake out claims vis-à-vis other competing organizations. The state for its part has good reason to supervise, infiltrate, and co-opt entities and activities it does not initiate or control to guarantee its survival. To argue, as many in the civil society discussion have done, that there is a clear distinction in the West between state and society; that civil society represents society against the state; and, therefore, that the concept does not work for China may be a case of mistaking the rhetoric of rights agitation in the West for substance. State and society are densely interactive realms everywhere, as much in the West as in China. Civil society might better be thought of, therefore, as a formation that exists by virtue of state-society interaction, not as something between, separate from, or autonomous from either.[1]

The presence of the state in Chinese society, although reduced from what it was in the Maoist period, is still strong and has heavy cultural sanction. The prospects for democratic outcomes to recent social changes, which the model of civil society might have predicted, do not appear promising at this juncture. Des Forges is the most optimistic of the contributors, envisioning a future Chinese version of civil society that may correct flaws in civil societies as they are now constituted in the West. Chan and Nesbitt-Larking express more modest hope for the emergence of democratic values among Chinese youth. Hayhoe and Zhong perceive a trend toward greater autonomy at least within universities, based on the experience of the Republican period, although they temper that prediction with an awareness that expectations about individual responsibility stretching back into the imperial era may limit the expression of autonomy in ways congruent with Western understandings. Brook and Zhang also invoke Republican traditions of local organizing to anticipate a strengthening of work- and fellowship-based associational activity. Frolic is more cautious about the prospects of seeing elements of civil society realized in China in the near future, although he sees embryos for their realization in the form of what he conceives as state-led civil society.

Whether or not these incremental changes should be construed as democratization, they are contributing to the building of a denser and more complex institutional infrastructure at the local level. This infrastructure is providing a greater measure of autonomy in some sectors. It is also providing substantial social capital from which the state benefits as much as society. By improving and increasing the linkages between state and society, such elements of urban life as auto-organization, autonomy, social representation, state-led civil society, and critical citizenship can contribute to what some Asian elites prefer to call "good governance," if not democracy. This observation may represent only a short-term perspective on the effect of this infrastructure building, inasmuch as good governance may require the scrutiny of society-based activists to prevent it from sliding to tyranny.

The Primacy of the Economy

We have already noted that civil society emerged in Europe in the context of the rapid commercialization and industrialization we associate with the growth of capitalism, when the production of wealth loosened the fit between political and social hierarchies. Political decisions in China today are driven by expectations for economic growth, and everything that is occurring there must at some point be referred back to economic factors. The state is promoting this development and is willing to postpone democratization as the necessary price for sustaining economic growth. For both, there appears to be considerable popular sanction.

In their search for nascent forms of civil society, some of our authors have been struck by their association with the emerging commodity economy. Hayhoe and Zhong attribute the growth of university autonomy and corporate identity squarely to the refinancing and partial privatization of universities. Zhang sees the shift from state corporatism to social representation in the work of trade unions as the result of new economic relations that have developed between managers and employees in Chinese enterprises and joint ventures. For Chan and

Nesbitt-Larking, the development of critical citizenship is linked both positively and negatively to the new economy: positively in terms of the autonomy implicit in capitalist relations, and negatively in the rise of materialistic desires and consumerism that may encourage indifference to civic culture. Economic factors have also clearly played a role in the emergence of social organizations noted by Frolic, as private funding underwrites activities formerly carried out by the socialist state, and as business associations form in response to the privatization of the economy.

In our haste to attend to social, political, and cultural forms, we have perhaps taken economics too much for granted. As Marx realized, the market in Europe changed everything. It produced a civil society in defense of property and mapped out an arena in which the bourgeoisie struggled for power, redefining relations between state and society. It empowered elites, promoted the embourgeoisement of culture, and established a society based in that image. Does this history provide any hints of what civil society, or something like it, could entail for China? The new economy in China is producing wealthy entrepreneurial and managerial social groups, even classes, that may eventually wish to remake society in their image, and the state in their service. The potential threat to existing bureaucratic and political elites could be enormous, particularly once mechanisms for mounting autonomous action in the political sphere are in place. So, too, could challenges from below: from industrial workers who, as Zhang shows, find themselves in structural conflict with management and capital; or from peasants who, as Dean tells us, are constantly devising means to manipulate and subvert the state and the global processes it seeks to harness, remaking their immediate worlds in ways neither the state nor we can fully anticipate.

Prospects

What seems certain is that these challenges will take place at the local levels of the economy and polity rather than at the top. It is not coincidental that the contributors to this volume focus on change at the local level. In part this is because the local is where the state first loosens (or loses) control. As the market economy expands, the reach of the state shrinks and its grasp weakens. New combinations of state and society, public and private, emerge at the most local points of interface. Township and village enterprises, for example, show themselves to be a transitional space, marked for experimentation and open to change: this is the terrain of fragmented authoritarianism in which state power is either reassembled or dispersed (Lieberthal and Lampton 1992). It is here, too, at the foundation of the changing matrix of local/national/global that future elites will coalesce and contend for power, although not necessarily in imitation of political developments in the West. Rather than collapsing China into the category of the exceptional, therefore, we believe that the time has come to reconceptualize civil society at least, and perhaps social theory as a whole.

This reconceptualization is already underway in part in discussions of civil society in the West. Many now argue that it no longer functions, if indeed it ever did, in the way it has been theorized. Ernest Gellner (1994) argues that the new civil society will be comprised of modular individuals, highly mobile, entering and leaving attachments almost at will, cutting across established borders with relative ease. The society we now inhabit, a consumer-driven, hollowed out society in which transactions replace citizenship and virtue is no longer the qualification for public voice, little approximates the civil society that social theory continues to preserve in ideal form. If this is indeed the case and civil society in the West has drifted into the realm of pure ideology, what has taken its place? Michael Walzer (1995) has proposed that we have entered the age of global civil society, "an international civil society the very existence of which raises questions about the usefulness of the state." National politics can no longer be conducted as they were. Transnational organizations such as Helsinki Watch, Amnesty International, and the United Nations peek over borders and communicate rights-based values, however idealized, to places where previously they were unspoken. Pop culture purveys notions of autonomy and resistance even as it inculcates obedience to consumerist consumption, and mass technologies like television and the Internet provide channels along which a confused mixture of liberation and discipline passes. No system can remain immune to these influences. This is not to say that states are ready to abdicate their power and surrender it to local or global bodies. They will hold fast to their systems of governance and integrative mechanisms even as transnational institutions spread the illusion of a global civil society.

Our year-long meditation on the fortunes and fate of civil society has led us to believe that we are on a threshold in the development of social theory. The predictive power of existing models of state and society are being rendered redundant, even inconsequential, by the explosion of forces on a global scale that the world has never before experienced. No economies are local anymore, nor are societies closed, and states that resist them may lose the footholds they still have to confront these changes and anticipate their effects. The Eurocentrism of the civil society model may discredit it, yet resistances to state power, whether frontal or devious, will continue to find points of escape from the enclosures that postwar states have learned with great skill to erect around the dwindling resources that sustain them. Whether this leads toward a new understanding of civil society, or away from it entirely, remains to be seen.

If there is one good reason for keeping the concept of civil society in play when we think about China, it is that the term has entered the discourse of some of the Chinese intellectuals who are currently striving to remake their state and society in new ways (Sullivan 1996: 15, quoting Dai Qing). Civil society is becoming part of their conceptual apparatus.[2] It affects their ways of thinking about society and the state, however much we may worry about its context or dispute its meaning. It will, therefore, continue to shape the language of critical engagement in China so long as some choose to resist the idealization of a communitarian Asia where the authoritarian state is allowed to stand in for society at every turn. In this sense, the concept of civil society marks a threshold of hope that our logical analysis may deconstruct but cannot dismiss.

Larger Perspectives

1

Auto-Organization in Chinese Society

Timothy Brook

The concept of civil society pivots on the post-eighteenth-century habit of distinguishing the realm of the political—"the state"—from the realm of the social—"society."[1] This distinction between state and society has grown out of the historical experience of state formation under European capitalism. It is explained as a process of social forces from below progressively limiting state power above: through elite challenges to the power of sovereigns (in the process of constitutionalism), through the ascendancy of market principles (in the form of capitalism), and through the pressure of public opinion on state decisions (in the realm of what has been called the public sphere).

The state-society relationship is regarded as a source of stability in Western societies; it is just as regularly viewed as a source of instability in authoritarian regimes in the Third World. Where democracy has failed, its failure has been attributed to blockages or imbalances in this relationship, and proposals to remedy these problems alternately identify the state (on a spectrum ranging from authoritarian to democratic) or society (ranging from vertical to horizontal) as the principal locus of dynamism—or as the barrier in need of removal—for broadening the political process and enhancing regime stability in the Third World. Among Western observers, pragmatists favor accepting the power of the state over society in their proposals for Third World political development; interventionists argue in favour of strengthening society against the state.

Analyzing the structure of power in China as a relationship between state and society can provide insights into how power is distributed and how its exercise is alternately publicized and hidden from view, thus creating the sort of instability that is essential for power to be effective. Yet, predicating power on a clear distinction between state and society poses difficulties in the Chinese context. The state has been a far more conspicuous element in constructions of the moral world in China than in the West, where the demands of society for representation both within and against the state have been strong.[2] A view that polarizes society against the state derives from a conception of society as larger and morally more legitimate than the state. In China, by contrast, the concept of society as a locus of legitimate public action has little moral terrain on which to stand that has not already been appropriated by the state or effectively delegitimized by state ideology.

The apparent weakness of Chinese society vis-à-vis the state may reflect an ideological blind limiting people's ability to recognize the full extent of their subordination to the state—a blind that only an externally situated analysis can raise. On the other hand, the notion that society in China is "weak" may signal an unwarranted assumption about universal norms regarding state and society that simply do not apply within Chinese political culture, leading us to conclude that what *is* there signifies an absence of what *should be* there. Both are misperceptions, and both affect how we think of China. Political regimes in China have indeed succeeded in building and communicating an effective ideological casing, in short, have instilled a conviction in the necessity and benignity of a directive state, that blocks an effective critique of state power from within the Chinese world view. That conviction has been formative in determining how actors within the setting imagine, broker, and pursue political opportunities. It can be left out of the analysis only at the risk of missing how Chinese orient themselves to issues of power.

The internationalization of human rights discourse since the 1980s has to some extent altered the terms through which the Chinese government must enunciate its legitimacy. International criticism of the government's human rights record over the past decade has exposed the regime to internal, society-based scrutiny that it has not been able completely to deflect by appealing to a culturally sanctioned tradition of the legitimacy of the state over society. Although this criticism derived originally from assumptions that may have had little to do with long-established Chinese notions of state and society, it is beginning to draw on alternative moral expectations and submerged historical memories within Chinese traditions that recognize the power of society and are not dependent on Western constructions of human rights or the rights of society against the state.

The concept of civil society not only derives from a European tradition of political thought, but has much to do with contemporary critiques in the West of the erosion of critical and communicative action in advanced capitalist society, and little to do, it would seem, with China. From another perspective, however, the concept provides a comparative ground from which to ask new questions. To broach the concept with respect to China, it is essential to bear in mind two cautions offered by China historians. One, put forward by Philip Kuhn, cautions that civil society is a model, not a reality. He points out that the "West" from which Jürgen Habermas, among others, elaborated the concepts of the public sphere and civil society is not the historical West but its theoretical double. Habermasian constructions of civil society and the public sphere are ideal types, not direct transcriptions of concrete historical formations (Kuhn 1994: 305–307). Since the concept of civil society is simply that, a concept, we should not think of Europe as "having" civil society; rather, civil society is a concept that provides a certain analytical perspective on Europe. In the same vein, China does not "have" civil society, however many of the elements associated with this European-derived concept can be traced in the Chinese past and present. Civil society in China is not a reality but a concept.

The second caution, which Bin Wong (1993: 44–45) has urged, considers the implications of importing wrong assumptions into the task of writing social theory. He advises that comparative history should not be undertaken on the presumption that similarities signify parallels or convergences. To avoid a Eurocentric unilinearity, comparative history must allow that profound historical differences can underlie similarities and must grant what is distinctive in the historical trajectory of Chinese society as much theoretical weight as what is distinctive about the history of European society. Otherwise, while picking out new historical possibilities as we look at China from a Western perspective, we may fail to see those that lie closer to the heart of the Chinese experience. The comparativist's task is to take the European and the Chinese historical experiences and read equally from both of them when constructing general models of state and society.

Auto-Organization

A recent definition characterizes civil society in part as "the realm of organized social life that is voluntary, self-generating, (largely) self-supporting, [and] autonomous from the state" (Diamond 1994: 5).[3] The present chapter has been written not to evaluate China in relation to this definition but, more modestly, to reflect on one element of that definition, the voluntary, autonomous organization of social life, as it might apply to China.

The Chinese state over the past three millennia has been active recurrently and conspicuously in organizing people into social units or "communities." An early ideal for the state modeling of community units, still alive in Chinese cultural memory, is the ancient well-field (*jungtian*) system. According to this system, arable land was divided into units of nine equal parcels distributed among eight households, each getting one parcel to cultivate and all holding joint responsibility for cultivating the ninth and tendering its product as tribute to an overlord/state.[4] Although the well-field model rested on the existence of natural communities predating the formation of the state in the second millennium B.C.E., it accepted the state's right to override social arrangements.

Not all organizing throughout Chinese history has been at the behest of the state, however. Chinese have recurrently formed communities that are neither under the direction of the state nor bound to such state functions as revenue extraction. This process of autonomous group formation, or auto-organization, has gone on within Chinese society since the emergence of the state, often out of its sight, and sometimes in tandem with (even in cooperation with) state interventions at the local level. Auto-organization has been an important factor shaping the lives of Chinese. It has contributed to the formation of the particular historical relationship between state and society that pertains in China today, rendering that relationship more complex and more disjointed than is usually acknowledged.

Auto-organization also testifies to the presence within Chinese society of horizontal integration, which political science scholarship tends to neglect. A common model of Chinese society, derived from the perspective of its elites, identifies local corporatism, the organizing of power among functionally differentiated groups (Fewsmith 1985: 163–65; Thompson 1995: 58), as the way in which Chinese usually group themselves in the local setting. Local corporatism stresses the vertical integration of ordinary people, who surrender their political voice to their elites. It minimizes the capabilities and opportunities that people exercise regularly to communicate horizontally and form cooperative bodies. Local corporatism has been a characteristic structure of Chinese society in the imperial period and beyond, shaping fundamental assumptions about social action, notably within kinship networks. But it does not exhaust the principles by which people group in China or anywhere else.

In his study of contemporary Italy, Robert Putnam has noted distinctive variation in the structure of local political life. At one extreme are the civic communities he tends to find in northern Italy, which are "marked by an active, public-spirited citizenry, by egalitarian political relations, by a social fabric of trust and cooperation." At the other extreme in southern Italy he sees places "cursed with vertically structured politics, a social life of fragmentation and isolation, and a culture of distrust" (1993: 15). Putnam regards the second type of local society, in which "force and family provide a primitive substitute for the civic community," as a "second-best, 'default' solution" to the challenge of building social integration (1993: 178). This negative evaluation does not induce him to elevate the latter to the status of what may be considered "typically" Italian. Both civic and uncivic communities exist in Italy, and do so across a range of possible modes of social integration that vary according to local habits and strategies for survival that Putnam traces back a thousand years. I would argue in a similar vein that, while the clientelistic fragmentation of local corporatism can be traced in Chinese society, it is also possible to identify over the same fabric consistent patterns of associative behavior based on voluntary cooperation. This chapter is intended to expose the presence of auto-organization as a more cooperative principle of social integration at the local level as it has been exercised and remembered over the past four centuries.

The case study for this chapter is Shanghai. Shanghai has had a well developed civic culture in the twentieth century, but it has also had something like a civic culture going back at least to the latter half of the sixteenth century. In a text written in 1606 to honor the restoration of the Confucian shrine at the county school, a local elder recalls a time when Shanghai was characterized by a higher level of distrust, gang justice, and fraud than any other county in the region. He asserts that the zealous administration of local officials in recent years has helped greatly to inspire popular trust in the gentry, who in turn have stabilized local society (Shanghai 1980: 467–468). As if to affirm the commitment of the next generation of gentry to this stabilizing process, the names of all 267 students registered in the Shanghai county school have been entered on the stele on which his text is inscribed. The way in which the author formulates his observation suggests that a transition from uncivic to civic community may have taken place during his own lifetime, although more evidence is needed to confirm this impression.

In the seventeenth century, the sphere of public commercial organization in the city of Shanghai developed rapidly, leading to a marked growth in formal trade and native-place organizations in the eighteenth. This growth not only continued but increased after Shanghai's designation as a treaty port in 1842, resulting in a productive mix of Chinese- and Western-style association building through the latter part of the nineteenth century and the first half of the twentieth. Because of its treaty-port status, Shanghai has been singled out as an exception to Chinese patterns of urban development, largely because of the transformation foreigners view as having been brought about by them. Prior to their arrival, foreigners considered Shanghai an insignificant town where the "feudalistic, seclusionist, and anti-commercial" character of China was faithfully reproduced (Barnett 1941: 11). By going back before 1842, I will show that a process of civic-community formation was already well underway. I will also argue that the later fluorescence of associational life in Shanghai cannot be adequately assessed without a recognition of the depth of historical experience that lies behind treaty-port Shanghai, although I acknowledge that we do not yet have a sufficiently dense body of research on Shanghai society to demonstrate this hypothesis conclusively.

I will begin by reconstructing, in brief outline, aspects of auto-organization in Shanghai during the late-imperial period, from the sixteenth century to 1911, to adumbrate the historical foundation on which associational life in the twentieth century came to be built. My focus, however, will be on the Republican period (1912–1949), when some of the political limits on auto-organization were removed. I will also briefly consider the submergence and resurgence of auto-organizational activity during the People's Republic. Empire, republic, and people's republic differ in their constitutions, each adopted distinct principles and institutions to order public life and distribute political

Table 1.1

Principles of Auto-Organization and Selected Historical Types

	Principles	Late-imperial types	Republican types
1.	Locality	Village society	Village committee, street union, district association
		Native-place association	Fellow countrymen's association
2.	Occupation	Guild	Trade association, chamber of commerce, occupational association, trade union
3.	Fellowship	Religious society	Religious society, church
		Benevolent society	Benevolent society, charity, improvement society
		Literary club	Dramatic society, choral society, book club, athletic club, women's association, youth group
		Academy	Private school, university, student union, alumni association, research society
4.	Common cause		Policy advocacy group, political party

power. What will be striking is the extent to which auto-organizational activity and types crossed the political divides of 1911 and 1949, as well as the degree to which Western practices of and discursive frameworks for social organization have played only a secondary role.

Based on a survey of sources from the sixteenth to the twentieth century, I have identified four principles beyond kinship by which Chinese have constituted groups: (1) locality; (2) occupation; (3) what, for want of an established terminology, I shall call fellowship; and (4) common cause.[5] These principles vary in their degree of voluntarism, with locality at one end of the spectrum creating associations assembled from largely pre-established ties, and common cause at the other end grouping people on a more voluntary basis. There is nothing absolute or final about this heuristic typology. I offer it merely as a way of summarizing under an extremely loose rubric certain characteristics of Chinese social life that appear to extend over time. The four principles and some historical types are listed in Table 1.1.

Late Imperial Practices

Locality was a basic marker of identification for all Chinese in the late-imperial period. Living together in the same place provided the most obvious foundation for the identity of the group. Based on that foundation, members of a village joined together as members of the village "society" (*she*), which was struck and dissolved as necessary to conduct religious festivals, organize local projects such as irrigation, and coordinate labor for crop watching. People did not choose their locality, though even as a nonelective identity, locality provided the core context for transcending the tighter ascriptive ties of kinship, tying the lived community together, and bridging the large horizontal gaps to outside villages.

Living away from a common locality also united people. As Chinese became more systematically mobile, sojourners from the same province or county formed native-place organizations in increasing numbers in the Qing dynasty. They did so to pool resources and provide themselves with social support and services that they otherwise lacked as sojourners. Such groups had existed on a less formal basis prior to the formation of corporate native-place associations. Sources from Shanghai indicate that, already in the Ming dynasty, out-of-county residents clubbed together in loose affiliations or "groups" (*bang*) of people sharing a common origin. Northerners tended to group by province—for example, we know that there existed *bang* of coprovincials from Shanxi and Shandong in Shanghai in the late Ming dynasty—while southerners, who were more numerous, associated by prefecture. In the seventeenth century, such groups began combining resources to establish such sojourner institutions as nonlineage cemeteries (Shanghai 1980: 194). By the eighteenth century, native-place associations in Shanghai were constructing "guildhalls" (*huiguan*) in which social and ritual functions made public declaration of the solidarity of the group and strengthened its authority in local society (Shanghai 1980:235). The term "public office" (*gongsuo*) came into general use in the nineteenth century to signify the offices that native-place associations maintained to handle their members' affairs, especially after 1850, when the number of native-place associations putting up buildings expanded conspicuously (Negishi 1951: 6). Although native-place associations acted to serve the needs of their members only, in doing so they contributed to the weaving of the increasingly dense network of public services that constituted Shanghai's urban public realm in the nineteenth century.[6]

Occupation was a second principle of group formation. It operated principally among urban artisans and merchants who belonged to "guilds" (*hang* or *hui*) distinguished by the goods they made or traded. Manufacturing guilds were well established before the Qing dynasty, but the institution of the "trade guildhall" (also *huiguan*) for merchants who were not from the same locality proliferated during that dynasty as commercial life became more complex. Shanghai's maritime merchants furnish an example of a commercial guild that declared a corporate identity not explicitly based on locality. These merchants enter the historical record in 1715, when they pooled their resources to construct the Commercial Shippers' Guildhall (Shangchuan huiguan). The stele recording the original building of the guildhall does not indicate whether these merchants associated as a guild prior to erecting this sign of their corporate identity (Shanghai 1980: 197); likely they did.

The state looked favorably on guilds as a means of guaranteeing its own interests, for it could off-load onto them such matters as taxation and urban control rather than trying to ramify its own control mechanisms into every nook of urban society, which was naturally resistant to the reach of the state. The state's interest in supporting this form of social organization was reflected in the willingness of local officials to intervene whenever the commercial interests of guild members were threatened by interlopers. When the chandlers of both the Ningbo and Shaoxing *bang* found their members being subject to extortion by self-appointed "heads of the trade" (*hangtou*), who fraudulently claimed they were collecting legitimate taxes, they appealed successfully to the Shanghai magistrate's office in 1868 for a writ of official protection (Shanghai 1980: 131).

Among merchants, occupational and native-place identities often overlapped, as did the institutional forms they constructed, guildhalls and public offices. Ningbo offers a good example. Sojourners from Ningbo who were prominent in Shanghai banking circles founded both the Shanghai Money Trade Guild (Shanghai qianye gongsuo) and the Ningbo Native-Place Association (Siming gongsuo) in the latter half of the eighteenth century. As institutions they were distinct, but their memberships overlapped extensively. Susan Mann has concluded that, by working through both associations, Ningbo bankers were able "not only to create an important monopoly in Shanghai commerce, but to exercise a powerful influence in the financial structure of all China" (Jones 1974: 78). More recently, Linda Johnson has argued from a broader perspective that guilds did not inhibit competition, serving more to broker trade than to monopolize it. She sees the cumulative effect of guild organization as positive in fashioning civic Shanghai in the nineteenth century. Guilds "created public spaces and served public interests" and "thus contributed to an evolving sense of a common civic identity quite distinct from paternalistic government supervision" (Johnson 1995: 154).

Fellowship, the third principle of group formation, was the basis of organizations formed on the strength of shared interests rather than non-elective ties. One was not born into a fellowship group, although the social situation of the fellowship group meant that ties of kinship, locality, occupation, and business all shaped and influenced membership. The fellowship principle produced the richest array of auto-organizational forms in the late-imperial period. "Devotional societies" (usually *hui*), which were organized to promote the worship of a particular deity, encourage religious devotion among members, and mobilize funds for temple building, became quite popular among local gentry in the sixteenth and seventeenth centuries (Brook 1993a: 103–7). Closely associated historically were "benevolent societies" (*tongshan hui*, *tongshan tang*), which were organized to carry out charitable work; these were increasingly popular with local gentry in the eighteenth and nineteenth centuries. The Infant Protection Bureau of Shanghai in the 1870s is a late example. Funded by local gentry with extensive experience in managing charitable enterprises, it was organized explicitly to compensate for the failure of local officials to take seriously or deal effectively with what local elites perceived to be unacceptably high rates of infant mortality, especially for girls (Fuma 1995: 51–52, 58).

The most common, and most characteristic, friendship-based association within elite circles was the literary club. Lu Shen (1477–1544), the leading figure in the local gentry of Shanghai in the 1520s, formed such a club or society among the leading Shanghai writers and calligraphers of his time. So, too, Dong Qichang (1555–1636), native to Shanghai and recognized as the greatest painter of the late Ming dynasty, formed a poetry society in his younger days and later in life was a member of a Buddhist Lotus Society with eminent scholars in the nearby prefectural capital of Songjiang (Dong 1630: 1.36a, 4.54a). A literary club could be no more than a trivial exercise in socializing among a closed class faction, but it could also be critical to the process by which a politically unenfranchised gentry built horizontal social ties, providing them with a forum for public discussion and giving them a presence in local affairs and influence with state representatives (Brook 1993a: 38–43).

Depending on the political climate, these groups could further formalize themselves into academies (*shuyuan*). Academies were unofficial institutions that offered private instruction to examination candidates, but also hosted academic discussions on pressing moral and political topics among the scholars of a county or even wider region. Shanghai was not the site of a nationally prominent academy in the Ming dynasty, although the famous Donglin Academy in nearby Wuxi became the focus for a conservative revitalization of Confucianism early in the seventeenth century and a base for challenging bureaucratic and eunuch factions at court. These "experiments in independent moral cultivation," as John Meskill (1982: 138) has described them, occupied a "precarious" niche in the political structure of late-imperial China, precisely because of the ease with which they could become bases for challenging state policies.[7] In times of intense competition for political resources, literary clubs and academies could become the building blocks by which "bureaucratic differences were articulated into extra-bureaucratic social movements" (Wakeman 1985: 92). This sort of politicization was strong in the last four decades of the Ming dynasty, when soft alliances among literary clubs led to the formation of vertically integrated factions interested in challenging the growing power of the eunuch establishment at court.

The fourth principle of auto-organization, common cause, was not available in the imperial era, for the simple reason that the state forbade people other than incumbent officials from discussing affairs of state. In actual fact, many fellowship-based organizations, from religious societies to academies, existed on the strength of a common espousal of public causes or a common aspiration for action. The Chinese state's monopoly of explicitly political resources made negotiating with interest groups within society inconceivable. The only recognized common cause was the cause of the state, and any group that positioned itself for political influence was automatically regarded as doing so for a cause less than that of the whole. Such a group was labeled a *dang*, which would become the term used for political party early in the twentieth century (by Japanese usage in the nineteenth).

Dang could signify nothing more than a tight group of like-minded people: painter Dong Qichang refers repeatedly to his cohort of gentry friends as "our party" (*wu dang*) (e.g., Dong 1630: 1.36b-1.37a, 2.1a). It could also have a derogatory meaning, as when Dong warns of "inferiors grouping together in a *dang*" (Dong 1630: 7.14a). Commonly, the term was used to disparage political cliques. When a eunuch faction within the Ming imperial household arrogated to itself the authority of the emperor, for example, officials were ready to condemn this takeover in terms of *dang*.[8] So too, though, did early-Qing dynasty commentators condemn late-Ming dynasty factions struggling to challenge abuses at court. Looking back at the disarray that led to the dynasty's fall, Tang Zhen refused to listen to the common defense of the reform faction as having been the only option for good men to battle evil. "*Dang* are the mortal disease of the state," he declared in his uncompromising essay, "Root Out Factions." "Fail to control them and the state will perish" (Tang 1984: 449). Tang allows no notion that auto-organization could be a foundation for stability. Stability's only guarantee is a strong state, even if it is a state headed by foreign invaders like the Manchus. The Manchu emperors in turn adopted this interpretation that the Ming dynasty had fallen because of internal factions. They published edicts against forming *dang*, taking brotherhood oaths, or gathering in clubs.[9]

The foregoing glance at social structure in Shanghai reveals a place where the fabric of social and commercial ties became more complex and dense over time. Some of these ties were vertical, as elites created and operated corporatist organizations through which they could dominate local opinion and mobilize the political support of their clients. But some were horizontal, linking together individuals into sociable circles and providing vehicles and scripts for civic action.

The Republican Experience

The formal ban on *dang* came to an end with the fall of the empire in 1911. Even before that collapse, however, the legal framework for auto-organization within Chinese society was changing. The cumulative burden of China's defeat by Japan in 1895, the collapse of the Guangxu reform regime in 1898, and the occupation of Beijing by foreign troops suppressing the Boxer uprising in 1900 pushed intellectuals, and eventually the Qing court, in the direction of limited constitutionalism. In 1902, the regime promulgated the first in a series of edicts that conceded to propertied individuals the right to associate for public purposes. The first such edict called for the organization, by urban officials, of chambers of commerce, although a national code governing their operation was not published until 1914 (Garrett 1974: 217–18). Recognition of the rights of assembly and association in other contexts followed. To tag the new public organizations, the state created the registration category of "legal group" (*fatuan*). It made this status available in 1903 to newly emerging professionals such as lawyers, bankers, and industrialists, who wanted to form associations to regulate their members' activities and promote the elite's ability to intervene with the state in civic matters that affected them.[10]

The forms that auto-organization had taken in the late-imperial period did not suddenly change with the endowment of legal status under a Republican constitution. The imperial-era types continued to exist, sometimes to mutate, and certainly to proliferate in the Republican era. If 1911 marks a shift in Chinese auto-organizational practice, it has to do first with the growth of cities as political centers, and second with the altered position of the state.

The founding of the Republic opened up urban politics. Compared to a century earlier, urban residents had greater opportunities to organize themselves and, through these organizations, to seek to influence municipal and national affairs. The Republican Revolution, the May Fourth Movement of 1919, the May Thirtieth strike wave of 1925, and the anti-Japanese agitations of 1931–1932 and 1937 were only the most prominent of the political crises that engaged large numbers of urban Chinese. Associations of all types proliferated in Shanghai in the 1910s and beyond: fellow-countrymen's associations, student unions, street unions, advocacy groups. Unlike the new political parties, these were not political organizations in the sense that they identified their goal as the capture of state power; rather, they were social organizations. Though *organized in society*, they were *organized for politics* in the sense of seeking to influence state policies in their favor. The presence of these auto-organizations created a new civic politics that changed the face of political life in the cities and further stimulated auto-organizational activity in a way that greatly altered the social landscape of urban China. It did so because of the continuities with the past, not the disjunctures. As David Strand has stressed, and as this chapter argues, urban politics in the Republic were pursued on the foundation of "a rich associational life which in turn was rooted in long-standing social practices in neighborhoods and occupational groups" (Strand 1994: 310).

The emergence of republican government also marked a shift in the state's relationship to auto-organization. The new state found itself obliged to respond to and interact with social organizations in ways that the imperial regime did not tolerate. A Qing magistrate had had to work informally with interested local groups—the local gentry, merchant guilds, native-place associations—to negotiate the state's concerns with their collective interests, a negotiation that was often obscured by his patronage of their institutions. The Republic did not leave the state's relationship to social organizations on such an informal, ad hoc footing. Anxious to channel public activism in ways that enabled it to direct and control the modernization process without opening political challenges from below, the Republican state recognized the right of people to organize but put regulations in place to set limits on the formation and power of social organizations. A formal registration process enabled the state to decide whether an organization should be allowed to exist and what activities it would be allowed to pursue. While Guomindang and Communist regimes registered organizations above ground, their parties and security apparatuses expended enormous efforts penetrating them from below or setting up rivals, particularly those espousing a common cause that could challenge the existing state. The political stakes in an unstable period were simply too high to permit the autonomy of society.

To provide a sense of the associational life of Republican Shanghai, I have surveyed social organizations that were sufficiently active in the late 1930s to have come to the attention of the Special Branch of the Shanghai Municipal Police (SMP). The SMP was a foreign police agency under the jurisdiction of the Shanghai Municipal Council, which oversaw the administration of the International Settlement. The Special Branch was charged with investigating political matters, such as dissent and sedition, as well as issues that could have international consequences. It became particularly interested in the activities of social organizations in the wake of Japan's invasion of China in the summer of 1937, when many such organizations in Shanghai mobilized to protest Japan's actions, but also used these protests to pursue domestic political goals. From the files of the Special Branch I have culled the names of 153 organizations: (1) eighty-six associations that

Table 1.2

Associations Active in Shanghai, 1937–1941

Type	Active organizations (July–August 1937)	National salvation associations (formed July–August 1937)	Organizations seeking/evading registration (December 1937 to January 1941)	Total
Locality	15	2	2	19
Occupation	34	14	12	60
Fellowship	36	22	7	65
Common cause	.1	7	1	9
Total	86	45	22	153

Source: Shanghai Municipal Police files of the Special Branch, 1894–1949: D-7994, 8002, 8039, 8157, 8157(C), 8166, 8350, 8679, 8692, and 8911. RG263, Military Archives Division, National Archives, Washington, D.C.

engaged in public protests or issued statements of opposition to Japan during July and August 1937 (SMP files D-7994 and 8002); (2) forty-five national salvation associations created by existing organizations to mobilize public opinion against Japan and raise funds to support the Chinese army (SMP files D-7994, 8002, and 8039); and (3) twenty-two organizations that either applied or failed to apply to the SMP for registration between December 1937 and January 1941 (SMP files D-8157, 8157(C), 8166, 8350, 8679, 8692, and 8911). In the discussion that follows, I refer to these associations by the English names recorded in the SMP files.

These three sorts of organization are broken down by type in Table 1.2.[11] The first set, comprising eighty-six organizations that came to Special Branch attention in the summer of 1937 sufficiently to be noted in Special Branch records, includes significant numbers of almost every type. Nine native-place associations are conspicuous, from prestigious groups such as the Ningbo Fellow Countrymen's Association (of which many of the prominent bankers of Shanghai were members) to provincial associations representing natives of Anhui, Shandong, Sichuan, and Zhejiang provinces, along with six local Shanghai district associations. The occupation-based associations include eighteen trade associations (as traditional as the Bean and Rice Hong Owners' Association and as modern as the Shanghai Film

Producers' Association), thirteen professional societies (of bankers, lawyers, dramatists, marine engineers, and wood sculptors, to name only a few), and three trade unions. Even more numerous are fellowship groups: five benevolent societies (including the Chinese Red Cross Society), five improvement societies, a sports club, two choral societies, two drama clubs, three reading groups, a vocational school, two alumni associations, ten research societies, and five women's organizations.[12] The sole common-cause group in this set is the Communist Youth League, which operated clandestinely in the region and could not register with the SMP.

The second set of organizations identified in the SMP files consists of national salvation associations that were established by existing organizations in July and August 1937. For this set, the distribution is slightly different than for the previous set. Only two native-place associations came to the attention of the Special Branch as engaged in this sort of organizing; one of these, the Cantonese Educational Circles' National Salvation Service Group, was, in fact, an occupational subset of a provincial group. By contrast, occupational, fellowship, and common-cause groups proved to be far more significant in mobilizing public opinion to pressure the Guomindang regime to oppose Japan.

Many organizations applied, or failed to apply, for registration with the SMC during the Japanese occupation. The twenty-two tabulated in the third column of Table 1.2 are only those for which I was able to find documentation (in most cases, the group's formal application for registration) in the files of the Special Branch. Registration had been required of Chinese public bodies operating within the International Settlement before 1937, and was reaffirmed by an SMP investigation of the status of all organizations in the summer of 1938 (SMP file D-8692).[13] The intention of this investigation was to limit the proliferation of national salvation associations, which the SMC judged as jeopardizing the modicum of independence that the International Settlement strove to maintain after Japan had established control over the rest of Shanghai. Only one application was submitted by a common-cause group, the "Unwilling to Become Slaves" National Salvation Association. It was rejected on 13 November 1937. The deputy commissioner of the SMP Special Branch went on record to declare that he did "not propose to register *any National Salvation Societies* [emphasis in the original], or [news]paper, in the Settlement at this time." He suspected them, rightly as it turned out, of being Guomindang or Communist fronts (SMP file D-8166). The SMC preferred to prevent auto-organization from moving into the volatile arena of common cause.

To those associations that could gain recognition, however, registration became increasingly attractive as the Japanese army pressured Chinese groups to show support for the occupation. Some had been in existence well before the occupation. Of the two native-place associations that applied (both for counties in the hinterland of Ningbo), the Fenghua association had been formed in 1924 and the Xiangshan association in 1935; presumably, they came forward to register in the summer of 1940 in the hope of gaining some protection through their status with the SMC. Most of the other associations seeking registration were founded in July 1937 or later. This was the month the "Three Lives" (*San Sing* or *Sansheng*) Dramatic Society came into existence, according to its application for registration, dated 20 June 1940. This dramatic society was not an amateur theater group, as the name might have suggested, but a workers' association set up by the managements of three cotton and flour mills, all with the character "life" (*sheng*) in their names, to organize after-hours activities for their employees. These three mills were all that remained of the great industrial empire of the famous Rong family after Japan occupied the parts of Shanghai where the Rongs' other mills were located.

Shanghai Municipal Police registration and surveillance records testify that native-place identity continued to matter as an urban auto-organizing principle in Republican Shanghai, as Bryna Goodman (1992, 1995, 1996) has fully demonstrated. They also indicate that occupation and fellowship were becoming even more prominent in the disoriented political climate of the Japanese occupation, suggesting that Shanghai residents were eager to create lateral social linkages to protect and advance their interests. Mutual aid and "friendship" societies, for example, like the Shanghai Municipal Monks' Adjustment Committee, which was formed on 5 June 1940 and registered seven weeks later, tended to be occupation-based. They assumed increasing importance among the unprotected who faced growing deprivations under the occupation.

Compared with origin and occupation, fellowship emerged as the dominant auto-organizational principle at the time. Shanghai during the late 1930s was a time and place when almost any interest espoused in common was sufficient to bring individuals together to share and protect mutual concerns or to promote ideas within society. The old-style religious and benevolent societies continued to function past the imperial period, but alongside them appeared modern organizations like the Chinese Red Cross and the YMCA. The old elite literary clubs left no traces in the SMP files, but in their place emerged drama clubs, choral societies, sports clubs, reading circles, alumni associations, and improvement societies promoting causes from Esperanto to literacy in Chinese characters. Many were specifically for women or youth, and most were founded before the emergency of 1937. These associations constituted an emerging structure of social cooperation and civic responsibility that was far broader than the associational fabric of late-imperial society, when membership in groups that extended beyond the confines of kinship or locality tended to be limited to those of elite status.

The principle of common cause was least invoked in the associational realm in the Republican era. As noted above, the only explicitly political organization that appeared in the first set of organizations for the summer of 1937 is the Chinese Communist Youth League. From another perspective, however, all of the forty-five national salvation associations could be interpreted as common-cause bodies, even though I have categorized all but seven according to the identity of their parent association. Their sudden appearance signals that common cause, suppressed by state authorities in periods of normalcy, could become an important organizing principle under conditions of sudden emergency or extreme political instability. In place of overtly political entities, the Japanese invasion stimulated the formation of higher-order associations of previously separate social organizations. Benevolent societies grouped together to form the Federation of Various Benevolent Societies for Famine Relief, women's associations joined forces to create the Shanghai Various Women's Organizations' Joint Office (under Guomindang sponsorship), and student unions linked to create the University Students' Friendship Society. Not surprisingly, given its desire to avoid offending Japan, the SMP declined to register any of them.

The State-Socialist Experience

Since taking state power in 1949, the Chinese Communist Party has been successful in stifling auto-organization in Chinese society. It has dominated associational life and disciplined most people to accept

Party-led organizations as the appropriate vehicles for mobilizing social action and public opinion. Until recently, all organizations that existed did so under Party tutelage. The leeway for such organizations (conceived and confined as elements of the Party's "United Front" with non-Party elements) was somewhat greater during the state-corporatist phases of the 1950s and 1980s. During the Cultural Revolution in the mid-1960s to mid-1970s, state and society were deemed coterminous. Briefly during the first year of the Cultural Revolution, socially based Red Guard organizations sprang up in Shanghai, although most existed by virtue of covert support from a Party faction and all were eventually suppressed. Under the extreme conditions of that time, any sense of legitimate space between state and society was eliminated. To argue for autonomy was to argue for the uncoupling of society from the state, a claim judged as treasonable to the nation.

The political reform program of the 1980s moved in the direction of distinguishing the Party and government, with the Party providing the rules by which the state would exist and the government charged with operating the machinery of state efficiently. This distinction was not one of state and society, but it did open some spaces within the flows of political power. One of these points of opening was the "mass body" (*qunzhong tuanti*). Prior to the late 1980s, these mass organizations were formed, directed, and managed by the Communist Party as adjuncts of state control. As part of the political reform program announced at the Thirteenth Party Congress in 1987, the relationship between Party organs and mass bodies was to be adjusted such that "each manages its particular functions and [the relationship] moves by stages toward systematization." More particularly, both the Party and government were called on to make fuller use of "mass bodies and basic-level autonomous organizations of a mass nature" in order that "matters concerning the masses are handled by the masses themselves according to law."[14]

That "masses" (*qunzhong*) and "autonomy" (*zizhi*) should be juxtaposed in this statement points to contrary lineages in the political reform position. "Masses" designates non-Party people whose political rights are determined by the Party; in the lexicon of Chinese Communism, the term is meaningless in the absence of the Party that gives it meaning. "Autonomy" on the other hand, indicates at least nominally the absence of higher authority in the decision-making process within the body. What it asks to be absent, more specifically, is the Party. The political reform removed the Party's right to intervene in social entities, however. Despite the reference to autonomy, it did not declare that power would be dispersed away from the Party. Rather, it rephrased the authority of the Party in the abstract form of "law," in accordance with which Party-created bodies were obliged to act. The rephrasing opened some space between Party organs and mass bodies without fully recognizing a civil society interposed between the masses-as-society and the Party-as-the-state.

However circumscribed, in Shanghai the reform program has seen the activation of occupational groups previously kept on close Party rein. Unions have become more vigorous in the protection of their members' interests, and trade associations have expanded membership as commerce and industry have grown. More visibly, the reform program has also seen the proliferation of legal organizations based on fellowship. Associations of common interest such as soccer clubs, photography clubs, and stamp-collecting clubs have blossomed since the mid-1980s, often by emerging from under the Party-dominated work units within which they previously nested.

Common interest has been accommodated by the reform regime, but common cause has not. Among the principles of auto-organization, this is the least easily invoked, inasmuch as common cause tends to proclaim an autonomy that can too readily serve to mark resistance to the Communist Party's hegemony over initiatives in the public realm. This potential came abruptly to the fore during the Democracy Movement in the spring of 1989, when students and workers formed "autonomous associations" (*zizhihui*) to promote calls for the reform of China's political system. Occupation and fellowship were regularly invoked as the principles governing this brief phase of auto-organization, yet the purpose of organization was consistently to promote not corporate interests, but interests in the public realm.

The process of autonomous organization began in Beijing during the first week of the Democracy Movement (the third week of April 1989) and extended to Shanghai shortly thereafter. Students first formed autonomous student unions by school that were distinct from those the Party organized for them, but quickly combined these separate bodies into the Autonomous Union of Shanghai College Students. Like the Beijing Federation of Autonomous Student Unions on which it was modeled, this organization was weakly integrated, vulnerable to factional splitting, and unable to firm up its goals. Even so, it succeeded through May and early June in mobilizing public opposition in Shanghai to the government's refusal to negotiate with the students in Beijing and in exercising a measure of coordination over the movement.

Students in Shanghai and Beijing were keen to mobilize worker support and distributed pamphlets praising workers for their support and reminding them of the heroic struggle of Polish workers to create Solidarity and remake the Polish state. A small number of workers responded by setting up the Shanghai Autonomous Federation of Trade Unions. This union aspired to occupy a structural position parallel in the movement to the students' federation, and indeed to enact the inspiration of Solidarity in China. This was the parallel that most alarmed Chinese Communist Party hierarchs, who feared the emergence of an independent working-class organization far more than they anguished over declarations of autonomy from students who, as future elites, could more easily be reincorporated into the state after the protests were over (Brook 1992: 85).

In addition to these umbrella groups, the Democracy Movement saw the proliferation of many more common-cause organizations in Shanghai: the China Youth Democracy Party, the Shanghai Patriotic Workers Support Group, the Chinese Autonomous Civil Rights Union, and the Patriotic Volunteer Army, to name only four.[15] By virtue of their declarations of autonomy from Party systems, all these groups marked a radical departure from the forms of occupational organization that had prevailed under the earlier state-corporatist and state-dictatorial phases of the People's Republic. In form and gesture they were strongly reminiscent of auto-organizational practices in the Republican era, although most participants were unaware of these precedents (Esherick and Wasserstrom 1990). They also proved to be painfully vulnerable to state suppression (Warner 1991: 228–29).

The suppression of June 1989 marked an abrupt setback to common-cause organizing. Continuing vigilance has meant that organizations such as the Shanghai Human Rights Association, which was suppressed as soon as it became public in 1994, cannot hope to secure legal status (Amnesty International 1996: 50). Outside of common cause, however, organizational life has not dimmed. Occupation in particular has gained ground as a principle of organization in the 1990s, attested to by the growing vitality of professional associations and trade unions. Indeed, it will be necessary for auto-organization to expand its presence within the emerging structure of state-society relations under China's current economic reform program for that program to work. This necessity arises not from the moral claim of the individual for the right to associate, but, more crudely, because horizontal social bonds, and the sense of civic investment they generate, contribute directly to economic and institutional performance by improving infrastructure and mobilizing subjective capacity. Both market and state operate more efficiently if economic growth is coupled to participation in civic life. As long as the government pursues development policies that demand this efficiency, it will be obliged to cede some space for the operation of independent corporate bodies. This cession is regarded variously as marking a resurgence of state corporatism, as signalling a departure from the state-corporatist model (as Yunqiu Zhang argues in this volume), and as generating a structural hybrid in which state and corporate bodies mingle (as B. Michael Frolic argues in his chapter). Where future auto-organizational impulses will lead remains not simply to be seen but to be interpreted and contested. That contest will intensify as "socialism with Chinese characteristics" emerges from behind its obfuscating label.

Some Characteristics of Chinese Auto-Organization

The evidence presented in this chapter suggests that we can identify four characteristics of auto-organization, derived from the Chinese experience but perhaps salient in other cultures as well.

The first is the responsiveness of auto-organization to crisis. The disruption of order provides an opening for initiatives from below, and associations have shown themselves to be responsive to that opportunity. This responsiveness produces impressive results at critical moments, but its corollary, the dependency of auto-organization on crisis, suggests that a consistent presence of auto-organizations has proven difficult to sustain on a day-to-day basis. This difficulty should be attributed not to the nature of Chinese society, but to the presence of sometimes violently repressive regimes during the twentieth century. That repression again need not be regarded as characteristically Chinese. It would be better traced to the instability of the modernizing state, which finds itself unable to negotiate with particular interests because of its constant fear that at each point of negotiation its legitimacy or hegemony will unravel.

The second characteristic of Chinese auto-organization is a readiness to combine into larger entities, again notably at times of crisis. Just as the Beijing Federation of Autonomous Student Unions was founded soon after the start of the Democracy Movement in 1989, so the Shanghai Students' Union emerged within four days of the May Fourth demonstration in Beijing in 1919 (SMP file IO-6691). It, in turn, became affiliated with a national students' association. (National combination proved hugely difficult seventy years later, in large part because of the state's more effective means of social control.) Street unions demonstrated a similar process during the 1919 movement, combining at the national level in the Amalgamated Association of Street Unions. Above these and other citizens' federations emerged the National Organizations' Union of China (SMP file IO-3524). Crisis had the same impact on the elaboration of associations during the May Thirtieth Movement in 1925, when the Shanghai General Trade Union was formed; and again during the crisis provoked by Japan's attacks on China in 1931–1932 (Henriot 1993: 66–78). Finally, as we have seen, the public outcry against Japan's invasion of China in 1937 generated a surge of alliance building with the creation of a national salvation association for almost every constituency in Shanghai: students, cadets, women, merchants, vocational workers, cultural workers, reporters, editors, professors, youth, even children (SMP file D-8122).

Combining of organizations takes place also *among* different types of association as well as *within* the same type, again at moments of crisis. This third characteristic of Chinese auto-organization was evident in the 1911 Revolution, and again in the May Fourth Movement in 1919, when student unions, chambers of commerce, native-place associations, trade associations, and even the Boy Scouts coordinated their efforts to a common purpose (Goodman 1992; Wasserstrom 1992; SMP files IO-6691, D-4656). Japan's invasion in 1937 led to even broader alliance formation, as the many national salvation groups pyramided into the "Unwilling to Become Slaves" National Salvation Association.

Although not free to be fully political, the auto-organizational sphere in the Republican era was nonetheless, to use a phrase introduced early in this chapter, *organized for politics*. This is the fourth characteristic. Social organizations understood that their purpose was to influence the state. They might not be able to work explicitly for the institutionalizing of a legal order, and they might wisely shrink from adopting explicitly political forms or platforms. However, they could intervene to scrutinize state actions in the public realm and to agitate for an improvement in governance. Aware of the political character of such interventions and the force of repression such politics can unleash, Chinese have shied away from common-cause entities in preference for bodies that did not declare political aims. Of the four different types of auto-organizations outlined in this chapter, those based on fellowship seem to have contributed most forcefully to the process of bringing the Chinese state within an accountability based on a shared set of rules (however much the rules themselves may have been contested), at least in the Republican period. Occupation-based associations by contrast have been least likely to mobilize citizens to make demands on the state. Craft guilds and workers' associations might do something of this sort when demanding fair treatment from employers, thereby nourishing an awareness of rights and their place within the larger structure of legal norms. But it is difficult to argue that they were able to make significant contributions toward establishing a larger structure of legal norms by which they could guard their autonomy, except insofar as they gave their members a taste of what collective action could achieve.

Auto-Organization and the Chinese State

The notion of civil society emerged in European social theory toward the end of Europe's absolutist phase. This was a time when intellectuals were looking ahead to understand the outcome of bourgeois challenges to the oligarchic state. It was believed that the failure of such challenges to occur—and China has been the popular example from Hegel through Marx to Weber and on to Deleuze—led to despotism. China's record as a warlord state during the first half of the twentieth century, and as a party-state through the second, seems only to confirm this analysis. And yet the Chinese state has not in this century, nor in any other, been successful at despotism for more than a few years. Despotism is a theoretical imaginary based on the unrealistic notion of absorbing all power to the center, an arrangement that can only be temporary and is always incomplete. Auto-organization is evidence of the incompleteness of Chinese despotism, and may provide some of the historical counterweight to its realization.

It is something of a commonplace to observe that Chinese political culture favors dependent relationships rather than assertions of independent moral decision, and that Chinese moral culture favors harmonizing the individual with society, and doing so within the larger moral goal of harmonizing society with the state. In a recent essay on the relationship of academies to the late-imperial state, Thomas Lee argues that Confucianism furnished intellectuals with the ideal of intellectual autonomy and moral independence within this larger framework of vertical harmony. The pursuit of moral independence drove academy intellectuals at moments of crisis to speak out against the moral failure of the monarch or those close to him. Lee sees the resolution of this tension in intellectuals' willingness to rate the omnipotence of the emperor more highly than the life of the critic, whose commitment must in the end be regarded, in Lee's view, as "irrational." The intention of critique was to remonstrate, never to stake a claim against the authority of the emperor over his subjects or, more abstractly, against the authority of the state over society. The academy movement, and most other expressions of auto-organization, should be viewed "in terms of successful involvement in moral government, rather than in terms of separation from it, and much less even in terms of a search for a legally sanctioned separate sphere of action." Lee is willing to accept that "something resembling a 'civil society' " existed in China before the eighteenth century, but "only briefly and only in difficult times." The occasional eruption of civil society signalled not a step toward something new, but a temporary systemic failure that only confirmed the more fundamental commitment to "mediation, harmony and unity in community rather than a carving out of an autonomous sphere for action" (Lee 1994: 118, 119, 133–35).

Such descriptions of Chinese culture may be sensible, and they are widely replicated by scholars who advocate a "China-centered" approach to questions of state power. But they conceal more than they expose and render themselves vulnerable to confirming ideological claims rather than probing the political basis on which such claims are erected. The recurring reversion to a fundamental commitment to harmony that Thomas Lee describes does not rule China out of an analysis that attributes this reversion to the instability of the Chinese state rather than to the "weakness" of Chinese society. Lee, after all, implies the instability of the state (in the unstable person of the emperor) when he observes that the Confucian commitment to harmony is ultimately "irrational" in exposing the official who is uncompromising in advocating of good government to execution.

Autonomous organization in the public realm has been construed by contemporary East Asian elites as potentially corrosive of the stability of the state. The analysis in this chapter suggests that the truth runs very much the other way. Auto-organizational activity increases in times of political crisis as a response to the breakdown or compromise of proper state functioning, not because society has somehow detached itself from the polity, but because a regime has failed to meet economic or political challenges. Auto-organization does not destabilize regimes. Destabilization occurs when the state acts in ways that cause its authority to appear merely oppressive and its legitimacy unsupported. Social organizations strive to reconstruct that stability, albeit on a basis different from that of state organs. Rather than polarizing society from the state, auto-organization patches ruptures between the two, anticipating breakdowns and rebuilding fallen bridges. It compensates for the recurring failures of the state, which are inevitable even under the most perfect of Confucian or communist constitutions.

The role of the state in China, thus, is crucial to social initiatives and social outcomes. To fault Chinese society for stubborn localist, isolationist, or corporatist habits that interfere with the formation of a mature public sphere or strong civic culture in the twentieth century (or earlier—in other words, for lacking sufficient vitality to sustain its own integration—is to ignore the terrific pressure that Chinese state bodies, by judicial and extrajudicial means throughout most of this century, have exerted to maintain political power when challenged by its elites to do better (Brook 1992: 204–9). If Chinese society appears riven by structural weaknesses, with the power of small organizations to combine more than matched by their tendency to factionalize and fall apart (Strand 1994: 321), we would do well to remember that groups in European cities prior to the full development of civil society were probably as vulnerable to factionalism, scandal, and repression. On the other hand, beating a retreat into the comfortable zone of historical comparison does not do away with the fact that the autonomy of civil society in Republican China was limited by "the absence of a reliable state to deal with," an absence that ultimately opened China to "illiberal solutions" (Strand 1994: 329). Nor does it cancel out the fact that the Chinese state today pursues a conscious strategy of incorporating those intermediate social organizations that bolster its position and repressing those it considers dangerous (White 1996: 219).

Despite the restrictions that state authorities have imposed on auto-organization during the past century, the memory of associational linkage has not been eradicated. With the current shift to close economic calculation, there is every reason to anticipate the reemergence of social organizations of the sort that thronged in urban China in the 1930s, although the conditions of their existence have yet to be fully negotiated. As these organizations reemerge, they will unavoidably come to act in ways that, at some point, will be construed as political; and the Chinese state will respond in ways intended to restrict their independence of action. The process of ramifying the organizational fabric and strengthening the social capital of Chinese life will be to the organizations' and state's mutual benefit, for it will multiply the bases of stability and link citizens more effectively to their state. Within the current political environment in China, this development will come only through a judicious balance between cooperation and critique. If the path seems narrow, it is one with which Chinese in this century have been made intensely familiar.

2

State-Led Civil Society

B. Michael Frolic

If the prospects for China's immediate democratization are uncertain, the vision of the emergence of a Chinese civil society, a sphere of activity marked by a growing degree of autonomy from state power, is more promising.[1] For some, the emergence of civil society is a slow process, linked to the social and political consequences of the opening up of China's economy. In this view, as economic reform causes the Chinese party-state to loosen its grip, civil society will take shape and gain strength. Others, less patient, look to more frequent instances of dissent and opposition, seeing civil society as a tool to be used by intellectuals for pressuring a "bad" state, rather than evolving in tandem with it.

Our interest in civil society was heightened by two events. The first was Tiananmen, which whetted expectations on the part of a substantial number of Chinese participants and Western observers that democratic reform was imminent in China. For many, the fifty-day confrontation at the Square should have produced if not dramatic political liberalization, then at least a measure of openness (*glasnost*) similar to the Gorbachev reforms, or a token loosening up of party-state control. Instead, the regime tightened its grip in the post-Tiananmen period. Those who expected a Chinese outcome along the lines of developments in Eastern Europe and the Soviet Union, where the party-state system quickly collapsed, were disappointed. The prospects for Chinese democracy, which seemed tangible before Tiananmen, evaporated in the retreat to political conservatism after 1989. The regime had demonstrated its capacity to stop political liberalization in its tracks. Thus, if democracy was unattainable in the short run, why not focus on civil society, on developing the infrastructure that is a vital condition for the realization of democracy? Setting their sights somewhat lower, proponents of political reform optimistically looked to signs of nascent civil society as a marker for emerging democratization.

A second event that turned our attention to civil society and away from democracy in the first instance was the end of communism in Eastern Europe. In Poland, Czechoslovakia, and Hungary, civil society seemingly had triumphed. Alternative society, "the parallel polis," "parliaments of the streets," "flying universities," *samizdat*—the deliberate opposition of society to state—had brought down a row of one-party states. Havel's Velvet Revolution and *Solidarnosc* in Poland could serve as models of a civil society strategy, in that democratic goals had been achieved in no small measure through the creation of networks of autonomous organizations in a space parallel to the state. They did not directly confront the state, but surrounded it with "a wide spectrum of activities, from cultural and religious organizations and human rights groups to independent economic activities ranging from trade unions to private enterprises" (Kiss 1992: 27). As Vaclav Benda (1991: 36), a leading Czech activist, put it:

> I suggest that we join forces in creating, slowly but surely, parallel structures that are capable, to a limited degree at least, of supplementing the generally beneficial and necessary functions that are missing in the existing structures, and where possible, to use those existing structures to humanize them.

These two events, the collapse of communism in Eastern Europe and the Soviet Union and the reaffirmation of the Chinese state's power in the face of Tiananmen, brought the civil society discourse to the center of Western political analysis. Yet the concept has proved difficult to define. Like "democracy," to which it has increasingly been joined in political discourse and rhetoric, "civil society" inspires a wide range of interpretations and individual agendas. For Westerners, it is a complex lens focusing on a wide range of activities, linking public and private, state and society, individual and collectivity, economy and polity. For example, consider the following definition of civil society by Michael Ignatieff (1995: 128–29):

> In civil society . . . division and diversity, checks and balances, are of the essence. Political power is fenced off from cultural power and economic advantage, office holders do not enrich themselves from office, power does not confer cultural authority, and social position does not entail cultural or political influence. A free society, acting through the press and its elected representatives, restrains the state, and the law restrains both.

Ellen Meiksins Wood (1990: 61) provides a different perspective, one that focuses more sharply on the emergence of capitalist economic relations:

> Civil society represents a separate sphere of human relations and activity, differentiated from the state but neither public nor private, and perhaps both at once, embodying . . . more specifically a network of distinctively *economic* relations, the sphere of the market place, the arena of production, distribution and exchange. . . . The full conceptual differentiation of "civil society" required the emergence of an autonomous economy.

This chapter presents four perspectives on civil society drawn from the substantial Western literature on the collapse of communism and on the nature of political change in China.[2] Each of these perspectives focuses on a central theme within the civil society discourse. The four are not mutually exclusive. Together they paint a portrait of a concept that is analytical, yet normative; a strategy that is associated with revolution, yet predicated on evolutionary change. In the second part of the chapter, I suggest that China may indeed be "different" and identify a fifth perspective, which is linked to the Chinese party-state's continuing control over the Chinese polity. This Chinese authoritarian "state-led civil society," created from the top down as an adjunct to state power, coexists with the more familiar Western "democratic" manifestations of emerging civil society. By state led civil-society, I refer to the hundreds of thousands of social organizations and quasi-administrative units created by the state to help it manage a complex and rapidly expanding economy and changing society. Depending on one's point of view, state-led civil society can be considered either a new form or just a temporary accommodation by the authoritarian state to forces that will overwhelm it soon enough. This Chinese version of civil society represents not only a government strategy, but may be conceived of as an

"Asian" type of political development, that is, a form of state corporatism or non-Western communitarianism that differs noticeably from the more conventional civil society of the West (Unger and Chan 1995: 29–54). In the third section of the chapter, I discuss four instances of state-led civil society: the new system of village elections; the rise of non-governmental organizations (NGOs); the beginnings of civil society in a Zhejiang municipality; and the opening up of "private space" for entrepreneurs in Xiamen. These examples show the diversity and scale of emerging state-led civil society in China, as well as its still tentative nature.

Will civil society provide the infrastructure for the democratization/liberalization of the authoritarian system? Will this process make China more like the West, or is there a particular synthesis occurring in which Chinese civil society is taking a path that will lead to a somewhat different experience from that in the West? Here we confront speculations about the enduring authoritarian nature of Asian life and politics, about cultural and historical limitations on the role and activities of individuals and the need for greater patience in awaiting democratic outcomes linked to the process of economic modernization. We should bear in mind that only a generation has passed since the death of Mao; it may be premature to speculate about the long-term direction of liberalizing trends in Chinese politics and society.

In looking for the emergence of civil society, we can make three assumptions: that there is a Western/Chinese mix of values and ideology that is producing a Chinese variant of civil society, that disengagement from authoritarian Leninist structures and norms will be slower than expected, and that nascent civil society should not be confused with the imminent democratization of China. We should also remember that civil society is about culture, values, and attitudes, which change slowly. When millennia of traditions still count, it is too much to think that fundamental transformation can occur within a single generation.

Civil Society as a Parallel Polis

The concept of civil society was reborn in the 1970s, primarily in Eastern Europe where it became an arena for dissent. Dissidents were able to create alternative structures outside the state, a polis that was parallel to the state. The latter did not, and apparently could not, eliminate these structures of opposition. Civil society emerged from the perception that the totalitarian state was no longer able to enforce its full control over society. Havel refers to a "post-totalitarian" system in which individuals "live within the truth," and "citizens' initiatives, dissident movements, or even oppositions, emerge, like the proverbial one-tenth of the iceberg visible above the water" (1991: 177). In Havel's view "good" civil society had been crushed by the "bad" totalitarian state. Now, alienated intellectuals and individuals with a true public spirit could recapture their institutions, ideologies, and values by setting up their own civil society in nonviolent opposition to this bad state. It was a citizen's duty to support good civil society against the bad communist state. According to Kuron, "Society organizes itself as a democratic movement and becomes active outside the limits of the institutions of the totalitarian state" (cited by Kiss 1992: 227). When these regimes imploded in the late 1980s, much of the credit was given to this parallel polis strategy: it was based within the society, produced a counterelite potentially capable of seizing power on behalf of the people, employed methods that were nonviolent, and was linked to understandings and perceptions of a civil society that had existed in the past and could now be used as a basis for the future democratization/liberalization of these postcommunist regimes.

The idea that dissidents and intellectuals in opposition could peacefully change a communist party-state was not lost on a small group of Chinese intellectuals and an even smaller group of dissidents in the 1980s. A part of the Chinese leadership appeared willing to permit a modest political opening. The economic reforms were creating potential "social bases for autonomy" (Kelly and He 1992: 28). This contributed to the perception that it was possible to pursue tactics similar to those in Eastern Europe. For example, the Beijing Stone Group, a computer company formed in the early 1980s, set up a think tank, the Social Development Research Institute, which promoted political liberalization through indirect means. Another organization, the Beijing Social and Economic Research Institute, was staffed mainly by academics who tried to open up the political system by advocating the extension of the rule of law and human rights. A variety of groups emerged to pursue activities to change the system primarily through soft, nonconfrontational tactics that "ranged from fund-raising concerts, suicide-prevention hot-lines, signature campaigns, Gallup poll-type social surveys, to political demands for freedom of speech and association" (Kelly and He 1992: 28–31).

But conditions in China were different. The activities of groups such as Beijing Stone represented a veneer of Chinese opposition to the authoritarian party-state. The idea of restoring a civil society that had been crushed by the state may have made sense in Eastern Europe, but it was problematic in China, which barely had a tradition of civil society in its past. Significantly, China lacked a critical mass of dissident intellectuals willing to challenge authority. Much of the energy of China's intellectuals and dissidents was consumed in trying to persuade the state to change itself, rather than overthrowing it through the creation of a parallel polis. This strategy was in keeping with the Confucian tradition that intellectuals should serve the state, and Communist practice that reinforced their subordinate position. "Neo-authoritarianism," advocated as a pathway to political reform in the late 1980s, essentially argued for modified authoritarianism, not for democracy. Civil society was seen as a future benefit to be bestowed by a benign authoritarian regime rather than as a vehicle for overthrowing a totalitarian state.

Civil Society as Citizenship

The concept of "civil society against the state" is relatively new. In its original usage civil society had another meaning, that of good citizenship. Benda refers to civil society as a parallel polis; in fact, we can say that civil society originally *was* the Greek polis, what men had created in opposition to the state of nature. In the polis, virtue and good citizenship reigned supreme. Civil society and the city-state were coterminous. This society was polite and civil, and it was elitist, since only a few men of virtue were citizens. It set the tone for all society, however. The community of citizens "is the source of morality which arises out of, and is sustained by the everyday interactions of persons within what is now called civil society" (Australian-Asian Perceptions 1993: 7). For Shils, a civil society is one in which the law binds both state and citizens together and they exercise the "virtue of civility," the hallmark of good citizenship. "Civility" means moderating particular, individual, or parochial interests and giving precedence to the common good. The citizen, a civil person, exercises the virtue of civility by giving precedence to the common good over individual feelings and needs (1991: 16).

This idea of good citizenship is at the center of the Western liberal-democratic tradition. Transposed from the polis to the twentieth century, it encompasses the individualistic, rational, and, until recently, elitist strands that comprise our political ideologies. Good citizenship can develop only over time and requires a community of rational, self-directing individuals who can elevate their private interests to a consideration of the greater public good. Trust and honesty are essential components in this process. In the long journey from subject to citizen, as from authoritarianism to democracy what counts is not only the development of individual and particular interests but the commitment of these interests to the public good.

Is China ready for this kind of civil society? The road from subject to citizen is long and arduous. Finding a critical mass of rational, self-directing individuals capable of joining their private interests in a broader consideration of the greater public good is difficult. China has differently constructed traditions of individuality and "the public" (*gong*). A recent Australian study identifies two types of citizenship, individualistic (Western) and communitarian (Asian), and suggests that the latter is strongly entrenched in China and in the wider Asian setting:

> In Neo-Confucian societies where the public sphere has been created by and from the state and not from the private sphere there remain few limits to the state and there are few opportunities for individuals to play multiple roles (such as the 'role' of the independent citizen) in Asian society. They cannot easily 'drop out.' They are always expected to behave as political participants in their communities, and the state has a right to intrude into their 'private lives' in ways which the hypothesized, individualistic, capitalist-liberal democrat citizen would not accept (Australian-Asian Perceptions 1993: 8).

If this is the dominant pathway for citizenship in contemporary China, what does this tell us about its emerging civil society? From a Western perspective, "communitarian" citizens lack the freedom of will, conditions of trust, and protection of law to act freely as rational individuals. Thus, the basic requisites of civil society are missing. But from a non-Western perspective, one might see this as a slow transition to soft authoritarianism, mediated by the state rather than by civil society. If Japan, Taiwan, and South Korea can make this transition over time, why not assume the same for Chinese citizens?

Civil Society as Political Development

The most common perspective on civil society is based on the great transformation of relations between state and society in the modern era in Europe. Specifically, the key events were, first, the separation of church and state; second, the rise of the capitalist economy; and third, the creation of the modern bureaucratic state. The separation of church from state created a space for multiple loyalties, for the separation of state and society, and for the evolution of the idea of a private sphere for individuals. The subsequent rise of the capitalist economy provided a different sort of space, based on the need to protect the individual's property. According to C. B. Macpherson (1962), the spread of "possessive individualism" in defense of private economic space contributed to the rise of modern civil society. A number of processes were occurring simultaneously. Individuals were acquiring wealth and power, and staking a claim to terrain independent of both state and society. The state expanded to fulfill its distributive and regulatory functions in an increasingly complex world. The multiplicity of private interests had to be integrated into a new concept of the public, one that could mobilize individuals in support of the common good. The relationship of individuals and state to society—the wellspring of values and, ultimately, change—had to be redefined.

The process of political modernization, therefore, demands a crucial space between a changing state and society, in which individuals interact and define themselves in relationship to the political. Civil society is that space and it serves to mediate political participation and change. It is this accommodation to change in multiple directions (economy, state, society, individual, political community) that characterizes Western civil society and explains its unique place in modern political analysis. In focusing on contemporary China, we can see the linkage between incipient civil society and economic modernization. The market economy has created a new economic space, within a rapidly differentiating society, in which central state political control cannot be sustained without increased reliance on mediating structures. Civil society is the most important of these structures, and its existence in China is predicated on the state's need to have such mediation. The state can use a civil society to govern more effectively. However, civil society also provides a realm in which individuals can protect themselves against both state and society in an ever-changing and increasingly complicated environment. In today's China, these are only emerging roles, existing in a weak institutional base, within a context of value conflict and change.

Civil society as political development is squarely based on the modern Western experience and has, it is fair to say, a Western bias. Aside from romanticized notions about the Greek polis, Western thinking about civil society is a relatively recent phenomenon, linked to the emergence of capitalism, the modern state, and democracy. China has barely experienced the separation of state and society, the powerful influence of capitalism, and the rise of the modern industrial state. Why, therefore, presume to look in today's China for a civil society that is linked to developed capitalism and democracy? Roger Des Forges in this volume argues that the various elements of Western civil society can be found in China over the past three millennia, in particular, in relatively autonomous social organizations at the local level. One can even find "civility" in Confucian practice. Yet, these were inchoate and episodic phenomena, which in my view differ fundamentally from the civil society that has taken shape in the modern West.

Civil Society as Governance

Ideally, civil society lubricates the political system and links the various parts together. To Havel and other East European dissidents, the "system" had become disfunctional under the communist party-state. It had to be restored by means of civil society, which could serve as compass and navigator for the new ship of state. Civil society is what makes the whole system work. It unites public and private, state and individual, disparate individuals within a community, and state and society. Civil society is both the energizer of development and its stabilizer. It comprises the main players and is at the same time their umpire. It provides structure and certainty, but also is flexible and accommodates change.

In "politically developed" Western systems, a civil society is vital for obtaining "democratic" governance. In other political systems, fascist, monarchical, or authoritarian, a functional version of civil society is essential just for providing effective management. According to Michael Ignatieff (1995: 128), "A civil society, as the eighteenth century theorists understood it, was not necessarily a democratic society." "Regular government" was the preferred goal, and it was best to commit key societal elements to the government by means of a civil society that was not democratic. Civil society was a mechanism which evolved to prevent disorder and maintain links between the new state and the changing society. In commenting on Robert Putnam's recent research arguing that northern Italy had a more developed civil society and was better governed than the south, because of the existence of "social capital," Fareed Zakaria observes that this has little to do with democracy. It has to do with the essential linking nature of civil society, however it is defined, and with the need for effective social and political management in the first instance. According to Zakaria,

> The Italian north has been better run than the Italian south for hundreds of years, during which the country was, to put it mildly, not always democratic. One might more reasonably conclude from Mr. Putnam's research that social capital makes any regime work, whether monarchical, democratic or fascist (1995: 28).

In searching for civil society in countries that are just now undergoing capitalist transformation and whose "social capital" is not the Protestant ethic, it may be more fruitful to look for linking mechanisms bound to the integration of local interests with the central state. "Linkage," which facilitates governance rather than democracy, is the short-term, utilitarian essence of civil society. In times of rapid change and during searches for new identities, civil society in its various interpretations and formations is an institutional and attitudinal linchpin uniting past and present, individual and collectivity, state and society.

To summarize, in this section I have presented four perspectives on civil society. My purpose was to indicate the range and complexity of the concept, which is rooted in the Greek polis, in the rise of capitalism and liberal democracy in the past three centuries, and in the events of East Europe in the 1970s and 1980s. Civil society is made up of many strands and perspectives. Some of these elements are present in today's China; most are not. Frequently we are motivated by the conviction that a fully formed civil society, linked to liberal democracy, must emerge from the cocoon of authoritarianism. More likely, however, is an incipient civil society tied to early capitalist development, that is, one based not on democracy, but on the building of infrastructure and values on the long road to political development. In analyzing China, we tend to look for democratic governance as if China were a highly evolved polity, rather than an emerging authoritarian political system, blinking into the light of political change and just trying to maintain order in the midst of constant chaos. Nor is it realistic to adopt a *civil society against the state* strategy for China when there is as yet no Chinese consensus about an alternative polis, and little institutional memory of a previous civil society.[3] To talk of a Chinese civil society based on citizenship is equally questionable, given that the rights of citizenship are still being negotiated as China moves from a subject political culture to one that is more participatory and autonomous. In the discussion, I intimated that the portrait of civil society in China presented through these four perspectives on civil society (parallel polis, citizenship, political development, governance) is not a satisfying one. Much seems to be missing. For a number of reasons having developmental, cultural, historical and ideological bases, civil society in China is likely to emerge along a different path, at least in the immediate future.

State-Led Civil Society

A fifth perspective is to consider China in terms of a state-led civil society. I see two kinds of civil society in today's China. One fits the pattern described above, which emphasizes the opening up of the political system, limitations on state power, and the advancement of the rights of autonomous groups and individuals. This civil society is still poorly developed and is struggling to maintain itself in China. But, there is a second civil society that extends the reach of the state into the new Chinese economy and community. This is state-led civil society. It is created by the state, principally to help it govern, but also to co-opt and socialize potentially politically active elements in the population. State-led civil society unites two strands of authoritarian politics: those of the socialist authoritarian state in transition, and those of the ascendant East Asian communitarian state (Unger and Chan 1995: 28).

By "state-led civil society" I refer to the recent creation by the state of literally hundreds of thousands of organizations and groups that serve as support mechanisms to the state. According to Jude Howell, in 1993 "there were reportedly over 1,460 registered national social organizations, 19,600 branch and local organizations registered at provincial level, and over 160,000 social organizations registered with county authorities" (1994: 97). Howell adds that the number of these organizations is probably much higher, because some have not bothered to gain official registration, while others are waiting for approval.

In the old Marxist-Leninist system, officially sanctioned groups and associations such as the Women's Federation, the trade unions, youth leagues, and writers' associations functioned as "transmission belts" for government policies. In the new Chinese political system, the number and functions of these "social organizations" (*shehui tuanti*) has soared. According to Gordon White, they are generally seen as occupying an organizational space between a state organ proper and an enterprise, an intermediate position that gives them, in theory at least, some degree of formally recognized status as a "popular" (*minjian*) or "people-run" (*minban*) organization as opposed to an "official" (*guanban*) organization. In Xiaoshan, a city of 1.153 million, there were approximately a hundred of these social organizations, divided into ten categories. Those in the categories of "political," "economic," and "science and technology" were the most numerous and important, constituting over half. Others were in the following areas: arts and culture, social welfare, social clubs, public affairs, health, and sports. The groups ranged from new social organizations such as the Individual Laborers' Association and the Private Enterprises Association, to old "official" organizations such as the Women's Federation and the Overseas Chinese Federation. Other examples included the Qigong Research Association, the Old People's Exercise Association, and the Dried Turnip Association (White 1993: 73–76).

Social organizations have multiple functions. According to White, they are "a crucial communications channel between a state organ and the organization's members, thereby helping the state to get across ideological points or specific policies" (1993: 79). In addition, they help to coordinate and focus state activity in particular sectors of the economy. They also take over functions formerly exercised by the state. They can serve a bridging function between the state enterprises and the private economy, and between collective and private interests. In an increasingly complex and more mobile society and economy, social organizations extend the reach of the state, providing a critical coordinating and participation mechanism. They are agents of administration and political socialization in the first instance. In addition, they are embryos of civil society as it is understood in the West. They also function as surrogates for a state that is devolving control, rather than serving as centers of citizen resistance to a repressive state.

State-led civil society is not only about helping the state to organize economy and society; it is also about the state acting as a powerful ally for individuals separating from society. Too frequently we focus on tyrannical states, forgetting that states emerged in the process of emancipating individuals from the tight grip of traditional societies. As Heath Chamberlain writes, "The 'rule of the folk' can be just as tyrannical as the 'dictatorship of the proletariat' " (1994: 117). Even the dictatorship of the proletariat at times can be more benevolent than the tyranny of semi-feudal society. He also reminds us that "Chinese society of the 1950s was a long way from being civil. It was essential that the state intrude rudely and violently to liberate people from the constraints of traditional family and social bonds, precisely in order to prepare the soil for civil society's future growth" (Chamberlain 1993: 210).

What the Communist state did so "rudely" against society in the past is negotiated more politely by maturing civil societies in the present. If China's civil society was absent or in an embryonic stage, it was up to the state, then and now, to disengage individuals from society. But one tyranny leads to another: the state becomes more tyrannical than the society that it has challenged.

State-led civil society is based on a number of assumptions. First, the new associations and groups are not against the state but a part of it. Second, they serve as training grounds for the development of civic consciousness. Third, they function as intermediaries between state and society. Fourth, state-led civil society is not riven by conflict between its civil society components and the state. It is a marriage of convenience rather than a catalyst for citizen resistance. Finally, mutual perception of strength and weakness plays a key role. Elements in the state perceive the need for change and regard social organizations as functionally useful, without threatening the state's hegemony. Those within the social organization perceive a slightly weakened state, but are more interested in short-term economic gains than individual autonomy at the expense of state power. Neither wants the state to collapse.

State-led civil society is a form of corporatism. The state determines which organizations are legitimate and forms an unequal partnership with them. The state does not dominate directly. It leaves some degree of autonomy to these organizations, but it does demand a disciplined partnership based on cooperation within specified sectors, usually in tripartite arrangements among business, labor, and the state. While corporatism is most commonly identified with fascist forms of government, corporatist mechanisms also have existed in liberal and socialist political systems. Anita Chan differentiates state corporatism from societal corporatism. The latter is a form of interest group politics. It functions at the grassroots level rather than at the peak of the system. It is less hierarchical and rigid than state corporatism, and is characterized by bargaining among the partners, rather than the dominance of the state. "At the other end of the spectrum from such societal corporatism lies what is variously called authoritarian or state corporatism, where the weight of decision-making power lies very heavily on the side of the state" (Chan 1993).

The Qigong Research Association and the Old People's Exercise Association are examples of societal corporatism. The Private Enterprise Association and the Overseas Chinese Association are examples of state corporatism. The latter deal with the hard issues of production and ideological matters. In part this is a legacy of state domination under Mao. But state corporatism is also viewed as a system of power relations that characterizes East Asian developmental states. Viewed from an "Asian" perspective, China's state corporatism bears similarities to the developmental states of Japan, Taiwan, and Korea when they were in the midst of rapid economic growth. Unger and Chan (1995: 33) have summarized the main features of what they call "the East Asian model of state corporatism":

> The East Asian states have shared a cultural bias favorable to corporatist structures. In the Confucianist teachings that pervaded all of the East Asian cultures, giving primacy to private interests had been viewed as equivalent to selfishness. The greater good was ideally manifested in a consensus overseen by the moral authority of the leadership, reflected in a moralistic father-knows-best paternalism.

It is tempting to argue that state corporatism is the natural pathway for Asian developmental states, based on the examples of first Japan, then Korea and Taiwan, and now China. Asian political cultures may indeed be more authoritarian and less concerned with individual needs and rights. State corporatism may be the preferred space between state and society, rather than conventional Western civil society. In China, "citizenship," "governance," and "political development" are more at the mercy of the state than in the West at a comparable period of economic growth. A double legacy of authoritarianism (Leninist and Confucian) may be more than civil society (in the Western sense) can bear. Still, while corporatist structures led by the state may be the present norm in China, societal corporatism is increasing at the grassroots. Andrew Walder writes of "local corporatism," wherein state and nonstate merge at the lower levels of production and management (1993: 311–15). We would be wise not to ignore the slow progress of more conventional civil society on the margins, expressed in nagging reminders of the potential for dissent; the slow drip, drip, drip of legal reform and electoral change; and the leakage from abroad of images and information about developmental alternatives. These are not antidotes to what is clearly an authoritarian developmental experience, but they are complements to the current mainstream of Chinese political development. What we see in China today are two types of emerging civil society, what might be called "dual civil societies," and it is state-led civil society that predominates.

Civil Society in China: Four Instances

I have argued that the identification and study of civil society in China is a recent phenomenon, inspired primarily by events in Eastern Europe and by the political consequences of Tiananmen. Evidence of the emergence of Chinese civil society is still sparse. We are dealing with a little more than a decade's experience. Yet such has been the pace of change in China, and such has been our thirst to document these changes, that we already have a number of case studies focused on civil society. This section of the chapter looks at four examples: a national NGO; social organizations in Xiaoshan city; village elections; and business associations in Xiamen. These four focus on "state-led" civil society, especially with respect to the growth of urban social organizations and business associations; however, the examples of NGOs and local elections remind us of the hesitant emergence of the other, more conventional (Western) forms of civil society.

"Project Hope" (*Xiwang gongcheng*), an NGO, was set up in 1989 by the China Youth Development Foundation (CYDF), which itself had been established only six months earlier by the All-China Youth Federation. The Project's purpose is to raise money to educate children in the poorest areas of China. It solicits funds from Chinese citizens and from abroad. As of mid-1993, it had established sixty-two primary schools and provided assistance to over 300,000 school dropouts. The Project serves an urgent need that the Chinese state seems unable or unwilling to meet: upgrading the very low level of rural education. Its nominal parent organization, CYDF, is controlled by one of China's oldest Communist Party front organizations, the All-China Youth Federation. The relationship among these three organizations is opaque. As a recent Western account observed, "It is unclear whether the CYDF has any authority over the distribution of funds and donations among the provinces and whether it can supervise the use of these funds when they are transferred to official organs" (*China News Analysis*, no. 1495, 15 October 1993). The National Committee on U.S.–China Relations questions "the lack of transparency in both organizational structure and accounting procedures (which) inhibits foreign cooperation and indigenous fundraising in China" (1994: 13).

The example of Project Hope tells us a number of things. First, the Chinese state has set up a number of NGOs to organize and direct private funding in areas of urgent economic need. A Chinese source notes that "China remains a poor developing nation. As a result, the government's financial capacity is limited. Therefore, various social groups and individuals have begun to provide notable charitable assistance to the poor and needy" (*Beijing Review*, 25–31 March 1996). As the state withdraws in favor of the market, Chinese authorities hope that private sources can take over. Second, these efforts, while ostensibly under the control of autonomous organizations, are monitored by a state parent tied to the old structure of power. This is a case of dual civil societies, a mix of state-led and conventional civil society, on the boundary between state and societal corporatism. Third, much of this NGO's activities remain confined within the orbit of secrecy that characterized the old way of management. These old habits predating the Communist regime are difficult to shed. Finally, there is no evidence linking this NGO to any group that is distancing itself from the state and manifesting any attributes of a budding civil society. It is probably too soon to make judgments about the success or failure of this NGO, based on the sparse reports of these visitors. A 1996 Chinese report on the China Charity Federation (CCF) provides a more glowing evaluation of NGO activity, pointing out that substantial numbers of citizens as well as influential foreigners, who are contributing funds, are actively involved in the CCF's work. The CCF "operates solely on interest income earned from its founding fund. No donations are used for administrative costs" (*Beijing Review*, 25–31 March 1996).

A second study looks at the proliferation of urban social organizations in Xiaoshan, a city of over a million inhabitants located in Zhejiang province. Xiaoshan is a new commercial center "on the make" in one of China's most productive areas (White 1993: 63–68). According to White, who visited the city several times in the early 1990s, "there appears to have been a flowering of associational life" in Xiaoshan during the Republican period. After 1949, the usual Communist-led organizations were formed, replacing these associations and functioning as transmission belts between the party-state and the population. In the post-Mao era, especially from the mid-1980s, the number of associations proliferated, "reaching a high point in 1988–89 and then declining drastically in 1990." There were ninety-nine social organizations in Xiaoshan in 1990. Their growth is attributed mainly to the economic reforms that opened up space for such organizations. Within the various categories of social organizations currently functioning in the city are the old-line "mass organizations" still serving as transmission belts for the party-state; newer organizations which have been brought by the leadership into the state-corporatist web, such as the Private Enterprise Association, which has a membership that is gaining economic strength in the community; and a number of "popular" (*minjian*) or "people-run" (*minban*) organizations, mainly in the fields of culture, education, sports, health, and religion.

Social organizations can be classified in terms of their relative autonomy from the party-state. White divides them into "official" (*guanban*), "semiofficial" (*banguan*), and "popular" (*minjiaxing*). The six official organizations such as the Communist Youth League and the Trade Union Federation have special links to the Party. The semiofficial organizations are primarily economic and technical in nature and constitute two thirds of the social organizations. These social organizations must be approved by a state agency in their sphere of operation. A social organization must be formally affiliated to a state organ or parent. Positions in a semiofficial organization are often staffed by persons who hold positions in the affiliated state organ in charge of that social organization. The more important an organization is perceived to be, the stronger the state control. The two types of organizations, state and social, "act as complementary parts of an evolving new network of management."

What does the example of Xiaoshan tell us about civil society? First, while organizations have proliferated, they are still directed by the state, to varying degrees. They function as intermediaries and possess limited autonomy, but they are not independent and offer no challenge to the state. Second, new relationships and networks are constantly evolving, and state and social organizations are working out new divisions of labor. One can hypothesize that in this process the social organizations will acquire more, rather than less, autonomy over time. Third, there is little evidence to support the emergence of Western civil society in the conventional Western sense. White observes that "one can detect only embryonic elements of anything that could be described as 'civil society.'" This is attributed to the state's having retained its dominant position in the economy. The distinguishing feature of organizational life in Xiaoshan is state corporatism and state-led civil society.[4]

Village elections represent a third case, one that looks at rural manifestations of civil society. Since the dismantling of the communes and the production brigades, which were the key units for managing village life, grassroots political institutions have been in flux. In late 1987, a trial Organic Law was passed by the National People's Congress to enlarge village autonomy and provide increased opportunities for political participation. The law was not designed to dismantle the state at the village level. Indeed, a strong state presence was deemed crucial to stop parochialism and the growth of "independent kingdoms." A study by Kevin O'Brien looks at the initial results of these measures, principally in Fujian province, in three areas: the holding of direct, semi-competitive elections, the creation of "villagers' representative assemblies" (*cunmin daibiao huiyi*), and the promulgation of "village charters" (*zhangcheng*) and "codes of conduct" (*cungui minyue*) (1994: 33–60).

By mid-1992, 80 percent of the villages had completed at least two rounds of elections, and villagers' representative assemblies existed in almost every village. While the new law encouraged electoral competition, often this did not happen, and leaders continued to be selected by local Party committees instead of by villagers. In poorer areas, there is less likelihood of democratic outcomes. While the percentage of non-Party members on village committees has increased, the key decisions, for the most part, continue to be made by the Party. Anne Thurston notes that, without the support of higher level leaders, the process will not work. As she points out, "There is no alternative to the Communist Party in the countryside" (Thurston 1995: 3).

O'Brien identifies four types of villages: up-to-standard, authoritarian, paralyzed, and runaway. In terms of successful implementation of these reforms, only a minority of villages have, as yet, attained up-to-standard status. Most remain authoritarian in that they prefer not to challenge existing authority patterns. Paralyzed villages are generally remote and backward, and have done little to implement the reforms. Runaway villages are those where village populist leaders have taken control and seek to gain maximum autonomy from the state. Party authorities worry about runaway villages, because they usually mean runaway cadres and weak Party organizations.

The rural sector comprises 75 percent of China's population. Political reform in the villages is a daunting task, not just because there are many peasants, but because their level of political development is low. It is encouraging that some villages have elected their own leaders, and observers note glimmers of change taking place. But this is not favorable terrain for the growth of civil society. The authoritarian cast of China's countryside is a tremendous burden. The contrast with the city reminds us that civil society has been an urban elite concept for most of its existence. Only in highly integrated societies can we think of a civil society wherein "the masses" play a central role. The Tiananmen crisis and its aftermath revealed that, if there is to be an emergent Chinese civil society, it will be found in the cities and not in the rural areas. Finally, some might question whether elections are part of civil society or whether this activity belongs more properly in the realm of the state, or of politics. My view is that, in the absence of multiparty politics and without a tradition of political opposition, village elections are mobilizing devices, exercises in the development of citizenship (and civility), a political green field site in which civil society and the political sphere can emerge in tandem.[5]

The fourth example focuses on business associations in Xiamen city, Fujian province. Xiamen has a population of 600,000, and it is one of China's five Special Economic Zones. It is a boom city and has strong ties with Taiwan across the Straits. According to David Wank, in 1988 Xiamen had 15,000 small private shops, mostly market stalls and family run stores, and 621 private trading firms. In 1988 the Xiamen City Chamber of Commerce (*Xiamen shi shanghui*) set up the Xiamen Civic Association of Private Industry and Commerce (*Xiamen shi siyang gong shang gonghui*) (1995: 55–74). This association sought to lobby the government on behalf of entrepreneurs' interests. Members wanted reduced taxes for all entrepreneurs and also lobbied on behalf of individual companies. The association ran afoul of the state Bureau of Industry and Commerce. The Bureau "saw the Civic Association as a challenge to (its) regulatory authority." It "moved to suppress the Civic Association, harassing its members by summoning them to meetings at short notice, raising their licencing fees, and warning non-members against joining." In 1990, the bureau set up its own private business association, headed by an exceptionally able and well-connected businessman.

Shortly thereafter, the Xiamen Civic Association was shut down by the state. Most of its members dissociated themselves from its demise. Wank had expected that Xiamen entrepreneurs would have a stronger self-interest as a group. He had hypothesized, based on the experience of East European marketization, that "entrepreneurs would seek alliances with other entrepreneurs, thereby enhancing their collective representation as a political interest group." He found this was not the case. In addition, he hypothesized that "entrepreneurs seek alliances with other subordinated social groups, thereby enhancing the collective capacity of civil society vis à vis the state." This, too, he found was not the case. Possible explanations include the following: that the Chinese traditionally have viewed interest-based associations as inherently selfish, that the entrepreneurs had a low level of political consciousness, and that the state was too strong and could always exercise its will if it chose to do so. But Wank found a better explanation: that there was no one "group" of entrepreneurs. These businessmen had different interests, depending on their social background, the size of their business, and relationship to the bureaucracy. Each entrepreneur dealt with the bureaucracy in his own way. Some sought to avoid contact with the state as much as possible. Others established patron-client relations with the bureaucracy to advance their own interests. Wank's conclusion is that this is a group caught in transition between a market and a command economy, for whom individual as opposed to group decisions or alliances are the norm.

Xiamen's experience raises a number of important points. First, it may be that entrepreneurs are too busy pursuing their economic interests to develop a sense of group identity. Second, the state has the power to limit the entrepreneur's activities, and the latter have no intention of challenging that power. Third, entrepreneurs cultivate or ignore the bureaucracy on their own terms when they deem it necessary. They see their relations with the state as instances of individual bargaining. Fourth, the state at the local level develops alliances with entrepreneurs to pursue its interests. This point has been forcefully made in a recent study by Christopher Earle Nevitt (1996: 25–43). The Xiamen Bureau of Industry and Commerce sponsored its own Association of Enterpreneurs in good part to "get a piece of the action" for itself. Finally, entrepreneurs are not advocates for civil society and prefer, for the most part, to be left alone. The Xiamen businessmen did not support the 1989 student movement. They felt that the students wanted too much too quickly. In the words of one entrepreneur, "We must go slowly, generation by generation. A country's stability is connected with order. Only by having normal order can people lead a normal life." When Xiamen entrepreneurs had a choice, they opted for the security of state-led civil society, rather than choosing to participate in a less authoritarian alternative.

Conclusion

The foregoing discussion of civil society (in terms of parallel polis, citizenship, political development, and governance) has shown that, in the Western literature, the concept has inspired a wide range of interpretations. These range from Greek ideas of citizenship, to the restructuring of state-society relations associated with the capitalist era, to the successful counterposition of civil society against communist regimes in the past decade. Throughout this discussion, it has been apparent that "civil society," as it is generally understood, is grounded in Western ideology and values. Most writing and thinking on the subject assumes a close linkage between civil society and democracy: the more developed a civil society, the more likely that it will become democratic. Western criticism of this linkage is generally confined to Marxists who argue that civil society is antidemocratic by virtue of its being part of the hegemony of the ruling capitalist class. Between these views is a functionalist perspective that sees civil society as a necessary linking mechanism between all states and societies, democratic or not, capitalist or not. This view opens a space for those who want to accommodate past and present China. It provides a modicum of justification for those who believe civil society was present in imperial China. It can explain the emergence of civil society under the aegis of the state in the form of state-led civil society. It also reinforces the concept of an Asian state-society linkage, Asian communitarianism, that departs, at least in the foreseeable future, from Western/democractic pathways.

Second, what I have identified as state-led civil society takes into account Chinese historical and cultural legacies and can be seen as easing the transition from totalitarianism. At this time Chinese are too absorbed in their economic lives to engage in the construction of an alternate polis. Unlike Eastern Europe, where disaffected intellectuals were willing to confront the state, Chinese intellectuals for the most part lack the desire to declare their independence from the establishment that has nurtured them.[6] Dissent and overt intellectual opposition have played a small role in the emergence of Chinese civil society. This does not mean that conventional Western expressions of civil society, such as increased local autonomy, development of an urban capitalist class, occasional outbursts of spontaneous group activity, the seepage from abroad of Western values, and segmentation and the growth of individual interests, are not present. Both types of civil society exist. But they do not represent a particular threat to the Chinese state. They do, however, represent an emerging infrastructure: a set of thickening linkages between state and society that can bring more autonomy and independence in the future, if not democractic processes and institutions.

Finally, these examples reveal growing activity by social organizations, particularly at the local level. Nationwide rural elections have been held with uncertain results. Nongovernmental organizations have emerged and are tasked with taking over for the state in certain parts of the rapidly diminishing social net, but their present role is still circumscribed. Urban business associations show some potential for shaping autonomy but little for actually achieving it.[7] These activities convey a mixed picture of possibilities and transitions rather than of systemic changes. We see a transformation in process, but it is difficult to visualize its path and velocity. In the short term, the state has the capacity to muffle or harness any concerted pressures for autonomy, and it is fair to say that no one has the capacity or the will to challenge that state by means of conventional forms of civil society. In the long term, this social formation could change, with a restructuring of state-society relations and the appearance of an effectively functioning civil society. For the present, however, expectations of the imminent emergence of Chinese civil society in the Western sense are premature if not misleading.

3

States, Societies, and Civil Societies in Chinese History

Roger V. Des Forges

> Every society . . . is continuously in change. . . . A conception of society should . . . contain within itself an explicit acknowledgment of the determinants of change. It should also offer guidance to the varieties of change and their major sequences (Shils 1975: 25, 33).

This chapter attempts to take the idea of civil society out of its modern Western context and place it in the larger context of Chinese history, and to relate Chinese perspectives on "civil society" to the conditions of the contemporary world. Three arguments are made: that antecedents of civil society are embedded in the states and societies of early Chinese history; that ideas of civil society live on consciously, or more often unconsciously, in the minds of Chinese today; and that the Chinese have long appreciated the values of moral community and public welfare, which are valuable complements to current Western ideals of liberal democracy and private enterprise.

Three Types of Civil Society

> To the extent that the moral dimension of civil society is crucial, the associations of civil society are not just interest groups, but communities. And communities are historically constituted, they are "communities of memory." The process of interpreting common symbols—asking what they mean for people today, arguing about them, putting them into new words, portraying them in imagery and performance—creates moral communities (Madsen 1993: 192–93).

The current popularity of the term civil society to explain recent changes in Eastern Europe, the Soviet Union, and the People's Republic of China (PRC) can be traced back to the late 1970s. Revived by Eastern European dissidents such as Vaclav Havel, George Konrad, and Adam Michnik, civil society was gingerly embraced by Chinese reformers both inside and outside the Communist Party as early as 1986 (Ma 1994: 180–85). In 1989, imbued with notions of democratic politics and civil society, Chinese demonstrated against Communist Party leadership, Eastern Europeans and Russians overthrew Leninist states, and American observers embraced a theory of the public sphere available through the timely English translation of Jürgen Habermas (1989). The relative failure of the movement in China compared with its success in Europe, together with Habermas' interpretation, fostered the impression that civil society and the public sphere were largely, if not entirely, products of the European Enlightenment and Western capitalism. Even Thomas Metzger, an American historian of China who has emphasized the dynamism of Chinese culture, could refer without fear of contradiction to "this purely Western concept of the civil society" (Metzger 1994: 1).[1]

Most observers associate civil society and the public sphere not just with the West but with the *modern* West.[2] Historians of China who describe the widening of the public sphere and the development of civil society in the Qing dynasty (1644–1911) and Republican times are quick to assert that these phenomena remained linked to what they call "traditional" forms of state-society relations and were thus fragile in comparison with European analogues under capitalism (Schoppa 1982; Rankin 1986; Rowe 1984, 1989; Strand 1989, 1990, 1993). The assumption that modern Europe produced the norms of civil society and the public sphere has led other historians of China to question whether these phenomena existed in China, since ostensibly similar Chinese practices actually diverged considerably from the Western model (Huang 1991, 1993; Wakeman 1993). One response has been to argue that a public sphere developed in China as early as the latter part of the Ming dynasty (1368–1644), although it was different from the public sphere in the West. Similarly, it has been argued that some characteristics of civil society emerged in the Qing dynasty, although, a "full" civil society never appeared and would have been quite different from civil society in the West if it had (Rankin 1993). Another response to doubts about the applicability of the concept of civil society to China has been to question whether historians should even try to find analogues to Western phenomena in Chinese history, but then to insist that the Chinese notion of "public" (*gong*) became "unprecedentedly energized in the late Qing." In this view, even though "there was no discursive counterpart in imperial China for civil society," one can find many signs of commercial capitalism, public management, civil law, publishing for profit, and even autonomous organizations from the late Ming on (Rowe 1993). The notion that the Ming-Qing transition in the seventeenth century was an important watershed in the development of a realm of local elite activism akin to the public sphere in late imperial China has been suggested in Timothy Brook's (1993a) recent study of late-Ming Buddhist patronage.[3] Brook nonetheless finds similar developments centuries earlier in the Southern Song, and concludes that a "gentry society"—not a civil society as defined within the Western intellectual tradition—persisted into the eighteenth and nineteenth centuries.

Whether or not civil society was exclusive to the modern West, it is clear that Europeans since the seventeenth century have defined it in different ways and have emphasized varying characteristics (Chamberlain 1993). The exile scholar Wang Shaoguang (1992) has singled out three important conceptions of civil society and has associated them with different Chinese translations of the term. I shall draw on his discussion and in the process suggest that these types had antecedents associated with different kinds of states and societies in Chinese history. These distinctions are summarized in Table 3.1.

The first of these three Chinese types of civil society arises in Europe from social contract theory or what R. P. Peerenboom (1993: 37–38) has called the "fable of the ascent of humans from a brutal and savage state of nature to the civilized wonder of a social life where each person's autonomy and dignity is safeguarded by a strong theory of rights."[4] Although prominent seventeenth- and eighteenth-century Europeans entertained different conceptions of the ideal state—Hobbes favored autocracy, Locke minimalism, and Rousseau majoritarianism—they agreed that life under a human state was preferable to life in a state of nature. From the perspective of Wang Shaoguang and many other Chinese, civility in this society resulted largely from the existence of a state. This form of civil society can be best translated into Chinese as *wenming shehui* (civilized or enlightened society). For Lawrence Sullivan and some other Western students of contemporary

Table 3.1

Types of Civil Society in Chinese History (after Wang Shaoguang 1992)

Chinese terms	English translations	Century concept was formulated in Europe	Eras in China of which it was characteristic
wenming shehui	Civilized/ enlightened society	Seventeenth–eighteenth	Zhou, Tang, Qing
shimin shehui	City people's society	Nineteenth	Warring States Southern Song, Republic
gongmin shehui	Public people's society	Twentieth	Han, Ming, People's Republic

Chinese society, however, contract theory in general and Rousseau's general will in particular envisioned a civil society that was organized in opposition to the state (Sullivan 1990).[5]

How is it that a Chinese analyst can interpret Western contract theory as an affirmation of the importance of the state in creating civil society, whereas a Western observer sees the same theory as a rationale for a civil society independent of the state? One answer is that the Chinese developed a durable conception of contract nearly three millennia before Europeans did and created an equally persistent myth of the state as a bulwark of civilization against barbarism. The case in point was the transition from the Shang state (ca. 1750 to 1100 B.C.E.) to the Zhou (ca. 1100 to 256 B.C.E.), when a frontier people invoked the mandate of "heaven and nature" (*tianming*) to carry out China's first "revolution" (*geming)* against an allegedly tyrannical state based in the central plain (*zhongyuan*, a synecdoche for China). Although the Zhou people had originally been considered barbarians by the Shang, they used a combination of "civility" and "martiality" (*wen* and *wu*) to claim the mandate to rule all under "heaven" (*tianxia*) (Creel 1970). Under the Duke of Zhou, the new state overcame opposition and governed a realm larger than today's France through a well-articulated patrimonial, feudal, and bureaucratic system (Hsu and Linduff 1989). The Zhou governed effectively for several hundred years and weathered attacks from other frontier peoples before gradually disintegrating. The dynasty won the praise of Confucius and became a model of statecraft for later generations (Hall and Ames 1987).

If civil society in its eighteenth-century European sense was anticipated in some ways by this ancient Chinese state, what of civil society in its nineteenth-century European guise? Here we encounter a rather different concept of civil society espoused by such thinkers as Hegel, Tocqueville, and Marx. They agreed with Adam Smith that the market was the prime generator of the civil society, which arose between society and the state and was in creative tension with both. This civil society was protected by a constitutional order, supported by autonomous organizations, and divided among national states. For Hegel and Marx, it was a transitional historical stage between one form of society and another. Western scholars have distinguished sharply among these thinkers, associating Hegel with a transcendent state devoted to the public good that would eventually merge with civil society; Tocqueville with individual liberties and voluntary associations that guarded against the tyranny of the majority; and Marx with a proletarian class that would eventually replace the bourgeoisie and witness the withering away of the state. Chinese, however, regard all three as emphasizing the legitimacy of the individual pursuit of profit in a commercial economy, the sanctity of private property and corporate independence, and the fundamental opposition between civil society and the state. Like Herbert Spencer and John Stuart Mill, they all embraced a form of civil society that put the commercial class (or bourgeoisie) in command. This form is implicit in the Chinese translation of civil society as *shimin shehui* ("city people's society") (Wang 1992: 6–12).

Although this kind of civil society seemed new to nineteenth-century Europeans, aspects of it had appeared in China as early as the Spring and Autumn and Warring States periods (722–221 B.C.E.).[6] During this age, the Chinese central state gave way to autonomous principalities that eliminated one another through warfare until they were reduced to a handful of powers vying for dominance (Lewis 1990). Life may have been hard, but this was also a time of cultural creativity, intellectual debate, social mobility, economic growth, and technological innovation. New commercial towns sprang up, merchants gained wealth and status, and society became increasingly autonomous vis-à-vis the state (Hsu 1965). Though one does not want to push the analogy between Warring States China and nineteenth-century Europe too far (the contexts and outcomes were quite different), China in this period was probably closer to a characteristic European-style society than it would be in the nineteenth century when it came into intimate contact with the West.[7] This period gave birth to such schools of thought as Mohism, which emphasized a kind of utilitarianism; Daoism, which stressed a form of individual freedom; and Legalism, which advocated the rule of law. These schools anticipated the concerns of nineteenth-century Europeans even though they conceptualized the issues quite differently (Schwartz 1985; Munro 1985).

If the dominant nineteenth-century European conception of civil society had some antecedents in China's early Spring and Autumn and Warring States periods, did the twentieth-century Western concept of civil society have parallels in Chinese history? This construct is an even more ideal type than the preceding two, since it includes a greater variety of competing ideas and has broader origins and applications. It holds that a civil society emphasizes self-development as well as self-interest, and the good of the community as well as the good of individuals. It posits that individual liberty must be accompanied by social equality, and political democracy by economic justice. The political process must include the popular masses; the resulting state must provide for public welfare; and nongovernmental organizations should restrain national governments, multinational corporations, and even international bodies. In short, this form of civil society is oriented toward social, economic, and global democracy.[8] By combining values from many times and places, and emphasizing public goods over private, it can usefully be associated with the now standard Chinese translation of civil society as *gongmin shehui* ("public people's society") (Wang 1992: 15–22).

The *gongmin shehui* ideal type of civil society has not yet been fully realized anywhere in the world, nor is it likely to appear in the near future. Wang Shaoguang refrains from advocating this third form of civil society and opts instead for the second form (*shimin shehui*). He argues that *gongmin shehui* will not produce the ideal societies posited by Confucianism and Buddhism, just as such a vision of civil society is likely to be dismissed in the West as utopian (Metzger 1994; Ignatieff 1995).[9] Nonetheless, some of the ideas associated with *gongmin shehui*, such as the Confucian "all under heaven as public" (*tianxia weigong*) and the Buddhist "pure land,"(*jingtu*) have been realized in Chinese history. As early as the Han dynasty (206 B.C.E.–220 C.E.), the Chinese constructed a polity which arguably included elements of this ideal type. The founder of the Han overthrew the extant Qin state (255–202 B.C.E.), which had attempted to rule China through excessive centralization and heavy requisitions. The Han modified the centralized system it inherited, returning some authority to a political nobility and recruiting men of merit to administer the realm on behalf of the masses (Ch'ü 1972). The Han did adopt the Qin goals of wealth and power and used military force to extend imperial frontiers in all directions, including parts of what later became the autonomous (and finally independent) states of Korea and Vietnam (Yü 1967). They ruled with sufficient skill and paid enough attention to common interests that the dynasty survived a brief interregnum under Wang Mang and lasted another two centuries. Whatever its defects, the Han acquired such charisma in the eyes of the Chinese people that its name was appropriated by the Chinese majority to distinguish themselves as *Han ren* from minorities within and foreigners without.[10] The Chinese writing system was standardized in this period and has ever since been called "Han script" (*Han wen*). Other significant elements of Chinese culture, from cosmology and urban design to rituals and agricultural technology, were regularized in the Han, confirming the polity's importance as a source of Chinese conceptions of civic order and cultural identity (Hsü 1980; Wang 1982; Henderson 1984; Ci 1994).

Three Types of Civil Society through Chinese History

Chinese polities adumbrating modern Western conceptions of civil society now popular among some Chinese intellectuals might have remained mere historical curiosities had they not spawned sequels extending to the present day. The Zhou state, idealized by Confucius, became a model for many subsequent states, especially the Tang (618–906). The second Tang ruler, Taizong, invoked the example of the Duke of Zhou to explain why he had killed his allegedly less capable and rebellious brothers and assumed the throne, thus bringing "security to the state and benefit to the people" (Weschler 1974: 24). Taizong's reign subsequently became the epitome of good government not only among Chinese, but among Koreans, Vietnamese, and Japanese. Another Tang ruler, Wu Zetian, rose from concubine to empress and declared her own Zhou dynasty, which adopted the calendar, rituals and architecture of that earlier state (Guisso 1979: 304). Empress Wu was an authoritarian but capable ruler who expanded the examination system to recruit more broadly and "who gave attention to women's religious status, welfare, education, and access to public office" (Wu Qingyun 1995: 8). The Zhou provided minatory as well as positive models for the Tang. For example, one Tang official warned the Tang ruler, Xuanzong, not to repeat the excessive refinement of the Zhou ruler Kang. Another Tang official invoked a late-Zhou exemplar to justify retiring from government to collect popular songs, viewed as voices of the people (McMullen 1973: 323, 328–29, 333). In the late Tang, regional governments "consciously posed as equivalents to Zhou feudal kingdoms that had owed no more than symbolic subservience to the Son of Heaven" (Peterson 1979: 505). In this period, the Zhou model was reportedly not just emulated but surpassed. A late-Tang official compared the Xianzong restoration favorably with previous ones, including that of the Zhou (Peterson 1979: 538).

A millennium later, Qing rulers and officials invoked both Zhou and Tang models to legitimate their authority and advance their policies. The first Qing ruler to govern from inside the wall, the Prince Regent Dorgon, reportedly aspired to live up to that model regent, the Duke of Zhou (Oxnam 1970: 44). When the Shunzhi emperor's beloved wife died, he was admonished by an official not to follow the bad example of Tang Taizong who allegedly spent too much time visiting the grave of his deceased consort (Weschler 1974: 198–99). On the other hand, Shunzhi's son, Xuanye, better known by his reign name, Kangxi, claimed to follow the example of Tang Taizong in dealing humanely with his officials (Spence 1974: 88). Kangxi in turn was praised by the Jesuits as one of the most enlightened monarchs in world history, and the civil tone of his reign helped to inspire the European Enlightenment (Adshead 1988: 243–44). His successor, Yongzheng, cited the Zhou model to explain how a frontier people like the Manchus could become civilized and thus earn the authority to manage society (Huang 1974:219). Yongzheng's son, Qianlong, frequently "turned back to the high years of the Tang and its archetypal dynastic accomplishments as if the very act of reading its record would enhance his own with some of the heroic qualities of that remote age" (Kahn 1971: 128).[11] In the 1860s, statesmen of the Tongzhi restoration recalled how the Zhou had allied with one frontier minority to suppress another and how the Tang had used the Uighurs to pacify the rebellion of An Lushan. Qing officials invoked those precedents to justify their policies of setting various Western powers against one another and using Westerners to suppress the Taiping rebellion (Wright 1957: 45–50).

Critics of the Qing also invoked elements of Zhou and Tang civil society in an effort to reform the system. Utilitarian thinkers such as Yan Yuan called for a restoration of the Zhou systems of decentralized administration and shared "public/private landholding" (*jingtian*) to replace the extant centralized bureaucracy based on private landholding. Ming loyalists such as Gu Yanwu and Huang Zongxi believed that the decentralized administration and public/private land system of the Zhou could no longer be revived in their entirety, but they called for restoration of the Tang system of central officials assisted by local appointees together with the Tang "equal-field system" (*juntian*) to complement the regular bureaucracy and "make the world more public" (*gong tianxia*). They recommended such changes as abolishing provincial-level governorships, allowing magistrates to serve in their hometowns, and turning schools into political as well as educational institutions for local literati. Opponents of such reforms, including such unlikely political bedfellows as the radical Ming loyalist Wang Fuzhi and the strict Qing ruler Yongzheng, went back to an alternative Tang tradition associated with the thinker Liu Zongyuan (Chen 1992: 95–96). Liu had held that the commandery-county (*junxian*) system was superior to the feudal (*fengjian*) system in selecting talent, benefiting the people, and defending the realm. This perspective won out and eighteenth-century proposals that sub-county officials be selected from among the local gentry were turned down (Min 1989: 89–102). Scholar-officials closer to the Qing political establishment also invoked models from the Zhou and Tang. The philosopher Dai Zhen clearly identified with the late-Zhou thinker Mencius; the poet Yuan Mei admired the Tang master Bo Juyi; the historian Zhang Xuecheng compared himself with the Tang historiographer Liu Zhiji; and the novelist Li Ruzhen satirized mid-Qing patriarchy with stories placed in the time of Empress Wu Zetian.[12]

The Spring and Autumn and Warring States periods, the classical locus of our second kind of civil society (*shimin shehui*), was less structured and coherent and never became such a positive model for later generations. Nonetheless, many features of that period reappeared in later times, transmitting certain models of how to behave in the time of cultural change and political disorder following the Tang. Although the Song dynasty, named after a regional state that had flourished in the Spring and Autumn and Warring States periods, achieved what has sometimes been called a "minor reunification," it failed to restore the far-flung frontiers of the Tang or to eliminate frontier states, such as the Liao and Jin, that competed for the mandate to rule the world (Rossabi 1993). It was under these conditions that the Song, like the Warring States, built up its wealth and power, increased the size of its bureaucracy and army, developed new industries and technologies, and carried out political and social reforms in an effort to strengthen itself and overcome its rivals (Liu 1959; Haeger 1975). In the end, like its earlier namesake, the Song was unsuccessful in this endeavor. But in its strengths as well as in its weaknesses it provided the context for political, social, and economic changes that are sometimes said to have resulted in the world's first modern society.[13]

To whatever degree the Song was "modern," it experienced a flowering of intellectual life that approximated the Hundred Schools of the Spring and Autumn and Warring States periods. Some of the Song thinkers were aware of the parallels between their age and that earlier one. The historian Ouyang Xiu, for example, wrote a history of the Five Dynasties period modeled on the *Spring and Autumn Annals* thought to have been edited by Confucius (Liu 1967). Scholar-officials invoked precedents from the Warring States period to explain their service to more than one government during the Song period (Liu 1988: 61). The philosopher Zhu Xi, among others, revived the tradition of private teaching and personal transmission of the Way initiated by Confucius and continued by Mencius (Ebrey and Gregory 1993). Attempting to recover the original Confucian vision, the Southern Song Confucians rejected Daoism and Buddhism as analogues to the heterodoxies of Mo Zi and Yang Zhu in the time of Confucius (Tillman 1992: 28). Suggesting the pervasiveness of this concept of historical recurrence as well as cultural continuity (which of course did not preclude innovation or even progress), the utilitarian thinker Chen Liang criticized Zhu Xi for failing to "wash clean" the Tang—as Confucius had idealized the Zhou—to serve as an effective model for Song times (Tillman 1982: 80).

With the fall of the Qing early in the twentieth century, China entered another period of cultural crisis and political disorder. Once again a variety of politico-military leaders (known by their critics as "warlords") failed to establish an effective central government in northern China. It was left to Guomindang forces to lead a Northern Expedition in 1926–1928 and impose another minor reunification, although large parts of China remained in the hands of militarists (Shanxi), declared autonomy from the center (Tibet), fell under the control of neighboring powers (Manchuria), or became independent (Mongolia). These conditions once again led Chinese to rethink their culture, strengthen their state, reform their society, and develop their economy.

Local gentry of the late Qing such as Sun Yiyan and Yan Chen turned to the Spring and Autumn period for models of "locally based social stability as the foundation of national order and unity, and . . . talented men moving upward from local societies to govern the country" (Rankin 1986: 124). Kang Youwei and Liang Qichao tried to reinterpret Confucianism to assume the roles of sages in a newly expanded, now global, world (Hsiao 1975). Republican-period dissidents, Guo Moruo and Wen Yiduo, identified with the Warring States' hero Qu Yuan, who was said to have spoken for the people against a corrupt state (Schneider 1980). Jiang Jieshi (Chiang Kai-shek) drew on models from the Warring States and the Song in devising his New Life Movement (Thomson 1969: 157–58, 173). One of Jiang's critics clearly identified himself with Su Dongpo, the literary giant of the Northern Song who opposed the reforms of Wang Anshi (Liu 1947). Republican historians such as Chen Yinque and Gu Jiegang were inspired by Song resistance to the frontier states of Liao and Jin and called for a strong defense against Japan (Yu 1970: 67; Schneider 1971: 280). Japan for its part followed the example of the Liao and Jin, which had claimed authority from the Tang, by justifying its rule in Manchuria as a continuation of the Qing (Chan 1984: 134–35).

Each of these three periods of cultural crisis and political disunity, accompanied by aspects of our second form of civil society, came to an end in a highly centralized and expansionist order that Chinese have on balance regarded as uncivil if not uncivilized.[14] The Warring States period was brought to an end by the triumph of its most authoritarian regional state, the Qin, in the third century B.C.E.. Using aggressive military force to overcome all opposition, that state's founder, known as Qin Shihuang ("First Emperor"), not only reunified the Chinese culture area after a long period of disunion, but also imposed a political system of centralized administration under an autocratic ruler. The Qin also overreached itself in suppressing unorthodox learning, establishing a royal line that presumed it would last forever, and demanding excessive labor services on public projects (Sima 1993). It governed all of China for only one generation before being overthrown in popular uprisings. With some important exceptions, the Qin was criticized in the historical record as "authoritarian" (*zhuanzhi*) or even tyrannical. Although the West knew China by a name derived from Qin, the Chinese preferred to name their polity "the central state(s)" (*zhongguo*), a more flexible image than that provided by the Qin or any other single dynasty.[15]

Like the Qin, the Mongol dynasty called Yuan reunified the entire Chinese realm for the first time since the Tang, extending the frontiers of China and, within those frontiers, exerting an unprecedented degree of control (Allsen 1987; Rossabi 1988; Endicott-West 1989). Whatever the tendency of twentieth-century Chinese and Western scholars to regard the Yuan as a "conquest" dynasty resistant to acculturation into China, the parallel between the Qin and the Yuan was recognized by contemporaries as well as by later observers. One official of the Southern Song opposed any negotiations with the Mongols, saying that they were bent on swallowing all other states just as the Qin had done (Peterson 1975: 221). Once the Yuan was in place, other scholars recognized its similarity to the Qin even while differing over the significance of the parallel. A leading Confucian scholar rationalized his acceptance of the Yuan with the assurance that the classical tradition would survive the Yuan just as it had the Qin (Lao 1981: 124–25). Indeed, since the Mongols lacked a complete and formal written code, Confucian literati found themselves in the odd position of counseling Yuan monarchs to follow the Qin tradition of relying on laws (Langlois 1981: 172, 175, 180; 1982: 100, 109, 119). Yet the Qin remained a flawed embodiment of the model. When one Yuan crown prince asked about Qin Shihuang, his tutor replied that he had been "cruel." He urged the prince to follow other models, including those of the Tang (Franke 1982: 165, 182). A Confucian scholar who refused to serve the Yuan expressed his hatred for both Qin and Yuan by writing a poem commemorating one of his townsmen who had tried to assassinate Qin Shihuang (Tu 1982: 255). If the Yuan commanded some respect for having restored China to its accustomed position of centrality, now arguably in all of East Asia, it failed to win the allegiance of many literati who were excluded from office and held in low esteem.

The Qin more than the Yuan remained influential as a model in twentieth-century China. Already in the late Qing and early Republican periods, there were some who hoped for, or feared, the appearance of a new centralizer like Qin Shihuang (Li 1974: xviii-xx; Friedman 1974: 156; Esherick 1976: 239). During the 1930s, some of Jiang Jieshi's supporters called on him to model himself on the Qin founder so as to eliminate inefficiency and corruption (Eastman 1974: 46; Li 1975: xxi, xxiii-xxvii). In the 1940s, some observers criticized Jiang precisely for having become another Qin Shihuang (Pepper 1978:146). In 1958, Communist Party Chairman Mao Zedong confidently accepted the analogy between himself and the Qin founder, asserting that he had even surpassed him in the number of counterrevolutionaries he had killed (Li 1975: xlix-l; Wilson 1979: 363–64). Mao was nonetheless aware of the risks involved in that comparison. In 1963 he suggested that the PRC needed a Qin Shihuang, and that Party Chairman Liu Shaoqi was playing that role (Terrill 1980: 302). Liu Shaoqi, of course, was soon overthrown by Mao in the Cultural Revolution. By 1971, Mao had come into conflict with his new heir apparent, Minister of Defense Lin Biao, who reportedly once criticized Mao for "implementing the laws of Qin Shihuang" and being "the biggest despot in Chinese history" (Wilson 1979: 471; Li 1975: l-li). Mao thereupon destroyed Lin Biao and sanctioned a campaign against Confucius which had the effect of elevating Qin Shihuang's status in official historiography. Nonetheless, in the April 1976 commemoration of the death of Premier Zhou Enlai, a poster appeared in Tiananmen Square criticizing China's contemporary Qin Shihuang (clearly Mao). In one of Mao's last recorded conversations, he acknowledged that "many," including Deng Xiaoping, had called him a Qin Shihuang. On his deathbed, Mao seemed to accept the analogy, musing that China might well "change color" after his death (Wilson 1979: 487).[16]

It is against this background of an uncivil society that we can understand the emergence, character, and continuing influence of our third form of civil society, "public people's society" (*gongmin shehui*), Like the Han that succeeded the Qin, the Ming that followed the Yuan was founded by a commoner who won broad support among the masses and recruited officials he expected to be dedicated to serving the people (Hucker 1978). Like the Han, the Ming pursued the goals of wealth and power and expanded its frontiers to include Mongolia in the north and, briefly, Vietnam in the south (Mote and Twitchett 1988). Like the Han, the Ming also imposed limits on the accumulation of wealth and power, relied principally on an agrarian-commercial economy for its revenues, required its military to support itself and allowed it to lose its capacity to fight, and relied heavily on ideology and ritual to govern for nearly three centuries (Huang 1981). Even the fall of the Ming, occasioned by eunuch abuses, literati factionalism, state deficits, and popular uprisings, resembled that of the Han (Wakeman 1985).

The similarities between the Han and Ming orders were not merely accidental or a figment of later historiography. Ming scholar-officials were clearly aware of the Han precedent and sought to fashion their own dynasty in its image. One late-Yuan literatus reportedly urged the rebel Zhu Yuanzhang, soon to become the founding Ming emperor (Ming Taizu), to "pattern his career after that of the first emperor of the Han" whose birthplace was near Zhu's own. Another advisor judged that the Han emperor Gaozu was "the best previous dynastic founder" but hinted that Ming Taizu would surpass him (Goodrich and Fang 1976: 384–85; Dardess 1983: 139, 172, 196). Those who patterned themselves on the past were not just imitating and replicating but learning and surpassing. After Ming Taizu took power, he reportedly read the history of the Han and tried consciously to follow Han Gaozu's example by balancing civil and military officials, curbing eunuchs, reducing taxes and labor services, and developing horse farms and military garrisons (Farmer 1976: 51, 66, 78–79, 87). Later historians noted that the Ming founder followed faithfully and in some cases transcended his Han model (Zhao 1799: 32/591; Wu 1948: 39, 132, 219, 224–25; Sa 1966–1968: 238–75). When the second Ming ruler succeeded to the throne, the historian Fang Xiaoru followed the example of the famous Han historian Sima Qian, who had dropped the Qin from the legitimate line of dynastic succession. Fang suggested that the Yuan be excised from the standard histories, to ensure its expansionist policies would not be admired and revived (Chan 1984: 129). Another advisor to the Ming founder advised that he check the authority of his princes on the model of the second ruler of Han who had tried to rein in the feudatories (Goodrich and Fang 1976: 399). Ming scholar-officials continued to invoke Han precedents through the rest of the dynasty (Farmer 1976: 102; Lo 1969: 58; Tu 1976: 36–38; de Bary 1970: 178).

Both the Han and Ming polities were attractive models for revolutionaries such as Sun Yat-sen in seeking to overthrow the Qing and establish a "people's state" (*minguo*) on the three principles of nationalism (*minzu zhuyi*, people's clanism), democracy (*minquan zhuyi*, people's rightsism), and socialism (*minsheng zhuyi*, people's livelihood) (Gasster 1969).[17] During the 1930s and 1940s when the historian Wu Han was writing his biography of the Ming founder Zhu Yuanzhang, he used it to level discreet criticism at the Guomindang (the Nationalist or "Citizens' Party") leader Jiang Jieshi (Wu 1948). But it was Mao Zedong and his cohort who, having never studied abroad, took the Han and Ming models most to heart. In 1920, a friend said that Mao aspired to be another Liu Bang, founder of the Han. In 1948, Mao himself recalled the lessons of Liu Bang's war against Xiang Yu as he pursued his war against Jiang Jieshi (Terrill 1980: 54, 189). As Mao planned his return to power after the setback of the Great Leap Forward, he reflected further on the history of the Han and the Ming (Li 1994: 440–42).[18] In 1964, on the eve of the Cultural Revolution, Mao remarked that the Han and Ming founders both lacked formal education but made good leaders, signaling his imminent assault on China's educational establishment (Schram 1974: 166). In 1965, Mao attacked the historian Wu Han, whose play about the dismissal of the honest official Hai Rui in the Ming dynasty he interpreted as an attack on his earlier decision to dismiss the outspoken defense minister, Peng Dehuai (Fisher 1993).

The campaign against Wu Han was the opening shot of the Cultural Revolution. During that time, Mao's wife, Jiang Qing, became one of the most powerful members of the government, just as Empress Lü had dominated the court in the last years of Han Gaozu's reign. After Mao's death, as part of an effort to retain authority, Jiang Qing commissioned historians to write favorable articles about Empress Lü (Terrill 1984: 312–13). Mao's immediate successor, Hua Guofeng, was reportedly chosen in part because he was, as a Han ruler said of a favorite official, "noble-minded and well-mannered but not pompous" (Terrill 1980: 407). During Hua's brief reign, articles appeared praising the "humane and just" policies of the third and fourth Han emperors, Wen and Jing, respectively, who allowed the people a respite after a period of heavy state exactions (Sun 1979). Nor was it wholly by chance, it would seem, that Deng Xiaoping's "open policy" and brief invasion of Vietnam were accompanied by favorable academic appraisals of Ming expeditions to the Western Ocean and Annam (Jinian weida 1985; Farmer and Des Forges 1994: 62–63). Far from being mere atavistic remnants of "traditional," "imperial," or "feudal" thinking, such historical parallels continue to be the very stuff of Chinese elite politics (Saich and van de Ven 1995: 200, 303).[19]

Contemporary Chinese Views of Civil and Uncivil Societies

> The process of relegitimizing the civilization-state (not the Party) with a strong civil society and a symbolically respectable and culturally influential center may turn out to be the most efficacious course of action. China's strong tradition of self-reliance at personal, familial, communal, and national levels, together with a richly textured social networking, provides valuable resources for this effort. . . . Predictably, in the Chinese case, even after the crisis in community becomes evident, the communal heritage survives not only in the economy and in social organizations, but in the intellectual ethos and in the minds of the people as well (Tu 1992: 279–80).

During the 1980s, some Chinese intellectuals embraced the second model of civil society that we have associated with periods of cultural crisis and political disunion. Shen Yue, apparently the first intellectual to publish in the PRC on civil society, argued in 1986 that Marx's German term *bürgerliche*, usually translated into Chinese as "bourgeoisie" (*zichanjieji*, capitalist class), should actually be translated by the broader term "townspeople" (*shimin*), including owners and workers. Shen suggested that there were townspeople's rights, including the right to equal economic exchanges protected by law, that were distinguishable from exploitative market relationships under capitalism (Ma 1994: 183). In 1988, two other writers in the PRC embraced the same concept of civil society, going even further to argue that individualism was the legitimate basis of "civic awareness" (Ma 1994: 184).

In 1990, Chen Kuide defined civil society to include "private enterprises, universities, newspapers and magazines, trade unions, churches, and other social organizations that are independent of the state" (Ma 1994: 187). Chen's concept of civil society, formulated and published while he was in exile, was clearly influenced by thinking in Eastern Europe: hence the emphasis on independent unions and churches. But in subsequent articles he found precedents for this kind of civil society in the Chinese past: (Ma 1994: 187).

> Returning to the source of history in China's axial age, the Spring and Autumn and Warring States period, all of the states (that were about the size of present-day provinces) were in competition. They developed unevenly in the political, economic, cultural, and military domains and

> thus provided sufficient spaces for the contemporary scholar-warrior class to demonstrate their capacities and ambitions in the forming and dissolving of horizontal and vertical alliances and in passing back and forth among the states. The result of such competition among talented people, the associations of personnel, the exchange of ideas, and the liberation of intellectual power was the most glorious period in Chinese history, characterized by cultural florescence and social development. Master thinkers appeared one after the other, the hundred schools contended, and Chinese civilization established a spiritual foundation and a moral system to which people are inclined to this day (Zhou 1992: 67).

Chen went on to argue that a similar kind of society, characterized by high mobility and spontaneous networks,[20] was emerging in the 1980s and 1990s to "create the foundation of a civil society (*gongmin shehui*)."

Because the Spring and Autumn and Warring States periods, like the Republican, were times of endemic military conflict, contemporary Chinese observers naturally differ over the relevance that *shimin shehui* may have for late-twentieth century China.[21] Chen argued that "purely economic organizations," such as town and country enterprises, secondary and tertiary schools, and urban small entrepreneurs, were the best guarantee against "chaos, warlordism, and banditry" (Zhou 1992: 70). Wang Shaoguang, however, reminds us that this kind of civil society has not led to democracy in China in the past:

> In Hegel's own theory, civil society (*shimin shehui*) and democratic politics had no necessary relationship. China from the 1911 Revolution to the war of resistance [against Japan] is an example. At that time there was a market economy (*shichang jingji*) since neither the central nor the local governments had the intention or capacity to exert complete control over economic activities. At that time there were autonomous organizations such as merchant associations, fellow–provincial associations, industrial and commercial enterprises, intellectual associations, theatre societies, independent newspapers, and private primary, secondary and tertiary schools, etc. In the third year of the Republic [1914], political parties were as numerous as the hairs on an ox, reaching 300 in number. But at that time no democracy appeared, not even the forms of democracy. In modern world history, examples of this kind are too numerous to count. This is to say that the full development of civil society (*shimin shehui*) is a necessary condition for political democratization but it is certainly not a sufficient condition (Zhou 1992: 19–20).[22]

While Chen Kuide characterizes civil society of the Spring and Autumn and Warring States periods as *gongmin shehui* and regards it as a model of "cultural fluorescence and social development" with continuing relevance today, Wang Shaoguang characterizes the analogous civil society of the Republican period as *shimin shehui* and distinguishes it from the democratic politics that most advocates of civil society currently hope to achieve in China.

Other writers raise issues related to this form of civil society in ways that resonate with, even if they are not consciously associated with, these earlier Chinese experiences. Zhao Suisheng, formerly of the PRC's Center for Economic Research, articulates the common idea that the Chinese state has been strong and the people weak, because there has been no middle class or bourgeoisie with sufficient independence or autonomy to offer a social counterweight to the government. With the weakening of the state during the reforms, various social classes did begin to stand up for their own interests, and intellectuals, organized into professional associations, used their intellectual capital to articulate the demands of an incipient middle class. In the end, however, they were too few and too weak to attain the goal of a strong state supported by a strong society (Zhou 1992: 171–92). In Zhao's view, this goal, which we may compare with those of polities in the Warring States and Song periods, can be attained only by a full-fledged bourgeoisie similar to that of the capitalist states that dominate the present international system.

Lü Xiaobo adopts a more jaundiced view of the process of embourgeoisement during the 1980s. Noting that tight organizational integrity was a chief source of the charisma of Leninist political parties, he remarks that the "post-revolutionary" Chinese Communist Party failed to transform the existing society but was instead transformed by it. With the weakening of that Party during the 1980s, civil society in the Marxist sense began to appear within it. He goes on to say that

> Marx recognized that so-called civil society was nothing more than the selfish interests and viewpoints of the petty bourgeoisie. That is to say, the most fundamental reason for corruption among the cadres of the Chinese Communist and other Leninist parties is the cadres' tendency to regard their individual, family, and small group interests as equal to or even higher than those of the party organization. The corruption is not, as many people suggest, a result of the influence of traditional

> culture, distortions introduced by the two-price market system, or the incomplete regimen of regulations and laws (Zhou 1992: 213).

From another perspective, exiled intellectual Wang Feng argues that personal relationships (*guanxi*) existed in traditional society but became more important and more utilitarian under socialism when they served as a substitute for a free market, a rational bureaucracy, and a democratic government. Under the reforms, this reliance on "personal relationships" should eventually diminish. In this view, apparently, China should be able to develop a market economy and an impersonal state without allowing utilitarianism to dominate personal relationships (Wang Feng 1992: 239–58). This defense of "traditional" *guanxi* and critique of its "modern" ("socialist" or "capitalist") utilitarian forms are rather reminiscent of the views of Confucius, Zhu Xi, and the "third stage" Confucians of the contemporary era (Tu 1985, 1993b).[23]

Similar ambivalence about individualism, an idea associated with civil society in its second form and with periods of dynastic decline and disunion in Chinese history, is evident in a survey touching on aspects of civil society in contemporary China. In a survey conducted in the Beijing area in 1988, most respondents favored two "negative freedoms": neither to assent to ideas propagated by nor to engage in activities sponsored by the state, the Party, and society. Respondents approved of two positive freedoms: to hold one's own beliefs, and to pursue one's own interests, even when they are inconsistent with state interests, so long as one does not infringe on the "rights" of others. These views reflected the influence of Western concepts, such as the freedom of speech, press, religion, and privacy, and respondents specifically distinguished them from early Chinese ideas such as Daoist eremitism and Confucian morality. Yet most respondents also criticized selfish motives and extreme individualism, in this respect following in the footsteps of their predecessors during the New Culture and May Fourth Movements (Lee 1985a: 239–58; 1985b: 282–307). Significantly, few if any of these respondents appeared ready to espouse the full-fledged egoism associated (rightly or wrongly) with Yang Zhu in the Warring States Period, the Seven Sages of the Bamboo Grove in the Wei-Jin period, and Li Zhi in the late Ming (Graham 1985: 73–84; Yü 1985: 121–56; de Bary 1970: 145–258).

Another area in which Chinese intellectuals feel ambivalence is autonomy for ethnic minorities. Gao Xiaoyuan points out that, although the Communist Party during its early years offered China's minority nationalities the right to self-determination and independence, it withdrew that promise during the war against Japan and organized 156 autonomous regions after 1949. Despite claims to the contrary, the Chinese central state strictly controls these "autonomous regions" through centrally appointed officials, local Party members, recurrent political campaigns, and continuous Han settlement. Democracy is not a panacea for nationality problems: witness the division in the Russian Federation of States, not to speak of the former Czechoslovakia and Yugoslavia. But Gao believes more room for debate is still an essential prerequisite to a peaceful solution of nationality issues in China. As China develops a more civil society, it will become possible to grant China's minorities, such as the Mongols, Tibetans, and Uighurs, the right to self-determination, including, if they freely so choose, independence. In Gao's view, this will not necessarily result in the break-up of the PRC any more than guaranteeing the right to divorce in civil law necessarily leads to the break-up of families (Zhou 1992: 271–90). Here we have an interesting compromise between the hoary Chinese ideal of the world as a single, supposedly harmonious, family and the twentieth-century Western principle of separate, presumably equal, nation states. Gao does not regard civil society as consistent with a system of states perpetually preparing for, let alone engaging in, warfare. Such a system may be considered a "world order" or even a "community of nations" by many Westerners, but it seems more like the global chaos of the Warring States period to many Chinese.

Given such mixed feelings among Chinese exile scholars about the second form of civil society, we may well ask why some advocated it for China in the 1980s and continue to do so. One answer is that many came to believe that the first forty years of the PRC had not been the originally promised New Democracy but rather totalitarianism (another Western concept). This view has been criticized for underestimating the extent of popular support for the Chinese Communist Party during its rise to power and the scope of quiet resistance to its will during the 1950s and 1960s (Shue 1988; Saich and van de Ven 1995). Mao and Deng did abuse theories of the people's democratic dictatorship and democratic centralism to cloak their personal, arbitrary power, hence the label of totalitarian. It was equally predictable that once the concept of civil society emerged in Eastern Europe as a potent alternative to Leninism, it would spread quickly to China. Therefore, to many

Chinese, civil society however defined seemed preferable to recently experienced alternatives: superior to totalitarianism in promising pluralism rather than uniformity, and better than democracy in seeming to safeguard the rights of individuals and minorities.

Having examined the appeal of this form of civil society to Chinese intellectuals of the mid-1980s, we now need to explore why some of those same intellectuals turned with such alacrity to the theory of neoauthoritarianism in the late 1980s (Ma 1990; Oksenberg 1990: 123–49). Neoauthoritarianism reflected frustration among certain members of the reform faction of the Party over seemingly intractable problems of state deficits, bureaucratic corruption, party factionalism, monetary inflation, and social unrest. The neoauthoritarians were impatient with "conservative" members of the Party who continued to uphold the ideals of socialism, often reduced to simple state ownership of the means of production. The neoauthoritarians were determined to use their dwindling authority to push through a new social system based on the private ownership of land and other forms of wealth. The translation of the term "neoauthoritarianism" (*xin zhuanquan zhuyi*) is closely related to the Chinese term for "centralized bureaucratic authority" (*zhuanzhi*), the system that originated in the Qin and has persisted to some degree ever after (Zhou 1992: 39–41, 44).[24] That system, we have suggested, was not a form of civil society but rather a recurrent Chinese antidote to the excesses of the second form of civil society, excesses such as inflation and unemployment that were reemerging in the China of the late 1980s. Without some foundation in earlier Chinese thought and practice, this solution to China's problems might never have been as readily invoked as it was in early 1989; this foundation in turn enhanced its appeal.

Sun Xiaoguang, formerly of the Planning Department of People's University, led a research team to conduct a survey touching on fifty-five townships in Fuyang, Anhui, in the mid-1980s. The team found that the Western notion of private property as "sacred and inviolable" was still weak in China, despite the perceived need to emphasize private enterprise as the key to China's development. They argued that strong state measures were needed to guarantee private property, even in the face of powerful special interests and adverse public opinion. "To eliminate excessive state intervention in economic matters and to establish a vigorous and stable civil society among the Chinese people who have lived under Communist Party rule for half a century is not a process that will be concluded quickly" (Sun 1992: 236). This view is quite consistent with neoauthoritarianism and the Legalist philosophy that lay behind it. That philosophy, after all, had inspired earlier authoritarian polities in Chinese history, including the Qin, the Yuan, and more ambiguously the Guomindang and Communist parties. Sun's use of the common term (*gongmin shehui*) that we have reserved for our third kind of civil society, emphasizing the public good, should not be allowed to obscure his penchant for our second kind of civil society based on private enterprise. Nor should his call to eliminate excessive state intervention in economic matters hide his willingness to use state authority to advance his own conception of the good society. His use of the adjective "stable" to describe the preferred form of civil society may hint at a degree of discipline consistent with authoritarian rule.

Given the ease with which the second form of civil society slips into authoritarianism in China as elsewhere, the Chinese may well have to adopt other modern Western concepts if they are to fashion a stable and durable civil society (Nathan 1990: 293–314; Kent 1991: 174; Peerenboom 1993: 51). Perhaps the ideas of Confucius, like those of Plato, and the experiences of the early and middle periods of Chinese history, like those of ancient and medieval Europe, are no longer relevant, and Chinese theorists must follow the lead of European philosophers in making natural, universal, and abstract human rights the foundation of civil society. Hobbes, Locke, and Rousseau in the seventeenth and eighteenth centuries; Hegel, Tocqueville, and Mill in the nineteenth century; and Rawls, Dworkin, and Nozick in the twentieth century have argued for fundamental and inalienable human rights as the only secure basis for a civil society and democratic polity (Peerenboom 1993: 30, 36–39). More recently, John Keane (1988) and Jürgen Habermas (1989) have provided seemingly authoritative analyses of the nature of civil society in the West, which are thought by many to provide useful standards for the rest of the world. Some leading Chinese intellectuals are aware of, and attracted to, these and other Western ideas and experiences (e.g., Fang 1991).[25]

Still, there are reasons to think that Western concepts and practices of civil society may continue to have a limited presence in China. Whether they are believed to be self-evident, God-given, natural, or man-made, human rights and individual freedom have always and everywhere been secondary to state interests and social survival, and are likely to remain so in the future no matter how democratic a polity or civil a society may become (Peerenboom 1993: 30). Second, Western ideas of liberal democracy and civil society, often honored in the West as much in the breach as in the observance, usually arrived in China from imperialist powers, such as Great Britain and the United States, that were intent on dominating China politically and exploiting it economically. Thus the legitimacy of the model of Western-style democracy has been undermined by Western-imperialist policies in China (Zhou 1992: 96). Some regard British and American reluctance to compromise lucrative niches in Hong Kong and Taiwan as further compromising Western efforts to propagate notions of human rights as universal.[26] Third, whatever the validity of current critiques of the political and social system of the PRC among Chinese intellectuals overseas, their ideas continue to have only limited distribution in China and are, therefore, unlikely to have much influence there (Ma 1994: 193). Finally, given the arguable failure or even counterproductivity of past efforts at complete Westernization and assaults on "tradition," from the May Fourth Movement through the Cultural Revolution (with the Maoist attack on the Four Olds) to the 1980s (with the Dengist advocacy of the Four Modernizations), some Chinese intellectuals are now intent on finding "ideological resources" for civil society within China's own legacy (Yü 1993; Su Wei, cited in Ma 1994: 188).

The question of which resources remain viable, of course, has been hotly debated. In 1990, expatriate Taiwanese intellectual Peng Wenyi argued for the continuing vitality of a specifically Chinese form of clan society (Ma 1994: 188).[27] Inspired by Confucianism, clan society had purportedly produced economic development in the four little dragons of South Korea, Taiwan, Hong Kong, and Singapore; presumably it could do the same if it were revived in the PRC. This thesis has come under fire from Chen Kuide, an early advocate of Western-style civil society, who has argued that the four little dragons are actually closer to Western-style civil society than they are to Chinese-style clan society. In his view, where clan societies are really strong (as he claims they are in India), they actually pose obstacles to economic development. Furthermore, the emphasis in clan society on political authority, social consensus, economic collectivism, respect for the aged, and human relations was present to an even higher degree under totalitarian socialism. In Chen's view, therefore, clan society will not appeal to citizens of the PRC, who are looking instead for the democracy, pluralism, individualism, equality, and rule of law associated with Western-style civil society (Zhou 1992: 55–59).

There is controversy also over the revival of sects, associations, and secret societies for the prospects for civil society in China. According to Su Shaokang, the producer of the television miniseries *River Elegy*, some eighteen hundred illegal secret societies have reappeared in China in recent years. Su sees them as part of a valuable counterculture that has taken the place of a loyal opposition. While Su does not shrink from calling these societies "civil," others wonder if organizations that smuggle arms and drugs, kidnap rivals and bystanders, and procure women and children can really be brought under the civil society umbrella, no matter how capacious (Ma 1994: 189–90).[28] Noting the variety of Chinese organizations that have grown up in the wake of the declining Communist Party, Richard Madsen remarks:

> Some scholars are calling this whole range of associations—everything from democracy salons to organizations of *getihu* to clan associations to *qigong* clubs—"civil society." But some are certainly more "civil" than others. . . . Those with the quality of "civility" might eventually contribute to the creation of a democratic public sphere. . . . Those without it may simply push China closer toward anarchic fragmentation (Madsen 1993: 190).

Several observers of the Chinese scene believe that Westerners forget the role of the state in helping to make society civil, positing an unnecessary opposition between the state and society and ignoring the distinction between civil society and society in general (Wang 1991; Chamberlain 1992: 205–9; Gan 1993; Ma 1994: 192; Diamond 1994). By contrast, most Chinese assume that the state has an important role in establishing and preserving civility.

These points take us back to our other two forms of civil society and to their continuing roles, conscious or unconscious, in the contemporary Chinese discourse on civil society. The first, *wenming shehui*, operates whenever there is discussion of civilization as opposed to barbarism, and civility as opposed to militarism. It unconsciously lies behind much of the current debate over various forms of centralization and local autonomy. Chen Kuide suggests that decentralization in the 1980s created spaces for local economic and scholarly activities that can ultimately give rise to economic autonomy and even political independence. He also sees intellectuals assuming the leading role in "selling political products to the people," thereby creating an independent cultural sphere that will eventually become legitimately opposed to the state (Zhou 1992: 66–67, 72–77). Su Shaozhi, Barrett McCormick, and Xiao Xiaoming, on the other hand, argue that the PRC was originally less centralized than the Soviet Union. Further decentralization of authority in the 1980s did not result in a real market economy and actually undercut the ability of the reformers to carry out their reforms. Nonetheless, they, too, believe that, once the fear of chaos inherited from past experiences with decentralization is overcome, a century-long trend toward an autonomous society in opposition to the state will continue despite the brief interruption of the 1990s (Zhou 1992: 80, 84–89, 101–5). Shi Zhengfu, for his part, notes that there were extensive decentralizations in the Great Leap Forward and the Cultural Revolution, and that decentralization went further under the reforms of the 1980s, resulting in rather autonomous enterprises. The simultaneous increase in the authority of local governments, however, has worked against the autonomy of firms. In his view, there is now a need for *recentralization* to ensure the state can obtain sufficient resources to allow firms to become autonomous (Zhou 1992: 139–44). However, as we have seen, Gao Xiaoyuan has called on the state to grant more real local autonomy to nationalities without fear that they will split from China and declare their independence (Zhou 1992: 280–81, 285–87). In sum, Chinese intellectuals intent on fashioning a more civilized relationship between state and society in contemporary China continue to be influenced, however unconsciously and variously, by the positive experiences of earlier elite-run polities such as the Zhou, the Tang, and the Qing, which were characterized by central administrations that permitted considerable local autonomy while staving off tendencies to total disintegration.

At the same time, contemporary Chinese scholars, including many living abroad, espouse the third form of civil society (*gongmin shehui*) that emphasizes the popular participation and social welfare we have associated with other Chinese polities out of the past. Wang Shaoguang notes that there is no such thing as elite democracy, because true democracy requires participation of the masses. Wang embraces the second form of civil society (*shimin shehui*) but asserts that it must be democratized. In his view, there must be limitations on the right to accumulate private property, broader social ownership of the means of production, more democratic planning, and reduction of the differences among social groups so as to increase the capacity of the people to realize their own destiny (Zhou 1992: 19, 21). While Wang continues to embrace the second form of civil society as the only realizable form at present, he seems to hope that it may some day be transformed into the third form, bringing social equality and solidarity along with individual liberty and autonomy. Ding Xueliang, for his part, even more openly advocates the third form of civil society in which the benefits of welfare socialism are retained as "social welfare thinking." This thinking includes guarantees of job security and a living wage, free health care and public education, low prices for essential commodities, and limited differentials in income and wealth. In his view, these values inspired some of the popular mobilization evident at Tiananmen and will continue to shape mass public opinion. They will, therefore, continue to influence Chinese politics no matter whether they become more authoritarian or more democratic (Zhou 1992: 37–38, 44–46).[29]

Along the same lines, Shi Zhengfu notes Keynesian economics emphasizes the distribution of wealth according to the market, but advocates state policies to promote price stability, orderly growth, and public welfare (Zhou 1992: 125–26). Such government policies are likely to enjoy broad public support in China. Fifty-one percent of older respondents to a 1988 survey worried about "who would take responsibility for the interests of the masses" if people had the right to abstain from state- or society-organized activities (Zhou 1992: 263). The younger philosopher, Gan Yang, is critical of the notion of *minjian shehui*, which he says posits too sharp a conflict between the interests of the state and the interests of the people. He argues instead for a *gongmin shehui*, in which the state takes responsibility for supplying whatever public goods society fails to provide (Gan 1993: 151). Reflecting, almost certainly unconsciously, the continuing force of, and choice between, the Chinese concepts of *wenming shehui* and *gongmin shehui*, Lü Xiaobo concludes his analysis of today's Chinese Communist Party by suggesting that there is a small chance that it may yet save itself from corruption and demoralization. In Lü's view, it can do so either by renewing its elite role as a vanguard dedicated to the interests of the entire society, or by popularizing itself by opening its doors to representatives of all elements of society (Zhou 1992: 214). These ideas of state leadership and the possibility of reform, and these particular styles of elite responsibility and popular participation, all have roots deep in China's past.

Toward a Global Civil Society and Moral Community

> If individualism understands only a part of man, collectivism understands man only as a part; neither advances to the wholeness of man, to man as a whole. . . . The perception of one's fellow man as a whole, as a unity, and as unique—even if his wholeness, unity and uniqueness are only partly developed, as is usually the case—is opposed in our time by almost everything that is commonly understood as specifically modern (Buber 1992: 36, 74).

In this chapter I have examined social changes and their sequences in Chinese history, and have appraised Chinese concepts of community based on common memories that transcend the modern Western choice between individualism and collectivism and focus on human beings both as wholes and parts of larger wholes. I have attempted to introduce an appreciation of what the Chinese still have to learn from the outside world concerning the constituents of a civil society, and what they have to offer the world based on their long-term efforts to create civil societies and moral communities. As Tu Wei-ming has noted, "The tacit assumption of the American public that what we have is what the overwhelming majority of the human race wants and strives to achieve is not groundless," and to this extent many Chinese will continue to look to the West for institutional models that defend individuals and minorities against the tyranny of the majority. Yet much of the American dream is neither plausible nor realizable on a global scale. The "reasonable quest for a legitimate modern style of living has made us individually and collectively . . . the most wasteful spender of natural and human resources the world has ever encountered." Despite a continuing assumption that we live in a civil society, many are increasingly aware that "there are no quick fixes for our problems in education, economy, crime, drugs, race relations, welfare, child care, and health" (Tu 1992: 251, 257). On the contrary, some observers clearly recognize that, far from being an impeccable model and teacher to the rest of the world, "the West itself needs to search for new ways to revitalize its public spheres" (Madsen 1993: 187).[30]

What I would suggest is that elements of Chinese social systems may have something to offer in the quest for a global conception of civil society. Consider, for example, the Chinese discourse on rights. However often it may not be observed in practice, the Chinese constitution does include guarantees of the rights to work, education, and an adequate standard of living, including food, clothing, housing, and medical care, rights that are not protected by the American constitution (Peerenboom 1993: 42–43, 49–50).[31] So, too, it assigns duties toward family members and fellow citizens as well as toward the state. Despite enthusiasm among dissidents for the second form of civil society, which is analogous to that espoused in the contemporary West, mainstream Chinese conceptions of human rights are likely to continue to reflect both a Confucian emphasis on harmony and a socialist stress on justice. Drawing on historical and legal evidence, Peerenboom (1993: 53–55) has induced a Chinese theory of rights, which holds them to be contingent on time and place, communitarian in theory and practice, ethically inspirational, socially relational, and with an emphasis on mediation over confrontation and economic benefits over political privileges. This long-standing Chinese view is consistent with a recent Western trend toward a more communitarian concept of personality (Taylor 1987; Avineri and De-Shalit 1992; Bell 1993). It is also consistent with Chinese realities, at least as these are presented in China's 1991 white paper on human rights, which argued that "no country in its effort to realize and protect human rights can take a route that is divorced from its history and its economic, political and cultural realities."[32] The Chinese state continues to assume a holistic cosmos in which all elements are interrelated.

The PRC has fallen far short of carrying on the best of China's own traditions of civil society, most notably in the crackdown of spring 1989 and in subsequent efforts to avoid outside scrutiny of its human rights record (Brook 1992; 1993b: 18–19). I would suggest that this has been in part because, imbued with essentially Western theories of Marxism and modernization, contemporary Chinese have underestimated the resources in their own past. Once they draw more creatively on their own history and shoulder again the responsibility to influence as well as to accept the contemporary world, they will be better able to realize their own forms of civil society that are in some cases more suited to present world conditions than those of the West. Increased Chinese awareness and acknowledgment of indigenous roots of current concepts and practices of civil society and human rights may help to counterbalance Chinese suspicions that the persistent Western rhetoric of a community of nations, based on universal human rights, masks the reality of great power hegemony based on economic and military might (Muzaffar 1995). Only then will they be able to attain their full potential in helping to establish a more global civil society and a truly universal moral community.

Particular Studies

4

University Autonomy and Civil Society

Ruth Hayhoe and Ningsha Zhong

The Chinese government is currently encouraging institutions of higher education to be more "autonomous" in an effort to stimulate their contributions to the economy. In this chapter we seek to convey a sense of the historical basis for university autonomy to better understand what such autonomy signifies.

Autonomy in the context of Chinese universities is most commonly expressed by the term *zizhu quan*, "the right to be one's own master." This right may be understood as that of having the authority to initiate action. In keeping with this idea, the new 1995 comprehensive education law designates universities as "legal persons" (*faren*) or corporate entities functioning in society in response to the market. The role of the state is limited to setting legal and policy frameworks. During the current (ninth) five-year plan (1995-2000), universities are expected to relate first to the state and thereafter to the market and society; in the twenty-first century, they will be expected to relate to the market, society, and the state in that order (Chen and Gu 1993). Congruent with this trend is the expectation that the university should operate as an independent "corporation" (*jituan*) that makes its own internal decisions in accordance with its own "charter" (*zhangcheng*) (Xu, Xiang; and Liu 1994: 32-33).[1]

These Western concepts of "legal person" and "corporation" are enabling Chinese universities to become more insulated from the vicissitudes of politics. Nevertheless, the notion of university autonomy in the Chinese context is different from the Western idea of autonomy. That idea is better translated by the Chinese term *zizhi*, or "self-governance," rather than *zizhu*, but *zizhi* is less commonly used in the official or legal literature. The choice of the *zizhu* concept reflects a long-standing concern over the individual's responsibility to the larger whole of society and state, in contrast to the more oppositional approach of the West that emphasizes the negative freedom of protection from state interference in the university's internal affairs.

In this chapter we begin with some reflections on traditional patterns of higher learning in China to consider what they may offer to universities in the present. We will then consider the combining of the tradition of the unofficial academies (*shuyuan*) with features of Western university models during the Republican period. Next we turn to the early Communist period, when Chinese higher education was totally restructured along the lines of the Soviet model. We see the current move to develop universities as corporations or legal persons as a conscious attempt to move away from internalized patterns of behavior, which were fostered through the Soviet model but have links further back to official institutions of higher learning in the imperial era.

Traditions of Chinese Higher Education

Our interest is in comparisons between European traditions of the university, specifically the concepts of autonomy central to those traditions, and traditional Chinese institutions of higher learning. Hayhoe (1984) has noted a polarity of values in the Chinese tradition regarding autonomy. Official institutions associated with the civil service examinations enjoyed not merely self-government but the right to govern the state through regulating and adjudicating its canons of knowledge. On the other hand, unofficial institutions such as the academies enjoyed a fragmented individual autonomy distinct from the corporate autonomy of the medieval European university community.

With regard to the autonomy of institutions and their capability of independent social action, we note that some medieval European universities were able to survive the vicissitudes of time and politics for seven or eight hundred years. Their survival was linked to their status as corporations, constituted by a charter and able thereby to maintain a corporate identity in the face of political and economic power. By contrast, official institutions associated with the Chinese imperial bureaucracy, such as the Hanlin Academy and the imperial academies at Nanjing (Taixue) and Beijing (Guozijian), rose and fell with each imperial dynasty, having no corporate existence separate from the state.

Unofficial institutions such as the academies were equally, if not more, vulnerable to political change, even though much of their land was privately owned and the scholars who taught there were often officials who had resigned or retired. They did not have a corporate identity in the sense of the medieval universities of Europe, and their fate was often tied to the reputation of a particular scholar (Walton 1989: 475–76, 482). Although the names of some academies have persisted over the centuries, none has enjoyed a continuous corporate existence (Chan 1989: 405). There were documents that defined the mission and role of particular academies, with Zhu Xi's "Regulation for Bailudong Academy" setting the pattern for many other academies (Gu 1992: 907); yet these documents did not give institutions lasting legal status or protect them from outside interference, as the charters of medieval European universities were supposed to do.

The Chinese concept of autonomy as applied to universities stresses the ability to initiate action rather than protection from external interference. This orientation may be linked to the Confucian concept of responsible action, rather than to the Western notion of incorporation that was introduced during the Republican period. In imperial China, institutions of higher learning had connections with the world of politics. Official higher learning institutions were part of the state and were governed variously by the emperor,[2] by the Ministry of Rites (Xue 1939), and by the Imperial Academy, which was the highest administrative body for education and the highest-level institution of learning in the country. Informal institutions such as academies were at some remove from the state; yet, by training students in the Confucian canon, they too were oriented toward passing on established knowledge aimed at endowing a sense of personal responsibility for social order, and by preparing students for office, they were reinforcing the authority of the gentry who supported the social system.[3] Our understanding of the concept of university autonomy in the twentieth century must take these traditions into account.

The issue of autonomy can also be raised in relation to students and university teachers, the two groups we focus on in this chapter. In Europe, each had its corporation, with the guild of students at Bologna and the guild of masters in Paris providing two influential models. In imperial China; students had a group identity and could at times exert influence on officials, but they never founded institutions such as guilds. The students studying together at the two imperial academies identified themselves as a common cohort, and there were enough of them that they could at times challenge policies at court. For the most part, however, their behavior was shaped by their vested interest in the system as officials-in-waiting, which inhibited their acting as a corporate group. Students experienced an even more restricted sense of community at the unofficial academies, where student life involved mainly the pursuit of individual learning and cultivation through the mentorship of teachers.

Teachers within traditional higher education were a less well-defined group. It is not evident that they had a corporate identity or the ability to act as a group. The basis for their identity as a group was weak insofar as they were not only teachers but officials as well, sharing the interests of other bureaucrats and hopeful of moving out of education and into more prestigious posts. Education held only moderate prestige as a vocation. The potential for group identity was also weakened by their physical dispersal: four to five thousand teachers worked in official schools during the Qing dynasty, at a rate of one or two per school. Only at the Imperial Academy in Beijing were they concentrated, usually numbering about thirty (Xiong 1983:294). Teachers at the academies had greater scope for independent action, yet their interests were split between those appointed by state intervention and retired officials-turned-teachers who often sought to use the academies as a basis for teaching that might well be critical of the state. In any case, many an academy was dominated by one scholar of distinguished reputation who set the tone for his institution rather than working together with other teachers to build a community of scholars.

Teachers in imperial China were both more powerful than their European counterparts, being members of the imperial bureaucracy who were able potentially to affect the political system through their actions, and less powerful, in terms of the limitation on their group identity. Students as officials-in-waiting were an important and privileged group who sometimes took part in oppositional politics, but their long-term interests lay with the stability of the imperial bureaucracy, which would provide them with lifelong employment if they were successful. Their integration with the bureaucracy meant that no group of scholars or students could maintain an identity through a dynastic change, as the bureaucracy was reconstituted each time. It was not until the twentieth century that a change of dynasty would not entail disruption. This has enabled some twentieth-century universities to survive several regime changes and still exist today.

The Republican Period

The hallmark of Chinese universities in the twentieth century was possession of a "charter" (*zhangcheng*), after the Japanese pattern. The first charter in China was for the imperial university, one of the few institutions conceived as part of the Hundred Days' Reform of 1898 that survived its suppression. It later became Peking University (affectionately known as Beida by generations of students and teachers). Its charter, drafted by the well-known reformers Kang Youwei and Liang Qichao, had eight chapters dealing with such matters as admission, graduation, the selection of teachers, placement, and funding (Zhu 1986). This document gained legal status in 1902, when the first national educational legislation was promulgated. Not only did it cover the administration of the university at its three levels (preparatory studies; undergraduate and graduate studies; and two associated institutions, the teachers college and the academy of scholars), but it also endowed the university with the role of being the highest administrative body in the state education system, much as did the Napoleonic University in France. According to this plan, the university was to administer a wide range of specialized institutions in all of the modern areas of knowledge, including agriculture, commerce, law, and engineering. With the educational legislation of 1904, however, this responsibility for national administrative leadership disappeared from the university's charter. The university was constituted as a state institution having a leading responsibility for higher education, but the administration of the new education system was conferred on a ministry of education.[4]

Although bouts of political turmoil (1902-1904, 1912-1913, and 1937-1940) tended to disrupt the continuity of specific institutions, as Liu Haifeng (1994) has observed, many universities after 1911 were able to sustain a corporate identity similar to that of their counterparts in the Western world, partly as a result of conscious emulation of Western models. Beida was in the forefront of this trend, and its position as the leading state university facilitated this emulation process. When Cai Yuanpei went to Beida as chancellor in 1917, it was with the intention of making the institution autonomous from the warlord government and instituting both autonomy and academic freedom. On the German model, autonomy for him was defined as "academic government by professors" (*jiaoshou zhixiao*), and the university senate accordingly was given an important role. Academic freedom took concrete form in Cai's efforts to appoint faculty from all political and ideological persuasions and encourage them to teach and research in a spirit of critical interaction. The price of autonomy and academic freedom was that faculty and students should refrain from direct political activism, a view Cai had adopted from his German university experience. He was also opposed to having the university serve as a cradle for training government officials. In keeping with this concern, he tried to remove the law school and make it a separate institution, since law was prone to attract young people who were ambitious for positions in the government (Duiker 1977).

The involvement of Beida students in the May Fourth Movement illustrates the degree of autonomy the university had achieved as a corporate body, although Cai was unhappy with the political activity of the students and resigned in protest when they would not listen to his request to refrain from collective political action. The students of other universities, both private and public, also participated actively, demonstrating their capacity to act more and more as corporate bodies. In fact, there was considerable positioning among institutions during the various student movements, with private universities such as Fudan University in Shanghai consciously striving to attract radical students who had been suspended from American missionary institutions.

After the Nationalist Party came to power in 1927, Cai Yuanpei made a failed attempt to establish a fully independent "National University Council" (*Daxueyuan*). The corporate identity of institutions that had come into being and thrived largely through the efforts of individuals and local intellectual groups with such financial help as they could get from official sources was subsequently curbed. Although the American model had extensive influence through a generation of scholars returned from the United States who took the leadership in these fledgling universities, the Nationalist government became increasingly interested in European models of educational administration because of their tendency toward centralization and their potential for keeping an increasingly radicalized faculty and student body under political control. Faculty members never became full members of the civil service as in the German and French models, but legislation was enacted that set strict academic standards for qualification and enabled the government to exercise political control under the auspices of maintaining standards.

Research on university students and student movements during the Republican period (Israel 1966; Schwarcz 1987; Wasserstrom 1991) has shown the extent of university and department identity of student groups and their considerable influence on political events from May Fourth through the anti-Japanese struggle to the civil war period. As Jeffrey Wasserstrom (1991: 80, 286) observed, university students perpetuated cultural patterns given to them from earlier imperial history, including the bureaucratic patterns of organization characteristic of their government, but at the same time they adopted new patterns and tactics. Particular institutions developed a group identity, which in turn meant that they were easily melded into higher-level municipal or regional student associations.

As for faculty, their group identity was less obvious and more vulnerable to Nationalist control. However, the academic profession emerged as a lifelong vocation in the Republican period, in contrast to the imperial period when teachers of higher learning were normally full members of the imperial bureaucracy who moved in and out of educational positions. While such distinguished Republican-era scholars as Cai Yuanpei and Hu Shi did hold high government positions for certain periods, they were mainly known as professors and university presidents and were part of this new professional grouping.

The propensity of faculty to struggle for a greater degree of autonomy than had been common in Chinese scholarly tradition was most evident in Cai's efforts to establish the university and subsequently the Academica Sinica as autonomous bodies able to initiate and lead activity based on scholarly rather than political purposes. This was a concrete expression of the notion of *zizhu quan*. At the same time, some dimensions of China's modern universities were shaped by the Chinese tradition of the unofficial academies, which were characterized by independent research, informal relations between scholars and their students, and flexible patterns of learning (Ding 1996). For the scholarly community, the development of universities was seen as an effort to give modern corporate form to institutions that had been a progressive force in Chinese tradition but had never attained the kinds of independence and continuity that a modern republican state made possible. For the political authorities, by contrast, elements of the patterns for knowledge regimentation and control that characterized official institutions in imperial times continued to be attractive.

By 1949, there were over two hundred higher institutions in China, most calling themselves universities. Some were private universities, others national or provincial-level institutions of higher learning. All operated within clearly defined and explicit legislation specifying their rights and obligations. Twenty to thirty of these, both public and private, had achieved a considerable academic reputation. Remarkably, all these institutions had managed to maintain their identities during the Sino-Japanese war (1937–45), when many had to relocate several times to increasingly remote hinterland regions, and some had to combine forces with other institutions (Zhuang 1979). The Nationalist government should be credited for both expanding higher education in order to be prepared for postwar reconstruction and providing such financial support as it could manage. This was also a triumph of what was now a professionalized community of Chinese scholars, many with degrees from abroad.

Their achievements during the war showed they had genuine ability, as corporate groups of scholars and students, to initiate action in terms of valuable research and training in areas such as aeronautics, wartime industrial development, agriculture, areas of basic science, as well as the social sciences and literature. Two Nobel-prize-winning physicists were nurtured at the famous "Southwest United University" (*Xinan Lianda*), and significant new literary and sociological research that related more closely to China's own conditions and culture than had the more Western-oriented work done when the universities were in the coastal cities was fostered (such as work by Wen Yiduo and Fei Xiaotong). With the defeat of Japan, these "wandering universities" were able to return to major coastal cities and reestablish themselves on campuses that had been destroyed by Japanese bombing or occupied by the Japanese army. In spite of amalgamation, their former corporate identities were restored in almost all cases. At the same time, they left behind foundations in the hinterland for the establishment of new institutions (Hayhoe 1996: ch. 2).

Communist Period

In her study of the Civil War period, Suzanne Pepper (1980) notes that most intellectuals were supportive of the Communist Party because of its efforts against Japan and because of some elements of its vision for

China. However, they were not convinced communists. They were hopeful for conditions of pluralism and a relatively independent role for the university as an institution that had proven both its loyalty and the practical value of its educational and scholarly mandate through the war. Such distinguished university-based intellectuals as Beida economist Ma Yinchu, computer scientist Qian Weichang, Beida philosopher Ma Xulun, and political scientist Qian Duansheng took this stance in the early years of the new regime after 1949.

There was considerable consensus among Chinese university scholars, including some of the non-Party intellectuals named above and sympathetic individuals within the Party who appreciated the achievements of China's major universities during the Republican period, that it was appropriate for the state to take over private universities, particularly those with foreign affiliations. This concern was magnified by the Korean War. However, it was agreed that the establishment of a socialist system of higher education and the determining of its institutional and disciplinary identities would best be carried out by Chinese professors who had dedicated their lives to higher learning as a profession and had proven their loyalty to the nation through many years of effort under difficult circumstances. Thus, the first higher education conference held by the new regime in June 1950, presided over by Ma Xulun, a leading non-Party intellectual, entrusted the work of revising the higher curriculum to four committees of scholars in the areas of humanities, law, science, and engineering (Mao and Shen 1988: 60-66). The initial intention was to maintain the institutional identities of the pre-1949 universities, while arranging for private missionary universities to be gradually taken over by the state. Within a very short period, however, this plan was abandoned in favor of a total restructuring of higher education according to Soviet patterns, with the direct involvement of a large number of Soviet advisors and academics. The Soviets were given positions in a newly established Ministry of Higher Education; in People's University, which had been patterned after the model of the Moscow Planning Institute to provide intellectual direction to the whole process of socialist planning; in the Harbin University of Technology, the leading university for introducing the Soviet polytechnical model; and in Beijing Normal University, which was responsible for establishing a whole new approach to teacher education.

The corporate identity and distinctive voice that universities had struggled for and won to differing degrees with great effort during the

Republican period were forced to give way to a system of higher education designed from above to fit into the vast machine of socialist planning.[5] Geographically, it was intended to cover the whole country in a rational manner, with the six major military regions—North China, the Northeast, the Northwest, East China, the Central South, and the Southwest—each having an appropriate number of national level institutions to serve their bureaucratic and economic manpower needs. Knowledge was reorganized in a hierarchical structure that gave first priority to major engineering universities serving heavy industry, both polytechnical institutions administered by the Ministry of Higher Education and monotechnical institutions under such powerful ministries as metallurgy and machine building. The second priority went to so-called national comprehensive universities, whose curriculum embraced only the basic sciences and humanities, a feature of the traditional German model that had been given a new lease on life in the Soviet Union. All other higher learning was organized by sector, including social sectors such as education, health, law, and finance, as well as productive sectors such as agriculture and forestry. At the head of the system was People's University, which had the dual function of training planners and economists to manage the whole socialist system and producing political theorists whose task was to inculcate absolute loyalty to the regime. By overseeing the work of regional institutions, the university extended this mandate of ensuring political orthodoxy at the local level.

The organic links among faculty members and institutions that had developed since early in the century were stamped out as the universities of the Republican period were broken up, department by department, and restructured according to the two parameters of geography and specialization. This process, known as "the reorganization of colleges and departments" (*yuanxi tiaozheng*), was carried out between 1953 and 1957. Each of the six major regions had a main center and one or two secondary centers, where the majority of national-level higher institutions was concentrated and from where they were to serve the manpower needs of the region and the central ministries that managed them. This system, with its notion of narrowly conceived modern knowledge specializations overseen and coordinated by a central ideological body, bears resemblance to the one that was outlined in the legislation of 1902, a system the Qing government never implemented due to scarce resources.

The system left no space for the initiation of action either by universities as corporate bodies or by individual scholars. The former universities of the Republican era were totally swallowed up within the newly established communist state bureaucracy. Many university leaders held important positions within the Party and state[6] and were moved around accordingly. Faculty members were assigned positions within the state cadre system. All students who graduated from the regular university system gained the right to state assignments as cadres. Most of the first generation of cadres in the new socialist system had gained their positions on the basis of their contributions to the revolution, but from this time forward graduation from the formal higher education system, or the restricted secondary specialist system for training technicians and teachers, was an important route for gaining the status and perquisites of a state cadre. The cost to the individual was taking whatever work assignment the State Planning Commission saw fit to hand down.

The higher education system formed between 1953 and 1957 could be described as a kind of Napoleonic-Soviet monster, organized on principles of narrow knowledge specialization and rational geographic distribution, and unsupportive of the integration between the old academies and the Western models of higher education achieved in the Republican period. The purpose of the new system was to offer direct service to the macroplanning processes of the socialist state by rationalizing manpower needs. It was envisioned as an efficient servant of socialist construction, not a location for either students or professors to shape a corporate identity or initiate their own courses of action. The last opportunity that professors and scholars had to reactivate a corporate identity was the Hundred Flowers Movement of 1956, when scholars like Ma Yinchu, Fei Xiaotong, and Qian Weichang criticized the rigidity and abuses of power of the Soviet model, both in higher education and in the wider socialist bureaucracy. The Anti-Rightist Movement of 1957 silenced these voices, and every academic department in the reconstituted higher institutions of the Soviet model was decimated through a quota system for identifying and punishing rightists. Little wonder that professors and scholars as a social group had neither an institutional base nor any possibility for self-initiated action after this period.

Students were in a different position. During the Great Leap Forward, a faction of the Party leadership was able to mobilize them to demand that the curriculum be changed in favor of more integrated and locally relevant knowledge. Many new institutions were established in 1958 by provincial-level authorities, reflecting the ambitions of local political figures who were able to enlist students to support their causes. This new level of provincially administered higher education included comprehensive universities, normal universities, and medical schools, as well as science and engineering institutions that brought together pure and applied fields. Most of these were newly created in 1958 (Yao 1996). These institutions tended toward more integrated and less specialized and compartmentalized knowledge patterns, with basic science linked to engineering and medicine, and social sciences connected to fields such as history, philosophy, and literature. A system of colleges of traditional Chinese medicine, established at a rate of at least one per province, reflected a revaluing of indigenous cultural knowledge.

In addition to the new institutions created during the Great Leap Forward, many national-level universities and institutes were demoted to the administrative purview of provincial authorities. We have been particularly fascinated with the fate of the national institutes of political science and law and of finance and economics, which had operated as a kind of extension of the influence of People's University. In a sense, they represented the long arm of the Soviet-style central bureaucracy in their role of training planners loyal to Beijing and Moscow at the regional and local levels. In Shanghai, both institutes were combined into the newly formed Shanghai Academy of Social Sciences; in Wuhan, they were made the basis of Hubei University, a local comprehensive university; and in Liaoning they provided the basis for Liaoning University, also a local comprehensive university. A kind of subversion of centralizing knowledge forces, whose tendencies to absolute control through knowledge had been reinforced by Stalinist patterns, was under way in these changes. However, it was certainly not professors and scholars as a corporate group that brought this about, but rather local political elites who were able to make excellent use of students in patterns rather similar to those of the imperial period. As cadres-in-waiting, students had much invested in the socialist bureaucratic system and wished to please local political figures who would have much to say about their future careers (Hayhoe 1996: ch. 3).

The Cultural Revolution posed a far more extreme, and less effective, challenge to Soviet patterns. Once again students proved extremely useful to the radical group around Mao Zedong. Whereas the Great Leap Forward had resulted in a proliferation of local institutions, many of which reflected local concerns and needs, the Cultural Revolution resulted in destruction rather than construction, leaving both national and provincial universities hollow shells of what they once had been. Republican and Soviet precedents were both wiped out, with nothing new created to take their place. When the higher education system was reestablished after 1976, the Soviet model was revived to lay the basis for the reform period.

The Reform Period

One of the first moves of the reform regime after Deng Xiaoping gained power in the late 1970s was to recognize the losses incurred by the suppression of professors and scholars since the Anti-Rightist Movement (a movement that, ironically, Deng himself contributed to launching), and to seek ways of restoring the scholarly community, first as individuals and later as a group. Their expertise in both scientific and social areas of knowledge was seen as essential to the modernization drive. A long series of memorial and reinstatement meetings was held in an effort to reverse the verdicts of the 1950s and 1960s, and scholars such as Ma Yinchu, Qian Weichang, and Fei Xiaotong were brought back from the political wilderness and given a voice in debates over the reform of higher education.

The reform of the urban enterprise system started in 1984. The importance of urban leadership in this process was reflected in higher education by the emergence of a new level of higher institution, the municipally based vocational universities which offered two- or three-year non-degree programs. About 120 of these were created between 1980 and 1985, often on the basis of branch campuses of national universities and with considerable assistance from their faculties. These institutions gained full financial support from municipal governments which were anxious to assure themselves of a continuous flow of qualified personnel for expanding urban initiatives. In many ways they anticipated the areas of autonomy that would later be granted to all higher institutions. They were free to recruit students locally, provided no housing and expected all students to pay modest fees. Their students were not assured employment under the state planning system but were expected to find their own jobs in the local municipality with the recommendation of their institution (Dai and Hayhoe 1991).

The popularity of these institutions often outstripped that of provincial universities of higher academic levels, and in some cases even of national universities. This was due to the entry they promised to urban job openings. By contrast, national and provincial universities were sending an increasing number of their graduates to less-attractive job assignments by the mid-1980s, when the most desirable positions that had opened up after the Cultural Revolution had all been filled. The greater autonomy of these vocational institutions came from the financial support they received from municipal governments on the strength of responding to local employment needs. While they did not have independent legal status, they did supplement their government income by forging direct links with local industry. The modest student fees they collected also contributed to a measure of financial independence.

The educational reform document of 1985 put out by the Party Central Committee and the state, not merely the Education Ministry, might be described as having a semilegal status. It assured greater autonomy to universities, allowing them to enroll a certain percentage of students outside the state plan, both private students who would pay full fees and students whose study programs were paid by direct contracts with industry. This document gave universities freedom to decide on the content of teaching and encouraged them to integrate research with teaching, an important element in moving away from the Soviet pattern by which each specialization had a uniform teaching plan defined by the ministry and research was assigned low priority. In the subsequent period, a series of reforms was initiated that enhanced the autonomy of universities, culminating in the educational law of 1995, which defined their status as legal persons and gave them full autonomy to initiate action within the parameters of the law. At the same time, it assured them a funding base that would increase at a rate somewhat higher than the overall national budget.

Some of these reforms favored the emergence of professors and students as autonomous groups. During the Democracy Movement in 1989, autonomous student groups emerged in ways similar to earlier student movements, particularly those before 1949. These groups tended to fall back on the bureaucratism and factionalism that characterize the Communist state, and to seek legitimacy by imitating official gestures and ceremonies, in keeping with pre-1949 student movements

(Wasserstrom 1994: 296). While the initiatives taken by organized students were remarkable as long as they lasted, the Party was able to dismantle and ban these student organizations completely once there was a consensus within the Party leadership that this should be done. Any claim to autonomy that the students had made during the movement disappeared.

The focus of attention from the West has been on the student leaders who were imprisoned or who escaped abroad after the movement, and little has been said about the large number of student activists who were punished through the job-assignment system. We met one of them in Guiyang, the provincial capital of Guizhou province. He was a local student whose high marks on the unified entrance examinations had opened the way for him to enroll in Fudan University's journalism department in Shanghai, and who had been promised on graduation a job posting to a major newspaper in Beijing. Because he had been on Tiananmen Square on the evening of 3–4 June 1989 and had brought back a report to Shanghai, he was punished by being assigned to return to Guiyang and take up a position as a reporter on political movements in rural areas for the provincial television station. Many other students faced the same kind of fate after Tiananmen.

While reforms in the job assignment system have been underway since the early 1980s (Hayhoe 1993b), encouraging universities to make direct links with employing agencies, and in some cases to include graduating students themselves in negotiations over job assignment, the Party was able to reassert control over this process and use it to punish student activists. In most major national universities, new Party secretaries were appointed shortly after the movement as part of their mandate to restore "normalcy." The position of all university students as cadres-in-waiting since 1949 has cast them in a role relative to the state that is similar to that of students in the imperial period. In short, their career interests have been intimately, if not exclusively, tied to the stability and progress of the Communist state. There has been no space for meaningful professional activity outside the state, and all higher education students have been destined to become "establishment intellectuals," a term coined by Hamrin and Cheek (1986).

What has changed fundamentally and dramatically by the mid-1990s, however, is the link between higher education and the state cadre system. Ever since 1986, World Bank advisors have been pressing Chinese officials to launch a massive expansion of higher education enrollment, mainly based on an efficiency argument, in the face of the low student-faculty ratio in Chinese universities. The Chinese response has been cautious, as it was clear that the state cadre system could not absorb hugely increased enrollments. (In the immediate post-Tiananmen climate, enrollments were cut back.)

The rapid economic growth of the early 1990s, however, made it increasingly clear that a much larger contingent of higher education graduates was needed by the economy. Provincial governments such as those of Guangdong and Shandong, where economic growth was particularly rapid, put pressure on Beijing to raise their quotas for higher education enrollment. By 1993, the policy research office of the State Education Commission abandoned the policy of "consolidation and replenishment" adopted in the immediate post-Tiananmen era and gave its stamp of approval to a movement towards mass higher education, anticipating enrollments of 3.5 million in the formal higher education system and 2.5 million in the adult system by the year 2000 (Hayhoe 1995). This means that about 8 percent of the age cohort will be entering higher education, in contrast to the 3.5 percent that entered both formal and nonformal higher education in the early 1990s. A massive increase in the number of self-financing students, and a move toward a blurring of the lines between students enrolled within and outside the national plan, with all students expected to pay a substantive fee of about 20 percent of actual costs (Hayhoe and Wu 1995), has led to a dismantling of the Soviet model and the kinds of control it facilitated.

The 1993 educational development plan signalled a clear move toward the end of the job assignment system. The plan stated that a certain number of excellent students would be encouraged to apply for positions within the state bureaucracy, in some cases taking examinations to qualify, but the majority would be expected to seek their own jobs. This change is seen by students as a mixed blessing, since it opens the way for considerable nepotism and the use of "connections" (*guanxi*); on the other hand, the pressure to compete in a global economy is causing employing agencies to become more sophisticated in their search for highly qualified people. The overall and striking change coming out of this severance of the link between formal higher education and the state bureaucracy will be the presence of an increasingly large contingent of university-educated professionals who are working outside of the state's reach and whose career advancement depends on knowledge, ingenuity, and a complex range of factors quite different from the political connections and conformity to Party norms that once determined professional career development in China. Some of them will be employed by joint ventures and will spend some of their time abroad, whereas others will work in township enterprises, many of which are competing successfully with state enterprises. Still others will work in various new economic and legal consultancy organizations which are quite separate from the state.

What will fundamentally change the position of university students as a group, we argue, will be the growing presence of a large number of educated professionals in the nonstate sector and the increasing variety of careers opening up outside the state. They are no longer cadres-in-waiting with all their expenses paid for by the state, but educational consumers selecting specializations that will best serve their independent career interests. In addition, they have a diminished need for the favor of the Party or university and state officials to guarantee their career prospects. The punitive actions taken against Tiananmen activists will no longer be available to the authorities, although the more obvious police tactics used against leading dissident individuals and organizations may survive. There may be some resonance at present with the Republican period. A completely new space is opening up for collective and organized action by university students now that the constraints imposed by the state in both the imperial and socialist periods are being lifted. What use Chinese students make of this new space remains to be seen, as students are likely to be an important component of what we might consider the newly emerging civil society.

What about professors? We have suggested that traditionally they were less able than students to form groups capable of initiating independent action. In the Republican period, however, universities had developed corporate identities, which provided a basis for professors to act as a group. This basis disappeared when the corporate identities of universities were stamped out by the reorganization of colleges and departments in 1952. In the present period, several interesting developments may substantively affect the relationship between professors as a group and the state.

We have noted the provision made for universities as legal persons in the new education law, passed in 1995, and the intention to provide conditions that will encourage them to respond directly to the needs of the economy, society, and state, in that order. We have also noted that universities have increasingly been diversifying their sources of funding from the mid-1980s, when they were totally dependent on state financial support through a kind of line budget system, which allowed for no discretionary spending, to the current situation in which they have a considerable funding base in student fees, research contracts with industry, and various productive activities (Yin and White 1994). Although state funding remains of crucial importance, if universities are to make a significant contribution nationally as well as gain respect in the international academic community, they must continue to diversify their funding bases.

In this regard, the State Council has been innovative in introducing a policy, nicknamed the "2/1/1 Engineering Project," designed to identify and support China's hundred best universities for their leadership role in the twenty-first century. The project was first announced in February 1993 as part of the Program for China's Education and Development (*Foreign Broadcast Information Service*, 3 March 1993). The project has been set up and will be funded by the State Planning Commission under the auspices of the State Council. It has established indicators based on international academic standards for first-rate universities. The project is intended to have two stages of development: a short-term phase for the period up to the year 2000, and a long-term phase to the year 2010. Through this initiative, the state hopes to reform universities in the areas of curriculum development, faculty upgrading and renewal, student quality, and funding.

An ongoing process has been set in motion for identifying the institutions that will be the future beneficiaries of the project, and hundreds aspire to find themselves among the privileged. Every province hopes to have one of its own institutions included, as does every state ministry. Over ninety universities, mostly national institutions, were designated as key-point institutions in the early 1980s and see themselves as natural entrants into this group. The prize of substantive and ongoing state funding at a priority level is worth considerable effort. It was reported at one point that the central government would commit 5 billion *yuan* (RMB), and it was expected that provincial governments would contribute the same amount of funding, altogether making 10 billion *yuan* (Bei 1995). So far the State Planning Commission has only allocated 300 million *yuan* to the project, much less than expected. However, among its first effects has been a loosening of the purse strings of provincial governments and ministries to enable their favored institutions to compete. All key-point universities under the jurisdiction of the State Education Commission have already passed the primary identification process, although not all have entered the first funding group. Sichuan Union University is one of the fortunate, partly because it is an amalgamation of Sichuan University and Chengdu Science and Technology University, two former key-point universities under the State Education Commission.

The 2/1/1 Engineering Project has stimulated voluntary amalgamations of institutions situated next to each other, even though they might have different programs as a result of the specialized approach to institution building of the Soviet model. Sometimes the institutions being merged are under the same jurisdiction, such as the three Shanghai universities under the municipal government that combined to form Shanghai University, now a megainstitution with an enrollment of over sixteen thousand students and a comprehensive set of programs (Hayhoe and Wu 1995). In other cases, mergers have been pursued under diverse jurisdictions, such as the gradual amalgamation of the Beijing Institute of Traditional Medicine, the Beijing Economic Trade Institute, the Beijing Chemical Engineering University, the Beijing Fashion College, and the Chinese Finance College, all of which are located in the northeastern suburb of Beijing (Guo 1995: 24).[7] As these amalgamations proceed and new and larger institutions emerge, the "reorganization" of 1952 will be reversed. This reversal reintegrates specialized programs and makes possible the renewal of identities from the Republican period. These restored institutions are currently writing their institutional histories, which should help enhance their sense of distinct historical identity. The formation of diverse funding bases and multiple relations with different constituents, in striking contrast to the linear, unifunctional role higher institutions once had within the Soviet-style planning system, will also militate in favor of greater autonomy.

Opposite to these multifunctional, large-scale universities emerging in the competition for priority state funding are the small-scale, vulnerable, yet increasingly active private institutions of higher learning, which have been given legal protection under the 1995 educational law. Earlier legislation defined "people-run institutions" as "non-profit educational institutions run by individuals, social groups or collective units, with private funding resources" (Xu, Xiang, and Liu 1993). Legal provision has also been made for jointly run institutions with private partners (*Zhongguo jiaoyubao*, 16 February 1995).

The new institutions are responding to market needs by offering practical training, but few are able to meet the stringent requirements needed to issue state-approved degrees and diplomas. Even so, they are attracting distinguished faculty from among retirees from distinguished state universities. Shanda University in Shanghai is such an institution, managed by retired professors from Jiaotong, Qinghua, Beijing, and other universities (Hayhoe and Wu 1995). All suffer from a lack of facilities, uncertainty about long-term funding, and difficulty in competing with state institutions for good students (*Wenhuibao*, 30 October 1994). However, they enjoy greater autonomy than state institutions, and as well can anticipate many opportunities for development, especially if they are able to gain support from foreign partners or from enterprises within China (Zhou et al. 1995).

At this point it is difficult to speculate on the future of these institutions, but the large and thriving private university sectors in Japan, South Korea, and Taiwan suggest that there will be cultural support for such a development. Will it be possible to develop private institutions with the kind of reputation for critical thought and action that have characterized institutions such as Waseda and Keio in Japan; Yonsei in South Korea; and Nankai, Yenching, and St. John's Universities in Republican China? The sudden appearance of universities of this quality is unlikely, given the abrupt character of the decision to close down private institutions in the early 1950s, but it is conceivable that in the future new Chinese private universities could become dynamic sites for collective action.

Two institutions of the recent period that give some sense of the possible role of private institutions are the Chinese Culture Academy (*Zhongguo wenhua shuyuan*), started by Beida professors in philosophy and related areas in the mid-1980s, and the Economic and Social Consultancy Center led by Chen Zimin and Wang Juntao. Both were disbanded as a result of Tiananmen, but the roles they had forged within the adult higher education system in the period leading up to Tiananmen gives some idea of how private universities might provide a basis for collective action by the scholarly community.

The Chinese Culture Academy focused its work on understanding the cultural change accompanying the modernization movement. It encouraged informed reflection through a well-developed correspondence program that reached forty thousand students at its peak, with the costs mainly borne by employers. The academy was also responsible for the publication of a series of volumes in comparative literature, comparative philosophy, comparative history, and comparative education which were used in this program. The basic assumption underlying the academy's work was that economic and technical modernization would never succeed without concomitant change in the cultural sphere. Its scholars wished to foster a self-reflexive understanding of social change processes in their students, most of whom were working professionals and technicians. The academy had great difficulty continuing the program after 1989, since employers were no longer willing to pay for their employees to take courses and fewer students were interested in this type of correspondence program at their own expense.[8]

The Economic and Social Consultancy Center took on the even more sensitive issue of political change. At one point around 200,000 correspondence students were enrolled in studies of political science through which they were acquainted with classics of Western political thought. In addition, the center carried out a series of surveys, which set out to document and interpret the political change process (Black and Munro 1993). After the 1989 movement, the Economic and Social Consultancy Center was disbanded and the Chinese Culture Academy was permitted to operate only under greatly reduced circumstances. However, these two institutions give some insights into the kind of role that might be played by private universities protected by law in the future. Features of both the traditional academies and of those private universities that were progressive and critical during the Republican period are evident.

The fundamental changes taking place in Chinese universities have affected the professional life and conditions of Chinese university faculty members, making them aware of their social and professional group identity in new ways. A great concern for university administrators in the present period is how to attract and keep good faculty in the face of new opportunities opening up in business and other areas, so that faculty members have some bargaining power. While faculty ranks were restored shortly after the Cultural Revolution and promotion processes that involved peer review and the application of academic criteria were established, salaries remained very low until the early 1990s (Johnston 1991), with pay scales the same throughout the nation and fixed to parallel levels within the state cadre system. In 1993, the salary scale for academic faculty members was separated from that of the cadre system and raised to a somewhat higher level, while provision was made to give special financial subsidies to those with outstanding academic achievements. This adjustment has resulted in a situation in which some professors have higher salaries than university administrators, although the level is still modest compared with those working in joint ventures or other new business areas.

In addition, professors have been able to gain increasing opportunities for consultancy work, involving so-called horizontal contracts with enterprises and local governments, which allow them to supplement their salaries. Often, consultancy earnings end up being higher than the actual salary, especially for professors in areas such as engineering, economics, and finance, and in geographical locations where opportunities for this kind of work are plentiful. One of the problems facing academic vice-presidents in many universities is how to strike an appropriate balance between the needed focus on applications for prestigious funding for basic research, and horizontal research contracts which require less strenuous academic efforts but provide important subsidies for individuals, departments, and research centers (Yin and White 1994).

Improved financial prospects have made the academic profession more attractive, as well as given it a more diversified social and economic base, but there are great differences by region and discipline. Universities in hinterland areas are having the most difficulty attracting and keeping qualified younger faculty, who are easily drawn to the coastal regions where salaries and consultancy opportunities tend to be higher (Bai 1993). Fields such as economics, finance, law, and engineering offer excellent opportunities for consultancy, in addition to being in high demand with students, which makes them attractive career areas for younger faculty. By the same token, however, there is a strong pull on these scholars to take up new business opportunities.

In basic disciplines, such as mathematics, physics, and chemistry, the situation is very different. There are few opportunities for consultancy work, and prestigious research grants for basic research are likely to be within reach of only the best scholars in national key-point universities. Teaching loads tend to be heavy, as a great deal of service teaching for other departments is required. Faculty members thus have fewer opportunities either to enhance their incomes or to engage in the kinds of research activities that will improve their promotion prospects. Faculty members in basic social science and humanities areas such as history, philosophy, sociology, political science, and literature face similar difficulties: inadequate support for research, few opportunities for consultancy, and a general undervaluing of their work in the present feverish concern with success in the market. Added to their difficulties is the cloud left by the post-Tiananmen investigations into theses and academic articles suspected of spreading so-called bourgeois liberal influences (Hayhoe 1993a).

These differences for academic faculty, by region and discipline, are further complicated by significant gender differences. University teaching has been a favored career for women under the socialist system, with the result that by the early 1980s, 29 percent of university faculty were women. In the 1990s, academic careers have become even more popular with women. By 1993, 37 percent of all faculty younger than thirty were women. It seems men are more inclined to accept the risks of new business opportunities, while women are attracted by the stability offered by life on a campus environment, including adequate housing, good educational facilities for children, and reasonable social prestige.

The disturbing elements in this picture are that a disproportionate number of women are found in the basic sciences and humanities, in which career prospects are more difficult and service teaching requirements are heavy, and that women tend to be less qualified in terms of graduate degrees than their male colleagues. A master's degree is now required for promotion to associate professor, and a doctoral degree to full professor, but women make up only 26 percent of all master's students and around 10 percent of all doctoral students. Women may be in danger of becoming an academic underclass, expected to take on heavy teaching and administrative loads at the basic level and less likely than male colleagues to qualify for promotion through the ranks or access to higher-level administrative opportunities (Hayhoe and Wu 1996). Thus, while the new conditions of the reform period have certainly opened up new opportunities for both students and professors to initiate corporate action, they have also thrown up new barriers to effective action linked to differences of gender, region, and field of knowledge in a context in which market forces play an increasing role.

Conclusion: University Autonomy and Civil Society

The debate about civil society in China has placed the issue of autonomy on the scholarly agenda, and this issue may help us to understand the profound changes taking place in Chinese higher education at the present time. As we have stressed in this chapter, the idea of autonomy in China has been shaped by values established before the twentieth century. This shaping is reflected in *zizhu quan*, which expresses the ability to initiate action, rather than *zizhi quan* or self-government, which carries the more negative sense of protection from external interference.

We noted that, in traditional higher learning institutions, neither teachers nor students had a corporate identity compared with their counterparts in medieval European universities. They never formed groups in the modern sense until the end of the nineteenth century. Modern universities, established according to Western patterns in the late-nineteenth and early-twentieth centuries, nourished a group identity among students and teachers. The latter created an academic profession quite separate from the state for the first time. Throughout the war period, universities enjoyed a considerable degree of autonomy, partly due to wartime conditions that gave them the space and opportunity to initiate their own contributions to China's development. There was a melding, therefore, of aspects of traditions of the *shuyuan* and other unofficial institutions in China with the European tradition of corporate autonomy.

Although universities in the Republican period had been patriotic and broadly sympathetic to the communist cause, their corporate identities were erased in the new system established under Soviet influence in 1952. They were thoroughly restructured and made to fit into the huge machine of socialist construction. On one level the new system was clearly influenced by Soviet patterns, but on a deeper level we might see it as a revival of certain autocratic practices associated with the imperial institutions of learning and the civil service examination system. The corporate identity of professors and students was stamped out as university members were once more integrated into the bureaucracy through the state cadre system. All students became cadres-in-waiting, while professors were given an appropriate position in the state system. Within a socialist planning process that radiated from the center to each locality, universities became subordinate parts of various ministries and had no opportunity to take their own initiatives in direct response to social or economic needs. What power they had lay in the authoritative status of the state, which defined and approved the knowledge they were allowed to transmit to their students.

Only in the period since 1978 have universities begun to regain forms of legal and practical autonomy that have parallels with the Republican period. Both the large multiversities that are emerging from the amalgamation brought about by the 2/1/1 Engineering Project and the small private universities that are now emerging have a corporate existence recognized in law. Professors and students can use the institutional base provided by the university to form groupings that take their own initiatives in the areas of the economy, society, and state. The importance of their contribution to the ongoing modernization process is more and more recognized by the political authorities, whose legitimacy depends in turn on the success of this process. We expect, therefore, that universities will be important institutions in the creation of a more diversified society, with different social groups able to make distinctive contributions.

These developments represent a tentative stop on the path to the emergence of a Chinese civil society. We recognize that university autonomy in the corporate sense of *zizhu quan*, "the right to be one's own master," is quite removed from Western conceptions of autonomy and incorporation. In today's China, autonomy of professors and students is still circumscribed and very much under state control. Privatization of universities may provide an impetus to nascent civil society, but this path is fraught with danger, as witnessed by the difficulties encountered by the Chinese Culture Academy and the Economic and Social Consultancy Center in the late 1980s. Still, privatization, a loosening of central controls, and the granting to universities of "the ability to initiate action" in law have provided Chinese universities with a framework for the exercise of broader autonomy that in time may be linked to the growth of a Chinese civil society.

5

From State Corporatism to Social Representation

Local Trade Unions in the Reform Years

Yunqiu Zhang

Chinese trade unions at the local (city and enterprise) level have been undergoing a gradual and largely unnoticed transformation during the reform years.[1] This transformation has been from the trade union as a state corporatist instrument or bureaucratic agency serving the state's purpose for social control and mobilization, to the trade union as a representative of workers as a social group. The basis for this change has been an increasing differentiation of interests, particularly within enterprises, and the growth of tensions between labor and management brought on by the economic reforms. It has been a dual process nonetheless. Workers have needed trade unions to protect their interests from infringement by managers, but the state has needed trade unions to alleviate the social tensions that arise between labor and management. To render them effective, the state has had to allow them to develop a certain degree of autonomy.

I would identify this change as a shift from state corporatism (Chan 1993; Unger and Chan 1995), by which trade unions represent the state's interests in society, to social representation, by which trade unions have come to represent the interests of a particular component of society. The transformation of the local trade union is significant, for it points to a change in the broader relations between state and society. The recent history of trade unions shows that the two sides have begun to separate as distinct entities and that societal forces have been growing vis-à-vis state power. Changes in the role and work of trade unions thus may shed some light on the disputed topic of whether civil society has been emerging in China since the 1980s. Civil society is not the same as social representation, however. The former concept implies a fully fledged autonomy of social organizations from state power, which the latter neither implies nor requires. It seems likely, however, that social representation, once exercised, could evolve into civil society.

What we are seeing in the trade union movement in China today may fall short of civil society, but the emergence of social representation does mark a significant development away from the state corporatism or socialist corporatism (Pearson 1994) that prevailed in the Mao years. The state-corporatist model continues to be useful in identifying high-profile, national-level mass organizations such as the All-China Women's Federation and the All-China Federation of Trade Unions (ACFTU). At the grassroots level, however, notions associated with the concept of civil society, which highlights the growth of societal forces, are more relevant to understanding popular organizations such as enterprise-level trade unions. Applying the concept of civil society does not necessarily mean that I acknowledge that a civil society "exists" in China, but I do find the concept useful in identifying trends of social change as well as in characterizing particular changes in state-society relations in the reform years. I will limit my use of the concept to changes at the grassroots level and within a certain sector (city- and enterprise-level trade unions), rather than applying it to the whole of society and its relations with the state.

This chapter has three sections. The first briefly looks at the relations of the Chinese Communist Party (CCP) with trade unions before 1949, then focuses on the fate of trade unions from 1949 to the mid-1980s, especially the rationale for their being neutralized by state power. The second section analyzes changes in local trade unions and the forces behind them since the mid-1980s, using the coastal city Qingdao in Shandong province as a case study. The final section offers some general observations about the changed relations between the state and trade unions and what these changes may mean for state-society relations in the future.

State Corporatism and Trade Unions before the Reform

The CCP had a long experience of working with trade unions before it took power in 1949. It had been infiltrating the ranks of workers in the cities and organizing trade unions from the day of its birth. The Party explicitly asserted its prerogative to lead the trade unions it organized in its founding documents of 1921, although in reality such leadership was limited. Because the cities came to be controlled by its chief adversary, the Nationalist Party, the CCP engaged in clandestine trade union activities. It faced intense competition from the Nationalist regime and capitalists in controlling trade unions, such that the Communist-led "red trade unions" were often neutralized by the "scab trade unions" organized by the Nationalist regime or manipulated by capitalists (Wang et al. 1992: 180–81, 195). Even within a red trade union, the CCP had to rely heavily on non-Party activists, many of whom were simultaneously members of other independent social organizations such as native-place associations and religious societies (Fu 1987). Usually, Party members cooperated with, rather than dictated to, non-Party trade union leaders. Moreover, the CCP recognized the legitimacy of the distinct interests of workers as opposed to those of the Nationalist government and its constituency of capitalists. It claimed that the primary function of red trade unions was to safeguard the workers' interests against encroachment from government and capital. It stressed the necessity for trade unions to engage in economic struggles to improve working conditions and raise wages as early as 1922. The communists were committed to this ideology and made great efforts to get red trade unions involved in economic struggles. Since protecting workers' interests coincided with the Communists' goal of overthrowing the existing state and winning national power, the CCP was ready to exploit contradictions between the (Nationalist) state and society (workers) and posed as the workers' ally or representative. Yet the CCP's influence on trade unions was offset and restrained by other forces before 1949. Even the red trade unions under CCP sponsorship enjoyed a considerable degree of autonomy from the Party. Concerned with workers' benefits rather than just with serving as the Party's political instrument, they functioned as workers' organizations.[2]

The trade unions did not abruptly lose their autonomy and importance when the CCP took over from the Nationalists in 1949. During the early years of its rule, roughly from 1949 to 1956, the Communist regime was lenient to trade unions and refrained from arbitrarily imposing its will on them. Such leniency was based on considerations of political expediency. The communists had been concentrated in rural areas before 1949. When they first moved into cities, they found themselves in a suspicious and even hostile environment. They faced the enormous task of restoring the urban economy and protecting cities from the sabotage of residual and hidden reactionary forces. The Communist regime desperately needed the close cooperation of workers and trade unions, especially in taking over the enterprises of the so-called bureaucratic capitalists. To forestall embezzlement, the regime recruited trade union members into the groups that were formed at the time to take over the operation of factories and monitor warehouses. As an expedient measure for stabilizing the urban economy, the regime allowed the national capitalists to continue their ownership and management of enterprises. Because this temporary arrangement meant that there still existed a proprietary class potentially hostile to the new regime, the latter found it useful to rely on trade unions to supervise this class and act as a mediator in labor-management disputes. The indispensability of trade unions for the CCP in dealing with urban problems earned unions high prestige, substantial influence, and a certain autonomy during this period. The regime treated trade unions more like a partner than a subordinate. The power of trade unions was partly manifested in the repeated protest activities of workers, such as petitions, strikes, and slowdowns. In the central and southern regions alone, fourteen such incidents were reported in the first five months of 1953 (ACFTU 1989: 172–75). Trade unions were most likely involved, or at least tacitly acquiesced, in these protest activities.

However, even during these "good days" for the trade unions, there were already ominous signs that their authority and autonomy would be restricted. In December 1951, Li Lisan, the Party secretary of the ACFTU, was removed from his position for "committing the mistakes of syndicalism and economism." Li insisted that trade unions, as mass organizations of workers, had different functions from the Party. They should retain organizational independence and the Party's leadership over them should be only ideological. To the central party leaders, Li was endorsing a separation of trade unions from the leadership of the CCP—what the Party called syndicalism. Li also acknowledged that within state-owned enterprises there were contradictions between "public" (state) interests and "private" (workers') interests, with the former represented by an enterprise's managerial authorities and the latter by its trade union. This distinction was the basis for the existence of trade unions in the socialist state: they should be primarily concerned with workers' personal economic benefits. The Party condemned Li's view of the role of trade unions as "economism." Li's removal did not affect the trade unions' position, however, for Li was succeeded by Lai Ruoyu as the principal leader of the ACFTU. Lai shared Li's opinions, although he had to join in criticizing his predecessor (Lai 1957).

Fundamental changes in the relations between trade unions and the Party (state) did not take place until after 1956. By the end of that year, China had completed the process of "socialist transformation." Private industrial and commercial enterprises had been taken over by the state and had become "public-owned enterprises." Gone also was the national bourgeoisie as a proprietary class, and as a potential threat to the regime. For the first time, the CCP firmly controlled the nation's economic resources and was without major political rivals. All of this was achieved with the cooperation of the trade unions. Now the party-state was able and ready to impose absolute authority over society, including mass organizations such as trade unions. From the party-state's point of view, trade unions had finished their historical mission of helping the Party win and consolidate power and, therefore, were no longer indispensable. If they continued to exist, they had to be incorporated into the state bureaucratic structure.

To justify this position, the regime took pains to stress the unity of interests of the party-state and workers and to downplay the contradictions between them. It claimed that, with the establishment of "socialist public ownership," enterprises belonged to all members of society including workers. Only on the workers' behalf did the state take the responsibility of managing these enterprises. In doing so, the state represented the workers' long-term and fundamental interests. There was simply no room for the kind of labor-management disputes and conflicts that existed in capitalist countries or in China before the socialist transformation. Workers did not need separate organizations such as trade unions to represent and protect them (Guo Zhefeng 1989: 123–29). The Communist regime was deliberately denying the distinction between the state and trade unions as social organizations, with the aim of neutralizing the latter.

The party-state's efforts to neutralize trade unions began with the criticism of Lai Ruoyu in 1958. It charged Lai with "not only repeating but also expanding the mistakes of Li Lisan," namely, syndicalism and economism. This time, the criticism was more hostile than it had been with Li Lisan. Lai and his associates in the ACFTU were branded as "rightist opportunists" who wanted to make the trade unions into their "independent kingdom," "placing them above the Party and the government," and "using trade unions as a base to seize power from the Party" (Liu Lantao 1958). Trade union leaders were regarded as anti-Party, antigovernment elements, and their contradictions with the party-state were defined as antagonistic. In retrospect, the above charges were excessive and far beyond the truth. But they indicated that trade unions were still a potentially influential force that had not been completely subordinated to the Party, and that they could be used by some factions in power struggles. The criticism of Lai also showed the Party's fear that trade unions might deviate from Communist leadership. Deprived of all their previous bargaining chips and confronted with an increasingly hostile and powerful party-state, trade unions were doomed to suffer.

In criticizing Lai, the CCP laid down its principles on the role of trade unions and their future relations with the Party. First, trade unions had "unconditionally" to accept the Party's leadership not only ideologically, but also organizationally. At all levels, they could become functional departments of Party committees and work under the latter's "absolute" authority. Second, the major purpose of trade unions was to serve the Party. Third, Party members working with trade unions represented the Party and not the trade union. They had to follow the Party's directives and could not assert their independence (Liu Lantao 1958).

This sounded the death knell for trade unions. To put these principles into practice was tantamount to abolishing trade unions. The Communist regime did not choose to make abolition an element of state policy, but allowed unions to survive as mass organizations in form while changing them into a tool of the Party in substance. This is the technique of state corporatism, a concept elaborated by Anita Chan (Chan 1993; see also Unger and Chan 1995). Chan has used it to analyze the ACFTU, the top layer of China's trade union hierarchy, in the 1950s and the reform years. She understands state corporatism as an arrangement by which a socialist state imposes vertical organizational controls on the population. The state either creates new organizations or incorporates existing ones, such as women's federations, youth leagues, and above all trade unions, into the state bureaucracy. The concept stresses the overwhelming power of the state versus society; accordingly, it is more useful for understanding trade unions before the reform than after, although Chan applies it to both periods. In the reform years, trade unions at the local level have been breaking away from official control and moving out of the state-corporatist mold. To understand this process better, we need to pay more attention to the growing power of society. This is not to deny the validity of Chan's application of the concept of "state corporatism" to the ACFTU in the reform years, when the national-level trade union underwent relatively little change compared with its local counterparts and still remained within the state-corporatist structure.

State-corporatist principles and techniques shaped trade unions from the late 1950s until the mid-1980s. During this period, trade unions lost their popular character and were no longer workers' organizations. They became appendages or bureaucratic agencies of the party-state and served the latter's interests. Trade union cadres were appointed by same-level Party committees to whom they were directly responsible. Their funds were provided by the government. Membership was compulsory. The primary tasks of trade unions were to cooperate with Party committees or administrative authorities in conducting such projects as "communist education" and the mobilizing of workers for "labor competition," "technological reform and innovation," and "increasing production and practicing economy" (Liu Lantao 1958; ACFTU 1989: 677–86). Sometimes trade unions were assigned the job of overseeing and organizing such trivial matters as recreational activities and physical exercise. They showed little interest in the issues that most concerned workers: wage increases and labor protection. If any trade union leaders had bothered interfering in such matters on the workers' behalf, they would have been rebuked by Party committees or enterprise administrators for "contending for power with the Party and government, which best represent the interests of the working class" (Guo Zhefeng 1989: 9–19). Without autonomy or power or a willingness to speak for workers, trade unions lost their trust. Workers felt that trade unions were too submissive to Party committees. In their language, the unions had to obey and serve the Party and government "as a daughter-in-law does to her mother-in-law." From the point of view of workers' interests, trade unions were just "skeletons" (Tian and Xu 1988: 58). They suffered severe setbacks during the Cultural Revolution, when most were paralyzed and some even abolished under the slogan of "strengthening the Party's unified leadership."

In sum, the period before 1949 and in the early 1950s was the golden age of trade unions in terms of the autonomy and influence they enjoyed as workers' organizations. This had been possible because of the diversity of social and political forces and the conflicts among them. By the late 1950s, trade unions lost their autonomous character and became "officialized" (*guanhua*). They operated within a state-corporatist structure and served the state's interests. Trade unions lost their former value as an ally, and their further autonomy could only hamper the regime's attempt to gain unified control over the whole of society.

Urban Reform and Changes in Local Trade Unions

Urban reform was formally set in motion in 1984 to enhance productivity by "enlivening" (*gaohuo*) enterprises. Among the major reform programs that were introduced were factory-director (manager) responsibility and various forms of enterprise contracting and leasing. The reform was basically a process of redistributing resources and power. An increasing differentiation of the population into distinct social or interest groups placed them in potentially conflictual relationships. In enterprises, the two major interest groups were the managerial elite and the workers. The latter were in a particularly precarious situation and vulnerable to encroachment from management on issues such as wages and bonuses. They needed some organizational means to protect their specific interests. This was the basis for the emerging changes in the responsibilities assigned to local trade unions. The state began to refrain from directly interfering in enterprise operations and became more tolerant of local trade unions as mass organizations. It required trade unions to share its burdens in mediating labor-management disputes and especially in redressing workers' grievances. To the state, the enthusiastic involvement of workers in the reform was a necessary condition for the success of the modernization crusade. After nearly 30 years of being tightly controlled by the party-state, trade unions had gained some room to maneuver, which allowed them a chance to champion workers' interests.

Under the director-responsibility system, the ownership and management of enterprises were separated. The state retained ownership while delegating management to enterprise directors. The latter were confirmed as the legal representatives of enterprises and assumed the central position in their operation. Directors were made responsible for the profits and losses of their enterprises. At the same time, they received a variety of powers over such issues as labor reorganization, rewards, and penalties. Directors or managers were usually technical professionals or former administrative personnel. They constituted a unique interest group, distinct from both the state bureaucracy and the workers. To enhance their interests and to safeguard themselves against state intrusion, they formed their own organizations such as directors' associations (*Qingdao ribao [QDRB]*, 27 January 1985). This managerial group was still in its infancy in the 1980s: it was not completely independent of state bureaucracy, nor were many of its members qualified for their positions as they lacked the expertise and skill needed to manage modern enterprises (An, Huang, and Cui 1990: 72–73). Vulnerable to interference from the state, managers were nonetheless in a powerful position relative to workers. Unlike the previous enterprise leadership, the new managers were more concerned with profitability than ideological issues. They used every means at their disposal to increase profit, sometimes at the expense of workers. Many managers resorted to strict labor discipline and harsh penalties, including heavy fines and dismissals for minor misconduct. For example, some managers stipulated that workers would lose a month's bonus for being late once. They tried to hold down wage increases, extend working hours, and even replace regular workers with cheap casual laborers (Zhang and Wang 1988). Such devices were especially common in enterprises operating under the leasing or contracting system. Concerned only with short-term results, managers frequently ignored their workers' situation, including worker safety. Some did not hesitate to abuse their power by giving priority to themselves, their family members, relatives, and friends in matters such as promotion and the distribution of bonuses and housing. According to a survey conducted in 1986, 45.35 percent of worker respondents felt that their relations with cadres and managers had deteriorated since the reform. Some workers complained that people in their enterprises were divided into two camps: the cadres, who made up the managerial elite, and the workers. The former enjoyed benefits far beyond the latter; the gap between them could not be closed (Yu 1987: 19–20; 190–91).

As a social group, workers were clearly at a disadvantage in the reform years. Their social status had declined from that of "masters of the state" and "leading class" to being mere hired laborers. Workers complained that "we have returned overnight to the pre-Liberation days after thirty years of working hard." Although their status as masters of the state had been little more than an illusion, workers felt that they had enjoyed respect under Mao's doctrine of "placing all under the leadership of the working class." In the reform years, that illusion was being shattered, and the former leading class sank into oblivion.[3] Workers were generally looked down on and regarded as ignorant and rough. Elitist elements in the reform faction, some of whom were proponents of neoauthoritarianism,[4] felt that workers were simply laborers to be dictated to, rather than a dynamic force that could be relied on to promote reform (An, Huang, and Cui 1990: 4–5; Yu 1987: 352–53). As the glory of workers faded, the previously despised professionals and technical experts were elevated to unprecedented high status.

Perhaps more important than the psychological blow of losing their status as the leading class was the workers' relationship to the new economic benefits. The urban reform endorsed the principle of material incentives and linked workers' rewards to performance. Pursuing individual interests was finally recognized as legitimate and was encouraged. Workers, like all other social strata, became increasingly concerned with personal economic benefits. Eager to get rich, they became ever more sensitive to infringements on their financial prospects. While workers were generally better off than before the reform, jobs and income were less secure. They felt more susceptible to forces beyond their control, facing strong competition in the job market, inasmuch as there existed a large "reserve army of labor" flowing from the rural areas into cities. Workers were living in the shadow of unemployment as some enterprises edged toward bankruptcy and were leased out to individual contractors without consultation (Guo Zhefeng 1989: 251–60). Workers found that the odds were always against them, and that their desire to get rich was unrealistic. Although the first blamed were their immediate bosses, workers did not realize the root cause of their problems was the transition from the planned economy to a market-oriented economy. The managerial elite served as an easy scapegoat in a situation that was essentially beyond the control of either group.

As employers and employees came to constitute separate groups within an enterprise, they found themselves in conflict. Workers felt they needed their own organizations to deal with the management. This placed the state in a dilemma. On the one hand, it had to guarantee the authority of the managerial elite on whom it relied to operate enterprises profitably and contribute to state revenue. On the other hand, the state had to find some way to appease workers who were in a particularly disadvantageous position in which their interests were being violated by the managerial elite. The state had to address these grievances and could not afford to alienate workers as a base of social power. Chinese leaders knew well the ancient admonition that "water can carry a boat and it can also capsize it." They realized from the example of Solidarity in Poland that a long-suppressed social group such as industrial workers could become an explosive force and a formidable political rival for a Communist regime (Tian and Xu 1988: 1; Guo Zhefeng 1989: 33–41). The regime's survival thus depended on redressing workers' grievances and alleviating tensions with the managerial elite.

The state turned to trade unions for help, stressing the need for strengthening their role as workers' organizations. In doing so, the state recognized the wisdom of permitting them to retain more autonomy. In 1987 Party Secretary-General Zhao Ziyang suggested that trade unions be distinguished from the Party and government in their functions: "Trade unions should represent workers' interests, speak for workers, and make them feel trade unions are their own organizations" (Tian and Xu 1988: 1). In the same vein, an enterprise law passed in 1988 clearly stipulated that "trade unions in enterprises represent and protect the workers' interests and operate independently and autonomously according to the law" (ACFTU 1989: 1603–1615). Such statements marked a fundamental departure from the regime's past positions on trade unions, which had come about in response to pressures from trade union leaders and scholars of workers' movements.[5]

The most vocal and persistent defense of workers' interests and appeals for trade union reforms came from leaders of the ACFTU, including Ni Zhifu, Luo Gan, and Chen Bingquan. They endorsed protecting workers' interests as the primary function of trade unions and the rationale for their existence. They emphasized that workers, as a distinct social group, had their own interests. Workers' "lawful interests could be violated by bureaucratism and corrupt practices of state organs and managerial personnel of enterprises." To defend their interests, workers needed to form their own trade unions based on the principle of voluntarism (Luo Gan 1982; Tian and Xu 1988: 50–55, 72–77). The ACFTU leaders argued that trade unions should be "independent and autonomous" rather than attached to Party organizations and subject to the dictates of the government. They should only follow the general policies of the Party while working as an equal partner of government. At the same time, the ACFTU reminded the local trade unions of their responsibility in this transformation. Local trade unions needed to overcome their "bureaucratic airs" and "administrative inclination" and become genuinely "mass-based" and "democratized" by concentrating on working at the grassroots (ACFTU 1988; Tian and Xu 1988: 2–19).

Some specialists on industrial relations suggested that trade unions should enjoy the rights "to participate in state and social affairs and enterprise administration," "to be involved in making important decisions concerning workers' rights and benefits," "to make proposals regarding labor legislation," and even to go on strike (Tian and Xu 1988: 330–39). Arguments for the rights of unions made by the ACFTU and labor scholars were popular with local-level union leaders and received wide support (Sun 1988; *QDRB,* 12 December 1987, 23 June 1988, 29 August 1988).[6] These appeals cannot be dismissed simply as rhetorical "pure talk" (*qingtan*), for they took place in a public context. The discussions about the changing role of trade unions from which the foregoing comments have been taken were all carried out publicly in open meetings and in newspapers and magazines. Thus, there did emerge in the reform era a kind of "public space," no matter how limited, that trade union leaders were able to use to press their case. This public space contributed significantly to making possible the advocacy of views that were a clear negation of the official doctrines on trade unions that had existed since the late 1950s. This exchange of views also constituted a search for a new ideology to justify the role of unions in society. Trade unions proved ready to take advantage of the relatively liberal political atmosphere, which was emerging as the Party loosened its controls, to argue for changes in the nature and functions of trade unions.

Such changes indeed took place, and are especially visible at the local (city and enterprise) level. In the 1980s, trade unions usually consisted of three layers: one general trade union at the city level; several general trade unions immediately below it at the level of districts or bureaus; and enterprise unions. In my research on the city of

Qingdao in Shandong province, I found that, in the reform years, unions at all levels were becoming more inclined to represent and safeguard the interests of workers; that they actively sought to have a voice in making policies affecting workers' interests; and that they were breaking away from direct official control and gaining a measure of autonomy, especially at the second (bureau) and third (enterprise) levels.

The Qingdao General Trade Union (QGTU) stated unequivocally that it and other trade unions represented the interests of the city's workers. To publicize this position and attract public attention to trade unions, it organized a city-wide discussion in 1988 on "how to build trade unions as the workers' own organization." The discussion lasted two months, and half a million workers were involved (Sun 1992: 43). The QGTU resorted to a variety of means to advocate on behalf of workers' interests. It strengthened the institution of "letters and visits" and established open telephone lines to union presidents to take workers' appeals. It set up a legal advisors' office to provide legal assistance to workers, notably in their disputes with management. The office actively exposed violations of workers' interests by management and urged the latter to follow the law and show restraint in imposing penalties on workers (*QDRB,* 15 September 1989). The QGTU frequently conducted investigations of workers' conditions and transmitted workers' requests to the city Party committee and government as well as to the upper-level trade unions. In 1988 and 1989, the QGTU completed fifteen special investigation reports and published eighty-seven issues of *Gongyun xinxi* (Information on the workers' movement). Sixty-three of the QGTU's proposals were adopted by the city authorities and the upper-level trade unions. Most of these proposals concerned workers' immediate interests, such as labor insurance, labor protection, and welfare.

The QGTU also became directly involved in the city's "leading group" for the comprehensive reform of labor, wages, personnel, and insurance, and participated in formulating policies and regulations. It requested that adjustments of wage increase rates in enterprises favor workers "on the front line" (those on the shop floor as distinguished from those in office jobs); that workers' medical welfare be protected; and that workers' congresses have a say in the process of distribution within enterprises. Most of these suggestions received a positive response from the city authorities (*Qingdao nianjian [QDNJ]* 1989:

220–21; 1990: 226; 1991: 158). The QGTU was particularly concerned with the "democratic administration of enterprises." It established a special organ, the Department of Democratic Administration, to encourage and ensure workers' supervision over enterprise management. The department helped set up workers' congresses, which were specified in the new Enterprise Law (see below), and it conducted frequent inspections of their operation. To make these congresses a formal and regular institution, the QGTU drafted an influential report on strengthening "workers' democratic administration of enterprises," and a regulation on the operation of workers' congress within enterprises (Sun 1992: 27). Furthermore, the QGTU guided trade unions in enterprises to set up special organs such as women's committees, wage committees, and mediation groups to serve as watchdogs of workers' interests (*QDNJ* 1990: 226).

It should be pointed out that the QGTU did not act on its own but was pursuing most of these initiatives with the support of city authorities. The close relationship between the two is not surprising. The QGTU president was chosen by the city Party committee, albeit with some public input; he was also a member of the city Party committee's standing committee. City Party authorities needed the cooperation of trade unions and intended to retain control over them; yet, this did not necessarily mean that the QGTU simply served as the Party's instrument. Trade unions expected to have their leaders recruited into policy-making bodies so that they could articulate their demands more legitimately. The QGTU was ready to use officially sanctioned institutions and channels to promote initiatives that served its interests and those of its constituency. Despite its official ties, or perhaps because of them, the QGTU behaved more like a champion of labor than a state agency, and its president could act as a representative of trade unions within the Party rather than just as the Party's representative within trade unions. It would be a mistake to assume a conflictual relationship between trade unions and city authorities, for they shared much in common. Both were concerned with maintaining social stability and economic development, and thus often proceeded in agreement.

At the enterprise level, trade unions played their role primarily through workers' congresses, for which they served as the executive organ. According to the Enterprise Law, the trade union committee was the "working organ of the workers' congress" in an enterprise and had responsibility for handling the congress' day-to-day work

(ACFTU 1989: 1610). By 1990, workers' congresses had been set up in 2,220 enterprises and institutions in Qingdao, accounting for 80 percent of the city's total enterprises (*QDRB*, 16 April 1990). The Enterprise Law empowered them to participate in enterprise administration, scrutinizing policies advanced by the management and supervising managers' performance. As popular institutions, their primary function was to safeguard workers' immediate economic interests against encroachment by management. The efficacy of these workers' congresses varied from one enterprise to another. Some succumbed to formalism and played only a marginal role. Others, however, were active and effective, especially in evaluating managerial personnel and enterprise cadres. In 1988, among 16,761 people subject to workers' congress evaluation, 303 lost their positions due to unfavorable evaluation results (Sun 1992: 28). Workers' congresses could also frustrate operational plans or proposals within the enterprise, notably those involving wage readjustment, distribution of bonuses and houses, and penalties on workers who had broken regulations. In 1990, 312 of 2,117 proposals challenged by workers' congresses failed to go into effect as a result of their opposition (*QDNJ* 1991: 158). Workers' congresses, therefore, provided workers with a channel to express themselves and served as a check on management. Backed by their own institutions, workers could be more outspoken in the reform years and so hinder the managerial elite from taking unpopular actions.

Compared with the Qingdao General Trade Union, trade unions at the enterprise level acquired even more autonomy. At this level, a system of direct elections for choosing enterprise union presidents gradually replaced the older appointment system. The experiment with direct elections started in six enterprises in early 1988. By the end of 1989, the system was extended to 690 enterprises. Candidates were recommended by members of enterprises, including workers and cadres; they could also come forward on the basis of self-recommendation. Often, ordinary workers were elected (*QDRB*, 27 November 1988; Sun 1992: 26). The elected leaders proved more responsive to workers' concerns than their appointed predecessors.

The degree of autonomy for enterprise-level trade unions also increased due to the erosion of the authority of the Party committees within enterprises. With the implementation of the director-responsibility system, Party committees retreated from administrative affairs and concentrated on ideological and political education. As the urban reform went on, however, ideology was no longer a concern for workers. Material benefits counted more than CCP membership, and the leadership of the Party was only nominal. Leading figures within Party committees watched helplessly as workers rejected their leadership. Their prestige and power faded away. For trade unions, this was something to celebrate: their "mother-in-law" had been removed and some free space had opened up.

As administration became streamlined, a number of industrial bureaus and bureau-level Party committees directly under city authorities were abolished, which meant that the corresponding bureau-level trade unions also died away. In their place emerged a new type of organization, the trade union federations. These federations were formed by trade unions at the grassroots level in enterprises within the same industrial sector. In Weifang, for example, a federation of trade unions for the textile industry was formed from most of the enterprise trade unions in this sector. Similar organizations were created in the sectors of heavy machinery, light industry, and chemicals. The initiative for organizing these independent federations came from enterprise trade unions rather than from the political authorities. Membership was voluntary, leaders were elected instead of being appointed, and their operating funds came from the members rather than from the government. The federations did not attach themselves to Party committees or governmental organs and were largely free from direct political interference (Xu et al. 1988). In Weifang and Changzhou, two cities experimenting with institutional reform, the federations were more autonomous than the unions at the enterprise level.

Immediately after the Tiananmen incident in 1989, the regime attempted to tighten its control over social organizations. Following a regulation from the State Council on the administration of social organizations issued in October 1989, the Qingdao authorities systematically investigated and registered social organizations in the city with the purpose of eliminating "disturbing elements." It stipulated that any unregistered organizations had to disband; that those with similar functions be combined; and that those breaking regulations be banned (*QDRB,* 26 March 1991). In terms of trade union work, however, there was no turning back. Although the regime repeatedly stressed the importance of the unified leadership of the Party, it recognized that trade unions were workers' organizations, and accepted the need for them to operate autonomously (CCP 1989). After a short period of retrenchment, the economic reform resumed and gained new momentum, especially after Deng Xiaoping's "southern tour" in 1992. In 1993, the regime officially endorsed the market economy and began the experiment with establishing "a modern enterprise system." This new round of reform aimed at transforming state-owned enterprises into independent economic entities with the status of a juridical person. It confirmed that labor was a commodity and virtually acknowledged that the relationship between workers and enterprises was a purely economic contract between wage laborers and employers. The latter had the power to hire or fire workers, while workers had the freedom to choose employers. In reality, however, the existence of a large surplus labor force meant that workers had little choice in the face of "rationalization." The scheme for developing a market economy in the post-Tiananmen period thus contributed to intensifying labor-management tensions, notably in the former state-owned sector. Both the regime and the workers still needed trade unions, albeit for different purposes, and the trend toward increased autonomy has not been reversed.

Two developments in the early 1990s confirmed this trend. First, the state made more of an effort to legalize the rights of enterprise trade unions as workers' representatives and as mediators in labor-management disputes, as seen in the Trade Union Law, the Regulations on Handling Labor Disputes in Enterprises, and the Labor Law, passed in 1992, 1993, and 1994, respectively. Under the Labor Law, enterprise trade unions could now supervise the implementation of labor contracts between workers and employers and intervene on the workers' behalf if employers cancel or break contracts without good cause. The law also stipulates that trade unions represent workers in signing collective contracts with management regarding wages, working hours, vacation, labor safety and sanitation, and insurance and welfare. The law puts enterprise trade unions on the side of workers (*Gongren ribao [GRRB]*, 6 July 1994).

Dispute mediation became a primary function of enterprise-level trade unions (*GRRB*, 8 April 1992). Each enterprise was required to set up a tripartite mediation committee consisting of representatives from the workers, management, and the trade union, with the union representative acting as director. Trade union representatives were also to sit in arbitration committees at the county, urban district, and city levels. If a dispute between labor and management were to arise in an enterprise, the two parties might first seek a solution by the enterprise-mediation committee. If mediation failed, they could apply for arbitration by the arbitration committees. The last resort was to bring the case to the People's Court (*GRRB,* 21 July 1993, 6 July 1994).

These laws and regulations have provided trade unions with legal means to defend workers' rights and interests and given unions a legitimate niche as mediators in enterprises, roles that demand a large measure of autonomy from state organs. Concerned with maintaining stable and harmonious labor relations in enterprises, the state hoped to forestall labor disputes at the enterprise level to reduce lawsuits and limit social unrest that might disturb production. If transferring part of the burden of settling labor disputes to trade unions meant granting some autonomy, it was in the interests of the state to do so. The state also welcomed trade-union involvement in mediation as part of its own disengagement from the direct supervision of class relations and its attempt to adopt a new role as the neutral representative of all the people. If the state was ready to disengage itself from labor disputes, it was not only to appease workers, but at least partly to avoid becoming a target of grievances from either workers or management. As of July 1993, 220,000 mediation committees at enterprises and 2,800 arbitration committees at the urban-district or city level had been set up, accepting and hearing a million labor dispute cases. Of these, 710,000 were settled by enterprise-mediation committees, and most of the rest were decided by arbitration committees. Only about a thousand cases went to litigation (*GRRB,* 21 July 1993).

A second important development in the early 1990s was that local trade unions began to penetrate private and foreign-related enterprises. These enterprises had mushroomed in China's coastal areas in the reform years. In the 1980s they were basically exempt from the intrusion of trade unions, not only by regulation, but also because private and foreign entrepreneurs objected to working with unions, fearing wage-hike demands. Some foreign investors threatened to suspend their investments when they detected signs of union organizing in their enterprises. At the same time, local authorities were too eager to woo foreign capital to encourage union organizing in foreign-related enterprises. In addition, most workers in these labor-intensive enterprises came from rural areas. Poorly educated, they did not understand the role of trade unions in the protection of their interests; some even did not know what a trade union was (*GRRB,* 20 August 1993, 23 March 1994, 17 February 1995).

The labor-management relationship turned out to be more strained in foreign-related enterprises than in Chinese enterprises. This was due partly to cultural barriers between foreign employers and Chinese workers, the latter, at least initially, being unused to the efficient but strict capitalist mode of management. The greater cause for conflict lay on the other side, however. Foreign managers often forced workers to work extra shifts without overtime pay. In some of Qingdao's foreign enterprises, workers were expected to work between nine and thirteen hours a day. In one electronics company, each worker averaged an extra hundred hours a month. In addition, some foreign investors neglected labor safety. In chemical enterprises in Qingdao and Guangdong, no dust and gas protection equipment was installed, and severe accidents resulted. Other foreigners hired labor without signing contracts or without stipulating what rights workers should have. Some Chinese even felt that foreign-related enterprises were reviving practices once prevalent (and thoroughly condemned) in the days before 1949, including corporal punishment and personal insult. For example, a toy company in Qingdao used male guards to body-search women workers to prevent theft (*GRRB,* 10 November 1993, 1 August 1994, 19 December 1994; Liu and Zeng 1994). Such treatment often provoked resistance from workers, such as slowdowns, deliberate wasting of materials, and strikes. In January 1993, Chinese workers in a Japanese-owned electrical machinery plant in Qingdao staged a strike to protest their treatment. The strike lasted eight days and was supported by workers from two other foreign enterprises (*QDRB,* 22 June 1994). From January through May 1993, strikes occurred nationwide in a hundred foreign-related enterprises (*GRRB,* 11 November 1993). Such disturbances happened more readily in foreign-related enterprises in part because there were no organizations such as Party committees to deter them. Chinese workers realized that militancy against foreign capitalists would not have political consequences.

These references to labor unrest are not intended to tarnish the image of foreign-related enterprises in China. Most have performed well and have made substantial contributions to China's modernization. But problems did arise, and where they did, they drew the attention of the authorities and trade union leaders, convincing both that trade unions were needed as mediators between labor and employers in foreign-related enterprises, perhaps even more so than in their Chinese counterparts. In 1994, the CCP Central Committee and the State Council transmitted a report by the ACFTU on creating trade unions in foreign-related enterprises, urging local authorities to place this on their agenda. Later, the ACFTU and five ministries under the State Council jointly issued a notice on strengthening the trade union work in foreign-related enterprises (*GRRB,* 21 October 1994, 2 November 1994). In Qingdao in 1993, the city Party committee put forward the so-called three-simultaneous principle: in negotiating foreign investment projects, the Chinese side should simultaneously explain to foreign business people and stipulate in contracts that workers have the right to organize trade unions according to the law; that preparations should be made for organizing trade unions while enterprises are under construction; and that they should begin to function simultaneously when the enterprises go into operation. In close cooperation with the city authorities, the QGTU and district-level trade unions made annual plans to establish trade unions in 85 percent of all foreign-related enterprises in the city by the end of 1993 (*GRRB,* 20 August 1993, 15 December 1993, 22 June 1994).

Trade unions have taken it upon themselves to harmonize relations between Chinese workers and foreign employers. They voice workers' requests and grievances to employers and act on their behalf in negotiations. Yet, trade unions also act as a useful partner of employers. They help foreign capitalists understand aspects of local culture that affect the workplace, and provide suggestions as to how enterprises might be better operated. They cooperate with management in explaining labor policies to workers, maintaining labor discipline, and modifying or curbing unreasonable demands from some workers, thereby preventing minor disputes from evolving into confrontations. The work of trade unions as mediators in foreign-related enterprises has proved to be constructive and indispensable. Most of the major labor-management disputes that have flared up in the wake of these changes have occurred in enterprises without trade unions (*GRRB,* 11 November 1993; Sheng et al. 1994).

Trade unions in foreign-related enterprises are usually started by cadres sent down by local Party committees or higher-level unions. Over time, their leaders have come to be chosen by elections. In the Shekou Industrial District of Shenzhen, for example, annual elections took place in 1994 in 99.8 percent of foreign-related enterprises. These unions operated quite autonomously and gained enormous influence within their enterprises (*GRRB,* 1 December 1994). Their autonomy can be accounted for partly by the absence of Party organizations. Ultimately, however, it stems from the multiple roles of unions as mediators in the complex new environment created by the reform. Workers look to trade unions as their representatives; foreign employers must seek their cooperation in dealing with workers; and the party-state relies on them to stabilize labor-management relations.

Trade Unions, the State, and Civil Society: Toward Social Representation

Local trade unions in the reform years have shaken off the status of being official agencies of the state. The changes have taken place gradually and quietly through the 1980s and early 1990s. Nonetheless, they have pushed trade unions in the direction of becoming autonomous social organizations. In the process, state-society relations have changed. During the Mao years, the party-state claimed it represented society and was able to maintain effective dominance over society. The state's power over society was manifested in its successful efforts to neutralize social organizations, including trade unions, stripping them of autonomy. In the reform era, however, as society became increasingly diverse and dynamic, the state was no longer able or willing to monopolize all powers within society. Instead, the state had to recognize the legitimacy of distinct interests within society. It accepted that some officially controlled organizations such as trade unions were slipping from its grip and gaining a certain autonomy. It even tolerated the formation of some nongovernmental organizations. The power of society was growing in a way that constituted a challenge to the state.

Although state and society were often in conflict due to their differences in interests, the two had common concerns that could make cooperation possible. The state had to rely on non- or semigovernmental organizations in carrying out certain programs. It chose to strengthen local trade unions and shifted to them the function of mediating labor-management disputes in the hope of appeasing an increasingly discontented workforce. Social organizations like trade unions could find resources in state organs that they could use for their own benefit. Local governments, no matter how meddling, could act as patrons for some social groups and their organizations as well as individuals. No wonder local trade unions usually considered it desirable to hook up with or attach themselves to government organs. They hoped to get the "benevolent" support of the state in dealing with the managerial elite. The latter, rather than the state, was the trade unions' principal target.

There is no strong consensus among China scholars about how or even whether to apply a European-based concept like civil society to China. Heath Chamberlain (1993) has rejected the dominant Western perspectives on civil society in China, while Frederic Wakeman (1993) finds the effort to apply Habermas' concepts to China "poignant" but ultimately unsatisfactory. Despite the risks, there is something to be gained by adapting the concept of civil society to the Chinese case. Most China scholars agree that the primary characteristics of civil society are the existence of voluntary, nongovernmental, and autonomous social organizations counterpoised to the state. Scholars such as David Strand have argued that civil society of this type was already in existence in the Republican period, and that after the state socialist interregnum of the Mao years civil society reemerged in the reform era (Strand 1989, 1990: 13–19). Strand's analysis has inspired the treatment of trade unions in this chapter. Trade unions once enjoyed some autonomy as social organizations before the establishment of socialism in China; later they were transformed into and remained a state agency until the early 1980s; and from then on they began to regain their character as social organizations enjoying some degree of autonomy from the state. The changes in local trade unions in the reform years, in combination with other developments (White 1993; McCormick et al. 1992), suggest that elements of a civil society are emerging in China.

Given the still immense power of the state, China has a long way to go to have a civil society characterized by social organizations with substantial and secure autonomy as currently exist in Western democracies. The nongovernmental social organizations that have emerged in China through the reform years are fragile and still vulnerable to state power. Traditional mass organizations such as trade unions, while having gained some popular appeal and a certain autonomy, remain under the general political supervision and ideological direction of the party-state. This does not, however, mean that the state has been undiscriminatingly hostile to social organizations and that it constitutes a long-term stumbling block to the emergence of civil society. The Chinese state's authoritarian nature in the reform era has undergone great modification and has by no means been immune to pressures from social forces. It frequently has had to adjust its policies to social changes and to respond to the demands of interest groups. The gradual transition from state-controlled trade unions to organizations that seek to represent social interests distinct from state interests has been the result of the state's positive response to the social problems produced by economic reform. In this sense, I agree with Chamberlain that both state and society can contribute to the formation of civil society. In the long run, the prospects for the emergence of a full-fledged civil society in China do not seem bleak. The deepening economic reform and the profound social changes it produces will create further conditions in its favor.

From this perspective, the application of the concept of civil society to China can furnish a useful vehicle for looking at state-society relations in China. Unlike the concept of state corporatism, which stresses the intentions and actions of the state, civil society induces us to think more about the influence of underlying social forces. This approach is particularly important for understanding the reform years, when China has undergone enormous social change and has seen a rapid growth of societal power. The applicability of the concept of civil society to China is not nullified by its Western origin and characteristics. After all, most concepts that Western and Chinese scholars apply to the study of China come from the West: capitalism, bourgeoisie, market economy, urbanization, democracy, and symbolic capital, to name only a few that have proved illuminating. These externally derived concepts help us to think comparatively about China, and in doing so to perceive what is specific to China. To assert that civil society does not apply to China is to work from an ideal type of Western civil society. Indeed, its use as an analytical tool does not even require that civil society exist in China. It requires only that we regard the comparative exercise as appropriate.

In any case, to argue that Chinese are so peculiar in their social behavior that there is no way for them to form something like civil society seems increasingly untenable now that China is being integrated into the world economy and sharing global influences with the West. Some prominent preconditions for civil society are already visible in China, including the emergence of a market economy, the rapid differentiation of social interests, the growth of a middle class, urbanization, and the loosening of state control over social life. Similar conditions once existed in Western Europe when civil society first emerged, although I make this comparison without assuming that a

Chinese civil society must replicate its Western counterpart. How civil society might emerge in China is subject to three considerations.

First, we cannot expect a unified civil society to emerge in the short run. Civil society in any country is internally divided, with voluntary and autonomous organizations representing different social interests and in potential conflict with one another. The tensions among them can sometimes be more serious than those between them and the state, and can be exploited by the latter. In this competitive environment, some social organizations may turn to the state as an ally. This is the inherent weakness of civil society in its confrontation with the state. I do not exclude the possibility that different social organizations may be united or reach consensus over certain issues, or at certain moments of crisis, as Timothy Brook shows in his contribution to this volume. But these moments of unity and consensus will prove to be the exception.

Second, civil society is elite oriented. Better-educated and more articulate, elites are more disposed to organize in protecting their vested interests or seeking more power, wealth, and prestige; and, they possess the resources and skills to assume the leadership of organizations. In the Chinese context, it is usually the intellectuals and entrepreneurs who first realize and exploit the advantages of formal organizations, whereas peasants are the last social group to do so. Here perhaps lie some limitations of civil society as a conceptual instrument for understanding China. It may lead us to pay more attention to the activities of the elites and cities where most of them concentrate, and to pass over the vast majority of China's population, that is, the inarticulate peasants in the countryside. It is not surprising that most Western studies of civil society in China have focused on cities and the activities of such social groups as merchants and intellectuals, including students. Closely related to this elitist bias is the narrowness of the concept of civil society. The concept is, as most studies show, particularly concerned with formal social organizations and their relations with the state. However, even in the most urbanized areas in China not all people or interest groups are involved in formal organizations due either to restrictions imposed by the state or to people's ignorance. For a comprehensive understanding of society and its relations with state in China, we need theoretical frameworks that are broader than the concept of civil society.

Finally, while the emergence of a civil society in China deserves to be hailed, the state may continue to play some significant and positive role. With the increasing diversification of social interests and the intensification of social contradictions in the transition to a market economy, the state must adopt a more neutral position to maintain social stability, to protect the inarticulate and the weak, and to maintain social equity. A social organization may be flawed with parochialism and primarily concerned with the interests of the group or population it represents, whereas the state has to consider the interests of the whole population, if only for the sake of maintaining its legitimacy. The common good of China's citizens may depend on the efforts—and on the cooperation—of both civil society and the state.

6

Chinese Youth and Civil Society

The Emergence of Critical Citizenship

Paul Nesbitt-Larking and Alfred L. Chan

China is a country of overwhelming youth.[1] Today there are no less than 300 million people between the ages of fourteen and twenty-five. Approximately half of the present population is not yet twenty-six years old, and if the category of "youth" is stretched to include those aged twenty-six to thirty-five, then young people in China constitute a substantial majority of the population (Hooper 1991: 264). They are hardly a homogeneous group, however, for there are important differences among them in terms of occupation, wealth, and residence. Despite these differences, China's youth of this generation share a common background of having been born in the late 1960s and 1970s. This was the cohort that spent its early childhood during the Cultural Revolution and was first socialized to the values of radical Maoism. By adolescence, however, the reforms of the Deng era were well under way.

As adolescents in a time of profound socioeconomic transformation, the 1970s cohort has experienced life as a series of contradictions, uncertainties, and disappointments. While promises of material gain and greater freedom have never been fully realized, the security associated with the Maoist system has disappeared. Moreover, China's youth no longer compare their material situation and the extent of their freedom to their East Asian neighbors but rather to the advanced industrial democracies. Not surprisingly, they find their own situation increasingly wanting. There is a sense of shame about China's continued political and social backwardness (Liu 1996: 167). Inflation and rampant corruption are their major concerns. In a 1994 survey, inflation was perceived as having caused a decline in living standards and increased income disparities (Lu 1995: 9–10). Chinese youth are confronted by the moral choice of whether to give bribes or "go through the back door" to get the things they desire (Duan 1995: 10–11). Corruption has added to the feeling that the social and political system is perverted. Only those with connections, notably, the children of high-level cadres, are well positioned to enjoy special privileges and to reap the benefits of reform. As the economy becomes more commercialized, there is the perception that money is omnipotent, but that the vast majority is unable to benefit. It is noteworthy that a recent issue of *Zhongguo qingnian* (Chinese youth), the official publication of the Communist Youth League, addressed the question: "What can one do if one fails to make a lot of money?" (*Zhongguo qingnian* 1996: 51–53).

The current leadership has responded poorly to the demands of young people and has countered their alienation with such irrelevant gestures as insisting on the "four cardinal principles" of adherence to Marxism-Leninism and Mao Zedong Thought, or requiring worship of outdated role models such as Lei Feng, the "socialist hero" of the 1960s who has been resurrected for political educational purposes once again in the 1990s.[2] Political education classes are still mandatory, although barely tolerated by the students, who regard them as confusing or useless. In one of these classes, the students burst out laughing when the instructor tried to teach them that the cadres were the servants of the people and that income was distributed on the basis of labor (Geng 1995). Recent efforts to arm youth with Deng Xiaoping's theory of building socialism with Chinese characteristics are proving to be little more than another futile exercise (*Foreign Broadcast Information Service*, hereafter *FBIS*, 16 May 1996: 45–46). The generation gap in China has become profound.

Given the aspirations of the young and the failure of the current leadership to meet such desires, the term "crisis" has been used to describe the relationship between youth and the Chinese state today (Rosen 1992; Kwong 1994). China's youth, it is said, are going through an ideological crisis; they have lost faith in the official ideology and are alienated from the regime. They no longer share the values and beliefs of their elders, and the generation gap is growing wider. From the perspective of the authorities, the inability to enlist the loyalty of the young and increasing episodes of restlessness and rebelliousness are matters of concern. Furthermore, since the May Fourth Movement in 1919, Chinese students have developed a long tradition of collective protest against the government. Their political actions have consistently had a more immediate political impact than those of workers and peasants. They have tended to create a "broadcasting effect" which has drawn other social groups to their cause. Student protests have often driven a wedge among the Chinese leaders, who have not been able to agree about how to deal with the protesters (Liu 1996: 142, 156–57).

From the perspective of the development of civil society in China, however, political aspects of the new mood among youth in China may be particularly significant. In sharp contrast with the strict socialization methods, ideological control, and cultural isolation of the Maoist era, Chinese youth of the 1970s and 1980s became increasingly exposed to a broad range of new ideas and have experienced opportunities for upward mobility which go far beyond those offered by the party-state. Even compared with their May Fourth predecessors, young people today are growing up in the context of monumental socioeconomic change. The results, in terms of future development, may prove to be even more profound. Youth in China today are more individualistic and materialistic, and they have increasingly become integrated into the international youth culture. Some commentators have complained about their indiscriminate worship of all things Western. Others have noticed the cynical, self-centered, hedonistic, apathetic, and nihilistic characteristics of Chinese youth (Rosen 1989a: 14, 34, 1990a: 265; Hooper 1991: 267; Kwong 1994: 252–53; Barmé 1995; Zha 1995). On the other hand, China's youth have already spearheaded several protest movements, including the Democracy Wall Movement of 1978–1979, the protest against alleged Japanese "militarism" and "economic domination" in 1985 (which demonstrated an important element of patriotism and nationalism), as well as the student movements of 1986–1987 and 1989.

For some analysts, these movements, which were vehicles for the articulation of demands for political and social change, are indicative of the arrival of civil society in China. However, as we shall argue, civil society means more than mere rebellion or discontent. We need to ask questions about the *particular* place of young people in the emergence of civil society. What role are they playing in nascent civil society in China? What kind of citizens are they becoming—notably in comparison with others in society? How profound was the political consciousness of youth in the 1989 protest movement? What changes in value systems and orientations, if any, can be detected subsequently? Do the hundreds of millions of Chinese youth today constitute China's first "thinking generation," or are they another confused, vacillating, and "lost generation"?

Civil Society in Modern China

The most important recent work on political culture and ideology in China is to be found in scholarship on the concept of "civil society." Our reading of the political consciousnesses of Chinese youth begins with civil society. We present a brief definition of the term, followed by a discussion of our place in the civil society constellation. Heath Chamberlain's (1993: 207–8) definition of civil society is both comprehensive and close to our own understanding of the concept:

> Civil society may . . . be understood as a community bonded and empowered by its collective determination to resist, on the one hand, excessive constraints of the society and, on the other, excessive regulations by the state. . . . By the term community I mean to stress that civil society coheres. It is more than an aggregate of individual producers driven by self-interest; it is more than a "floating population" suddenly uprooted from home or workplace. . . . Civil society is animated and sustained by widely shared beliefs and attitudes . . . concerning relations among individual citizens, and between this community of citizens and the state. These attitudes and beliefs touch upon such crucial matters as resolving conflicts, setting the outer limits of dissent and deviance, and determining proper modes and style for pursuit of particular interests—all largely "private" matters, handled openly, in the "public" forum, in a "civil" manner.

A fundamental matter addressed in the literature on civil society is whether civil society actually *exists* in China. Some argue that China, either historically or at present, contains clearly defined elements of civil society (Rowe 1984, 1989; Rankin 1986; Strand 1989; Nathan 1990a; Halpern 1991; Kelly and He 1992; McCormick et al. 1992; Whyte 1992; Chamberlain 1993.) Others reject this interpretation and see in China little more than the political-cultural continuity of a system alternately fragmented into narrow and parochial shards of familial power or dominated in an authoritarian manner by the elite at the center (Pye 1988, 1990; Fu 1991; Wakeman 1993).

We have not adopted a definitive position in the "continuity versus change" controversy, nor will we undertake here the detailed historical analysis such enquiry would demand. Instead, we offer an operationalization of selected attitudinal aspects of civil society, which we call *critical citizenship,* and we assess the degree of critical citizenship among Chinese youth by means of data drawn from a 1987 empirical study of Chinese attitudes on key political issues. To be a *citizen* in a civil society implies a fundamental commitment to the good health and continuance of one's political community as well as a basic trust that others share the same commitment to stewardship. To be a *critical* citizen is to go further. It is to claim part ownership in the organization of public life and to insist on the right to be heard and express genuine political choice. Critical citizenship is present in a society, therefore, to the extent that individuals in a political community exhibit stewardship over—as well as a proprietorial and discriminating orientation toward—their society and political system. We will return to these themes later in this chapter.

One key element of critical citizenship is a propensity to discriminate among three objects of political orientation: the broad political community, the regime, and the authorities. Our research has already demonstrated substantial levels of critical citizenship among Chinese people (Chan and Nesbitt-Larking 1995). Moreover, there is evidence of strong levels of critical citizenship among Chinese youth, levels that decline progressively with each age cohort. Despite evidence of this growing phenomenon, it is possible that aspects of critical citizenship have deeper roots in traditional political culture. Irrespective of the precise longevity of these characteristics, their prominence in the reform period is noteworthy, and confirms the relevance and usefulness of thinking of these changes in terms of the emergence of civil society.

To construct an analysis based on the concept of civil society, one should not gloss over the range of nuanced approaches to the concept. These are already well represented in this volume. Without adding to the substance of this discussion, we will identify the point at which our version of civil society may be located in the spectrum of distinctions. We start this investigation from the point of view of the citizen in society, but do not base it on an unreflective imposition of Anglo-American political sociology onto the complexities of Chinese political life. Our analysis and the work of Min Qi, the principal investigator of the empirical study of Chinese citizens on which we base our findings, have been informed by Western social scientific theories and methods, but these have been employed in a manner that remains open to the lived experiences of those under investigation. It is important to recognize the historical context of contemporary Chinese state and society, in particular the long traditions of state-led and corporatist tendencies. While acknowledging these traditions, this chapter demonstrates the extent to which these are now being challenged from below. We strive to remain both antiteleological and antifunctionalist, inasmuch as it is almost impossible to know in advance the direction of political change in China. It would be unwise to rely on the concept of civil society too greatly to suggest that contemporary China is undergoing changes that are substantially analogous to those in seventeenth-century England or eighteenth-century France. Rather, we are making use of civil society as a framework that is at our disposal. It is no more than a heuristic device.

Political Community, Regime, and Authorities

In Chinese political culture before the twentieth century, state and society were regarded as essentially the same, and individual interests were thought to be indistinguishable from those of the state-society. Politics was regarded as a matter of ethics or moral conduct, and the ideal leaders were an exemplary elite who achieved legitimacy through high moral standards (Pye 1985). The Communist Revolution, with its emphasis on a Leninist vanguard party and complete domination of the state over society, ironically reinforced the traditional facets of Chinese political culture. To serve society meant to serve the state and, by implication, the Communist Party. By the same token, loyalty to the country meant loyalty to the Party and its leaders (Goldman et al. 1993). It was unpatriotic to criticize leaders and government policies. In other words, the boundaries between the political community, regime, and authorities were blurred.

In the Maoist era, Chinese intellectuals tended to view their role vis-à-vis the state in traditional terms. Their ultimate mission was to serve the party-state, and most regarded the Communist authorities as progressive revolutionaries working toward similar goals. In their minds, the notions of community, regime, and authority were inextricably intertwined. In this context, it is not surprising that in the 1980s, when some writers began to articulate openly the need to distinguish between "the motherland and the people" (*zuguo*) and "the government or the state" (*guojia*), this was regarded both as a breakthrough and as something of a political challenge.[3]

Beginning early in the 1980s, Deng Xiaoping introduced a series of reforms in China that, in an economic sense at least, facilitated a more liberalized society. The introduction of market forces and a new openness to the West ushered in an era of rapid economic and social change. These developments were accompanied by accelerated urbanization, the spread of means of communication and transportation, and closer contacts with the outside world. In addition, the role of the state has somewhat diminished, and the distinction between public and private is now more clearly drawn. New voluntary social organizations have been formed, and with the emergence of many new social and economic relations, Chinese political culture is undergoing transition.

Chinese youth manifest the greatest shift away from traditional culture. They have recently developed an intense cynicism about the regime's ideology, goals, and values (Hooper 1991: 264–69; Rosen 1992; Rosenbaum 1992: 24; Kelly and He 1992: 31; Lu 1995). For them, the official ideology, goals, and traditional channels of upward mobility have simply lost their appeal. Chinese youth are beginning to make distinctions among objects of political attention and to evaluate them differentially. Illustrative of their propensity to discriminate among political objects is the slogan, "We love our country, but we hate our government," which appeared in the demonstrations of May and June 1989. Recent data reported in the journal *Lilun yu shijian* (Theory and practice), based on a 1994 survey of young people, show a generalized support for "traditional Chinese culture," as well as decreasing levels of trust in "the government and the leaders" (*Lilun yu shijian,* in *FBIS,* 5 January 1995; Goldman et al. 1993: 125). While loyalty to China as a political community remains of paramount value, as was evident in the protests against Japan in 1985, Chinese young people are increasingly prone to divorce such loyalty to their country from their orientation toward the regime and the authorities, despite the intense efforts of the authorities themselves to limit criticism and dissent.[4] As Stanley Rosen has observed, contemporary Chinese youth no longer automatically equate patriotism with blind loyalty to the regime or strict obedience of the party line (Rosen 1989a: 23; 1990a: 270–71). Such a critical and discriminating mind-set toward the political community, the regime, and the authorities was demonstrated in the national survey of young people conducted by the China Youth Research Center and the School of Political Studies for Young Chinese in 1993. Their national survey of educated young people between the ages of 18 and 35 reported that, after the elimination of corruption and the establishment of democratic institutions, the "separation of the Party and government" was the most desired reform of the political system. Moreover, the findings made clear the powerful feelings of distaste for the corrupt and self-serving practices of the authorities, a low level of faith in socialism, and mixed feelings toward the political regime, with criticism tempered by a measure of patriotism.

In a comparative study of political cultures, Ronald Inglehart (1990: 155–57; see also Rosen 1992) observes that, in China, while younger respondents show a materialistic drive for "personal gratification," older respondents stress "social duty" and a kind of premodern lack of interest in materialist values. Through their adoption of these modern and materialistic socioeconomic orientations (but, of importance, not postmodern or postmaterialistic), China's younger generation is developing a commensurate individualistic and liberal civil culture in which the roles of the state and the regime are diminishing. Inglehart's interpretation must be treated with caution, as it is based on a small database of ninety-four respondents drawn exclusively from an area of China adjacent to Hong Kong. More recent studies have also unearthed high levels of materialism and individualism among Chinese youth (Hooper 1991: 265–68; Lu 1995; Wu Zhong 1995).[5] Our empirical findings, discussed later in the chapter, offer partial support for these characterizations.

Despite the economic changes in Chinese society, the Deng leadership has, in effect, taken up where Mao left off, by insisting on equating patriotism with "loving" the socialist new China under the leadership of the Communist Party (Pye 1993: 127). Ideologically, the four cardinal principles introduced by Deng Xiaoping in 1979 and later enshrined in the constitution not only establish the limit between what is admissible and what is not, but are also the benchmark for determining loyalty to the country. Although the leadership conceded that officials can be corrupted and that citizens are allowed to express a certain degree of disapproval, the regime still insists that loyalty to the Chinese people and the motherland cannot be separated from loyalty to the ideology and goals of the Communist party-state.

Official intransigence notwithstanding, there are indications that a nascent civil society has been emerging in China since the early 1980s. A number of scholars have recently drawn attention to the acceleration of political participation, protest, and efficacy, notably among China's urban population (Zhu et al. 1990: 995; Halpern 1991: 38–59; Rosenbaum 1992: 9–11, 17; Whyte 1992: 85–96; Nathan and Shi 1993). The concept of civil society, however, remains elusive, value laden, and ambiguous (Shils 1991; Chamberlain 1993). Chinese seem to take two divergent approaches to the issue of civil society. Theorists residing in China are concerned with the creation of a modern citizenry with "civic consciousness," but this notion has quickly been co-opted by the officials to stress the law-abiding citizen and "socialism with Chinese characteristics." Exiled dissidents, on the other hand, are so disenchanted by the party-state that they are anxious for a private realm separate and independent from the state (Ma 1994). For instance, immediately after the events in Tiananmen in June 1989, several writers took the sudden solidarity of the protest movement which united different social groups in a common front against the authorities as evidence of the emergence of a civil society (Sullivan 1990). Subsequent research, however, shows that this solidarity and heightened social consciousness may have been vastly exaggerated (Cheek 1992; Perry 1992; Nathan and Shi 1993). As already mentioned, there are difficulties inherent in attempting to evaluate critical consciousness in an environment of control and censorship, so caution must be exercised when interpreting signs of post-1989 levels of consciousness.

Another much-vaunted indicator of an emerging civil society in China over the past fifteen years is the ostensible separation of state and private entities and the proliferation of associations, clubs, unions, and mutual aid societies (Whyte 1992: 78). Given the powerful corporatist (Yang 1989; Miller 1992; Chan 1993) and interventionist traditions of the Chinese state, however, this indicator alone is insufficient. Even "semiofficial" and "unofficial" nongovernmental organizations may be lacking in true autonomy from the state. It is for this reason that our research is based not on the mere *existence* of separate private and public institutions and associations, but on young people's differential orientations toward them. Our reservations about the inaccurate uses of civil society in the literature have prompted us to favor Chamberlain's definition. What is critical about this definition is that his formulation enables us to transcend isolated events and superficial changes.

From Chamberlain we have been able to develop our key understanding of critical citizenship: What distinguishes a civil society from an authoritarian or totalitarian one is not merely the *existence* of a separate and formally free domain of private association, but the emergence of a voluntary *political community;* a *regime* of choice and deliberation; and *incumbents* of that regime who are open to scrutiny, criticism, and replacement. Richard Madsen (1993: 189) rightly criticizes studies that indiscriminately label any separation of state and social activity as civil society. In a key sense, then, civil society is defined by its refusal of the authoritarian or totalitarian propensity to meld party, state, and people. Citizens in a civil society, therefore, are critical because they exhibit a propensity to discriminate among levels of the political system. Citizenship emerges from the collective consciousness of a shared political community. Turner (1993: x) defines citizenship as "a bundle of rights and duties relating to an individual as a member of a political community." For Beiner (1995: 1), the problem of citizenship is "what draws a body of citizens together into a coherent and stable organized political community." Grounded in this sense of cohesion built on a shared political community, citizens are critical, to the extent that they exhibit a propensity to regard their political institutions, practices, and personnel in a discriminating manner. The critical citizen exhibits confidence about shared ownership of the regime and stewardship over it, as well as a constant vigilance toward the political authorities. Highlighting the efficacious aspect, Simeon and Elkins (1974: 409) describe critical citizens as "those who do not really trust the government, but who have some confidence about their ability to affect it." From the normative perspective, Kymlicka and Norman (1995: 284) argue that democracy itself depends on the desire of citizens "to participate in the political process in order to promote the public good and hold political authorities accountable."

In *A Systems Analysis of Political Life,* David Easton (1965) distinguishes among the political community, the regime, and the political authorities.[6] In brief, the political community consists of the citizens of a political system; the regime consists of the underlying ideologies, behavioral norms, and constitutional and institutional structures in a system; and the authorities are those individual and collective incumbents who occupy political roles. Following Easton, it seems reasonable to anticipate that, if China is developing a civil society, citizens will manifest a propensity to differentiate critically among the objects of political support. Table 6.1 on page 161 summarizes data in support of this contention. Table 6.2 on page 162 demonstrates that the propensity to differentiate among levels of the political system is inversely related to age: the younger the citizen, the greater the manifestation of critical orientations. Both tables, as well as a detailed discussion of their implications, are to be found in our earlier work on critical citizenship (Chan and Nesbitt-Larking 1995). The analysis in this article builds on these foundations. Having demonstrated the overall higher levels of critical citizenship among Chinese youth, it is now possible to explore their relative levels of cynicism, potential for protest, materialism, individualism, and trust. Are young people in China more cynical, less trusting of the state, more materialistic and individualistic, and more supportive of acts of protest than their older fellow citizens? Taken together, these characteristics reflect a belief system closely associated with critical citizenship and a vibrant civil society, even if, taken to the extreme, any one of them can also serve to undermine civil society.

Empirical Analysis of Chinese Political Culture

To explore the above question, we have employed data gathered in an extensive national survey of Chinese political opinion. In 1986–1987, Min Qi (1989) collaborated with a group of young Chinese intellectuals who had recently returned from a period of study at the University of Michigan. Taking advantage of the climate of open enquiry at the time, they conducted a survey of public opinion in China in which they asked some five thousand respondents questions inspired by the landmark civic culture study of Almond and Verba (1965). There is little information about the administration of the questionnaires. It is apparent, however, that they were administered face-to-face, and that, in employing a quota sampling technique, there was some discretion on the part of the field researchers as to who would be interviewed. Min acknowledges certain problems of validity and representativeness (Min Qi 1989: 240–45).

It is not known how many interviews were refused. All that was reported was that, of 5,000 interview forms administered, just over 3,000 were returned in a completed and usable form. On the whole, the entire country seems to have been well represented in the sample.[7] The data do show regional and socioeconomic gaps. The southwest was seriously underrepresented with only 14 of the total of 3,204 respondents (Min Qi 1989: 246, 250). So, too, the poorer areas of China were underrepresented. Just over 3 percent of the respondents come from "poor and remote border areas," while nearly 39 percent come from "large cities" (Min Qi 1989: 248, 252). Perhaps the single most serious problem in using data drawn from this study is the lack of information about the details of the survey's administration. There might well have been serious problems of acquiescence and response-set bias. These are always potential problems, but they might have been particularly acute in China, among individuals accustomed to quiet obedience who are often fearful of speaking their political minds after years of "cultural revolution" and other political dangers.[8]

Although we lack access to the original data, the 114 tables contained in Min's book based upon the study contain much usable information. The tabulated data do not always permit the disaggregation necessary to perform further statistical analyses. We are frequently unable to break down political orientations by age or age cohort, and this clearly restricts what can be learned from the data. But, even in their tabulated form, the data permit a satisfactory assessment of our main considerations. Provided the results are treated with caution, they are illuminating. Despite its shortcomings, Min's survey remains a precious resource for understanding political culture in contemporary China.

Immediately following the suppression of the students at Tiananmen in June 1989, all public opinion research institutes were either closed down or forced into dormancy. The Party has continued to produce "surveys," but with data which tend to justify and support the Party line. For instance, officially sponsored polls are said to show youth support of the socialist-market economic system, opposition to "radical democracy," satisfaction with current reforms, and opposition to the West's interference in China on the pretext of human rights. In the still politicized atmosphere regarding political surveys, the Chinese Academy of Social Sciences has provided the Party with polls that suggest that 78 percent of respondents want to be active in politics (*Xinhua,* in *FBIS*, 7 July 1994, 13 July 1994; *Lilun yu shijian,* in *FBIS*, 5 January 1995; *Renmin ribao,* 21 March 1995). In exploring the massive amounts of officially sanctioned data, it is possible to read between the lines and detect some useful clues to the popular mood. But Min's survey was conducted in a spirit of scientific objectivity and administered in a time of relative openness, and very little has become avail-

Table 6.1

Orientations Toward the Political Community, Regime and Authorities: A Comparison of Overall Means

	Mean support (%)	Mean opposition (%)	Standard deviation	No. of items[a]
Community	85.0	15.0	9.7	(3)
Regime	62.2	37.8	20.0	(44)
Authorities	48.8	51.2	15.6	(15)

[a]Refers to the number of questionnaire items within each category.

able since 1989 to equal its importance. Attempts have been made by individual researchers to revive survey research, but their organizations have been banned once even mildly sensitive questions are posed (*Ming pao,* 15 August 1994).

Comparing Orientations Toward Political Community, Regime, and Authorities

The data in Table 6.1 set out the overall empirical pattern discussed earlier. Among all respondents, irrespective of age, support for the political community is higher than for the regime, and support for the regime is higher than for the authorities. The standard deviations of each of the three categories indicate greater variation among the regime items than among either the political community or the authority items. This pattern lends support to the contention that respondents manifest a greater ambivalence toward the system and structures of government than they do toward either the political community or the authorities.

Age and Political Orientation

Table 6.2 illustrates the propensity for Chinese youth to discriminate among objects of political support to a greater extent than their elders and, therefore, indicates their higher levels of critical citizenship. Because Min's original data on the authorities were not broken down by age, this category is not included. As anticipated, support for the politi-

Table 6.2

Differences Between Average Percentage Support Data for Political Community and Regime by Age Cohort

	≤25	26–35	36–45	46–55	56–65	≥66	No. of items[a]
Political community	85.6	84.3	84.2	86.3	81.3	89.0	(3)
Regime	55.4	56.0	58.5	62.0	64.5	64.0	(12)
Difference	30.2	28.3	25.7	24.3	16.7	25.0	—

[a]Refers to the number of questionnaire items within the category.

cal community did not vary in any consistent manner with age cohort, and it was high among the young and old. There were too few respondents in the oldest cohort to make any definitive statements about this age category (the number of cases varied from nine to sixteen). Although not too much should be made of the finding, the penultimate cohort, those aged fifty-six to sixty-five, seemed consistently to be somewhat lower in support for the political community. This is the generation that reached their age of adulthood just before the Communist victory, in the tumult of the civil war. They are the only respondents who seemed prepared, even slightly, to question their own commitment. Table 6.3 lends further support to this interpretation. The penultimate age cohort scored substantially below others in the highly affective matter of "love" for the country. While it might not be more willing to rebel than other cohorts, the quality of this cohort's emotional bond to the political community is more contingent.

Line two of Table 6.2 displays the mean averages of the twelve items assessing each age cohort's support for the regime. If the unrepresentative "oldest" age cohort is removed, there is a monotonic increase in support for the regime with age cohort. The differences are substantial enough (9.1 percent from youngest to the penultimate oldest cohort) to be interesting, if not overwhelmingly conclusive. However, if the small, and maverick, oldest age cohort is removed, the diminution in the gap between support for the regime and the political community, shown as "Difference" in line three, is monotonic and substantial. Among the youngest cohort, it is over 30 percent. For the precommunist cohort aged 56 to 65, it diminishes to a relatively inconsequential 17 percent. Here, in a nutshell, is evidence of an emerging

Table 6.3

Items Assessing Support for the Political Community by Age
(% expressing support for the political community)[9]

	≤25	26–35	36–45	46–55	56–65	≥66
"If the country disappoints you, you have cause not to love it." (% disagree)	76.0	73.4	74.7	76.4	68.6	76.9
"If the country disappoints you, you have reason to rebel against it." (% disagree)	86.3	85.1	84.6	87.1	85.1	90.0
"The fate of the country is everyone's responsibility." (% agree)	94.6	94.4	93.4	95.4	90.1	100.0

civil society in China. Those who are disinclined to distinguish between political community and regime are being replaced by younger, progressively more discriminating and critical citizens.

Table 6.3 illustrates the relatively uniform and high level of support for the political community for each age cohort across the three items. Of note, while differences are small, middle-aged citizens are more likely to support contingent rebellion against the political community.

Tables 6.4, 6.5, and 6.7 assess portrayals of Chinese youth as cynical, lacking in trust for the regime, materialistic, individualistic, and supportive of participation in acts of protest. (These items take us well beyond the range of the twelve items directly related to the assessment of the regime, which are summarized in Table 6.2. While these twelve items are presented in full, they are joined by another fifteen items not included in the assessment of "orientation toward the regime.") The data presented in Tables 6.4, 6.5, and 6.7 record the scores for each age cohort which *contradict* these profiles.[9] In other words, each score measures the percentage of respondents in each age cohort who are *not* cynical, who are *trustful* of the regime, who are *anti*materialistic and *anti*individualistic, and who *do not* support participation in acts of protest. If our expectations of Chinese youth are valid, we should see these scores increase with age cohort. A glance at the tables shows that the general trend is indeed upwards, and that only two of the twenty-seven items contained in the three tables display even a modest trend in the opposite direction.

Cynicism and Trust

Table 6.4 displays the results of fifteen items reflecting cynicism and trust. Key age differences occur in those items which assess trust in the government. Youth do not trust their government and want it to interfere less in their private lives. When asked, "What kind of attitude do you hold toward the government—trust or not trust?" a *relatively* small 71.7 percent of those under twenty-six trust the government, while a comparatively substantial 90.1 percent of those aged fifty-six to sixty-five express trust in the government. In seeming contradiction, however, responses to the statement, "We should trust and obey the government because it is always working for our good," show 64.1 percent of those under twenty-six in agreement, while only 50.6 percent of those aged fifty-six to sixty-five are in agreement. One explanation for the discrepancy is in the implied degree of generality. While the question about attitude toward the government seems to be specific, the question about trust and obedience connotes both a longer time and a more idealized scenario. While the young do not trust the regime of the day, they are somewhat more likely than the older cohorts to believe that governments in general "work for our good." This interpretation is supported by the data on the question, "Are you satisfied with the majority of the government's policies?" While 83.3 percent of the under-twenty-six age group are satisfied, fully 97.1 percent of the fifty-six to sixty-five age cohort are satisfied. Similar trends are apparent in the item "Are you satisfied with the many things government does on behalf of the people?" Responses to the question, "Are you satisfied with the efficiency of the government?" are mixed. Overall rates of satisfaction are low among each age cohort. Surprisingly, perhaps, the youngest age cohort is somewhat higher in satisfaction than those aged twenty-six to forty-five.

Although a large majority of each age cohort expresses satisfaction with the political situation in China "in the past ten years," it is apparent that the youngest age group is the least satisfied. Despite high levels of satisfaction in general, few respondents believe that either "reforms" or "democracy" are unnecessary "at present." Intriguingly, it is the youngest age cohort that is most likely to state that reforms are

Table 6.4

Items Assessing Cynicism and Trust by Age (% expressing trust or the absence of cynicism in the regime)

	≤25	26–35	36–45	46–55	56–65	≥66
"Do you feel proud living in a socialist country?" (% proud)	74.7	70.6	81.5	82.3	84.4	88.9
"Do you have faith that the National People's Congress would implement democracy?" (% great deal of faith)	71.8	70.4	75.6	80.0	88.9	87.5
"What kind of attitude do you hold towards the government—trusting or not trusting?" (% trust)	71.7	72.3	78.6	81.8	90.1	100.0
"Are you satisfied with the many things government does on behalf of the people?" (% satisfied)	79.3	86.6	89.8	89.4	90.4	78.6
"Are you satisfied with the majority of government policies?" (% satisfied)	83.3	89.5	90.7	93.1	97.1	83.3
"Are you satisfied with the efficiency of the government?" (% satisfied)	28.2	22.2	22.9	31.0	22.5	30.3
"How would you evaluate the effectiveness of the regional people's congresses?" (% very/somewhat effective)	68.4	69.3	77.6	80.7	80.3	77.8
"We should trust and obey the government because it is always working for our good." (% agree)	64.1	68.0	64.5	57.2	50.6	40.0

(continued)

Table 6.4 *(continued)*

"Satisfaction with the political situation in the past ten years." (% satisfied)	83.6	90.6	91.7	94.6	96.9	85.7
"Do you think China needs reforms of the political system at present?" (% no need)	25.7	22.6	21.0	19.9	13.6	25.0
"Does China need democracy at present?" (% unnecessary)	20.6	17.4	21.1	21.2	22.0	9.7
"Political struggles are filled with treachery and hypocrisy." (% disagree)	51.0	48.9	57.4	61.7	70.9	90.0
"Politics is noble." (% agree)	65.2	67.0	66.6	70.3	82.5	90.0
"Do you agree that in politics one must be unscrupulous?" (% disagree)	55.6	52.3	57.1	64.1	72.7	81.8
"The Party and the government can manage this country well; we do not have to be involved." (% agree)	52.4	55.6	57.3	59.2	59.0	90.0

not necessary. It is difficult to explain this finding inasmuch as the other data in Table 6.4 portray the youngest Chinese as relatively cynical, lacking in trust and suspicious of politics.

The cynicism is clear in the responses to the items "Do you feel proud living in a socialist country?" "Do you have faith that the National People's Congress would implement democracy?" and "How would you evaluate the effectiveness of the regional people's congresses?" Although all age groups score relatively high, there are clear differences between those under thirty-six and those older than thirty-six. Young citizens are less proud of the ideology and have less faith in Chinese political institutions.

Three items on "politics" as an object of orientation display a clear age-related pattern of cynicism and distrust. The younger the respondent, the more likely the respondent will regard politics as treacherous, hypocritical, ignoble, and unscrupulous. Employment of the referent "politics" suggests that these items are tapping into the "authorities" end of the regime spectrum. If this is so, then the clarity of the distinction between the age cohorts suggests that there is relatively greater dissatisfaction with state personnel among the young vis-à-vis other age groups than there is with reference to institutions, ideologies, and offices of state.

Materialism and Individualism

One of the most striking features of Table 6.5 is the absence of substantial age-related differences in the final three items, each of which is related to the theme of "materialism." Inglehart's research, discussed earlier, concludes that younger Chinese respondents are more materialistic than their elders. Our data do not entirely support this conclusion. Most respondents are tolerant toward the "influx of Western ideas," with a slight tendency for younger respondents to be more tolerant. However, the distinctions are not as clear as might be expected. Most respondents also agree with the contention that the political system has retarded "development" in China. However, there are no consistent patterns according to age. Similar comments are applicable to the final item, in which "adherence to principles" is counterpoised against "the quickest possible development of the economy." The data display mixed feelings about this choice, but no meaningful patterns according to age.

Patterns are somewhat clearer in the first two items. In these items, the relative individualism of younger respondents is apparent. There is a clear tendency for older respondents to accept the notion that "everything I can have is given to me by the government," and they are substantially more comfortable with the notion of government interference in an individual's private life. The fifth item, assessing trust in the leaders, also exhibits a clear age pattern. Those over thirty-six are substantially more likely to defer to their leaders than those thirty-five and under. On two more stringent items, measuring attitudes toward government interference in questionable or even harmful private affairs, substantial age differences disappear. Most respondents adopt a laissez-faire attitude toward government

Table 6.5

Items Assessing Materialism and Individualism by Age (% expressing anti-materialist or anti-individualistic attitudes)

	≤25	26–35	36–45	46–55	56–65	≥66
"Do you agree that 'everything I can have is given to me by the government'?" (% agree)	46.0	50.4	51.4	58.4	69.6	72.7
"The government should not interfere in an individual's private life." (% disagree)	30.3	28.1	30.1	40.7	42.5	54.5
"The government should not interfere with affairs not harmful to others." (% disagree)	15.4	13.7	11.7	20.0	17.3	9.1
"The government should not interfere with affairs that may harm people if there is no complaint." (% disagree)	62.5	59.4	59.3	62.1	61.7	72.7
"When there is no consensus, I would listen to the leaders." (% agree)	27.0	27.8	34.1	30.0	36.4	50.0
"Attitude toward influx of Western ideas." (% not tolerant)	12.0	6.7	13.2	14.1	18.6	26.7
"Problems with the political system are the main reason for the slow development of China." (% disagree)	27.7	25.0	25.2	32.6	27.4	40.0
"In China what is important is not adherence to principles, but the quickest possible development of the economy." (% disagree)	42.2	37.7	48.7	54.6	44.8	33.3

interference when affairs are "not harmful to others," and each age group is equally in agreement that the government should not interfere under such circumstances. A substantial majority, however, agrees that the government should interfere to prevent harm to people even if "there is no complaint." These views are approximately equal for each age cohort.

The Communist Party

Table 6.6 contains two items which assess respondents with respect to the Communist Party. Having already established that Chinese youth are lower in support for socialist ideology, detest political education, and are more cynical and individualistic than their older fellow citizens, it might appear surprising that it is Chinese youth who aspire to membership in the Communist Party. However, the paradox is more apparent than real. Until there is a substantial change in the regime, membership in the Party remains one of the best vehicles for upward mobility and material success. Tolerance for "stern criticism" of the Party is universal, and almost 100 percent across age groups. Just because Chinese youth aspire to join does not imply that they are more likely than others to defend the Party.

Participation and Protest

Table 6.7 supports the proposition that younger citizens are more inclined to support political protest. This characterization is clearest in the first and the third items, in which those aged twenty-five and under are substantially stronger in their support for student demonstrations and movements than are all other age cohorts. Additionally, in the first and third items, there is a trend upward for each of the remaining age cohorts. The second and fourth items are interesting in that they record behavior rather than attitude or predisposition.

It is apparent that younger age cohorts are more likely to join "spontaneous activity organizations" than are older groups. However, there is little distinction in age when it comes to joining government or official organizations. This finding is in keeping with the data on the propensity of Chinese youth to join the Communist Party for instrumental rather than ideological reasons.

Table 6.6

Items Assessing Attitudes Toward the Chinese Communist Party by Age

Item	≤25	26–35	36–45	46–55	56–65	≥66
"Do you want to join the Chinese Communist Party?" (% yes)	48.6	41.1	38.4	39.8	32.0	66.7
"How do you treat people who criticize the Party sternly?" (% tolerant)	94.6	95.0	95.8	95.0	95.7	95.0

Table 6.7

Items Assessing Attitudes Toward Protest by Age
(% expressing attitudes opposed to participation in protest)

	≤25	26–35	36–45	46–55	56–65	≥66
"Attitude toward 1986 student movement." (% not understand and not tolerant)	9.6	28.4	36.2	34.0	40.1	50.2
"Group membership in spontaneous activity organizations." (% not joined)	73.5	84.9	93.5	86.3	85.7	87.5
"I will never take part in activities similar to student demonstrations." (% agree)	48.7	62.8	68.0	71.9	66.7	72.7
"Group membership in government/official organizations." (% joined)	22.3	17.4	16.8	15.4	21.4	37.5

Conclusion

The data gathered by Min Qi create an overall impression of substantial age-related distinctions in political orientations in general and in critical citizenship in particular. There is clear empirical evidence of a generational change as younger cohorts manifest a more critical profile than older cohorts. While sustaining high levels of support for the political community, younger Chinese are substantially more critical of the regime than their elders.

This profile is further explicated and supported in the empirical analysis of levels of cynicism, distrust, materialism, individualism, and support for political protest. To summarize our findings, younger Chinese are substantially more cynical, more individualistic, and more strongly supportive of acts of political protest. Younger citizens are also less trustful of the regime and politics in general than their elder compatriots. There is also evidence to indicate an even greater degree of criticism among youth toward the authorities. Of interest, they do not appear to be more "materialistic" than other citizens, in the limited sense of supporting the rapid development of the economy. This finding lends some support to our earlier contention that the onset of rapid economic development in recent years has not, in itself, constituted the emergence of a civil society. It is possible to support economic development—and that development may or may not be "capitalist"—and also be strongly supportive of the regime, the authorities, the dominant ideology, and the political system. The model of the critical citizen in a civil society, which has been reflected throughout this chapter, portrays the critical citizen as diffusively supportive of the political community, efficacious in the expression of "ownership" of the political system, and discriminating with respect to both the regime and the authorities. This model fits well with the information on the attitudes of Chinese youth that we have found in Min's data.

One of the demands of the Democracy Movement in 1989 was to end the corruption and inefficiency of public officials. The yearning to be incorporated into a "modern" political system—which may be democratic to varying degrees—has always been part of the vision of Chinese student activists in this century (Liu 1996: 143–44). In a democratic society, the authorities are temporary incumbents in office, and there are institutionalized and regularized procedures for selecting and removing them. The Chinese have consistently been blocked from the exercise of this kind of political influence. The evidence derived from Min's study indicates that Chinese youth are dissatisfied with their officials and wish to see reforms in the conduct and structure of their government. Attempts by the government to indoctrinate the current generation of Chinese youth are proving futile. It remains to be seen whether the contradiction between the established leadership and the critical citizenship of the masses, notably China's youth, can be resolved gradually and peacefully, or whether the events of Tiananmen Square were a precursor of greater conflict in the future.

7

Ritual and Space

Civil Society or Popular Religion?

Kenneth Dean

This chapter discusses the multiple spaces opened up by the rhythmic performance of ritual events in contemporary rural China, and contrasts these kinds of contingent, contested spaces with the concepts of public sphere and civil society introduced to Chinese studies in recent years.

Beginning in 1979, an extraordinary renaissance of reinvented traditional forms of ritual activity has transformed China, particularly rural China, still home to three-quarters of its vast population. Hundreds of thousands of temples have been restored, rebuilt, and reconsecrated. Millions of people have taken part in ritual events which have become more frequent each year, as well as more complex and multifaceted. This activity has been most intense in southeast China, particularly in Fujian, Guangdong, and Zhejiang, but there is increasing evidence that local religious practices are spreading all across China, especially in the south.[1] This is not to say that the Chinese state has revised its definition of much of popular religious practice as "feudal superstition." In many areas, arbitrary decisions are made on the acceptability or allowable scope of religious activity, leading in some instances to the banning of processions, the tearing down of temples, and the arresting of priests and temple committee members. Cadres of the local office of the Bureau of Religious Affairs and Public Security personnel in provincial capitals and urban areas in general discourage large-scale ritual events, and sometimes actively intervene to prevent such occurrences.[2]

From one point of view, these tensions might be interpreted in terms of a split between state and (civil) society, with the renaissance of local cultural forms paradoxically playing the role of a force for greater liberalization. There are, however, certain fundamental difficulties in adopting such an approach. This chapter begins, therefore, with a critique of the concepts of civil society and the public sphere in the writings of Jürgen Habermas, and of the ways in which they have been applied to the study of China. The second part of the chapter discusses local cultural circuits within distinct areas of China and the opening up of different kinds of "public spheres" through the performance of repeated ritual events.

Critique of the Concepts of Civil Society and Public Sphere

In *The Structural Transformation of the Public Sphere* (1989), Habermas describes the emergence of a public sphere generated by the rise of bourgeois liberal institutions in Europe, and the subsequent demise of this public sphere with the growth of consumerism and mass media and the expansion of the state into the intimate space of the family. Although vigorously applied to the study of China, particularly with regard to the rise of provincial and regional chambers of commerce and parliamentary bodies in the late-imperial and Republican periods, the appropriateness of the framework has been questioned by a number of China scholars (Rowe 1993; Wakeman 1993; Kuhn 1995). The impetus for its increasing application to China appears to have been the sequence of events leading up to the 4 June 1989 massacre, and the desire on the part of many observers of China, and many Chinese students and intellectuals, to see the emergence of a "public sphere" in China. The example of Poland, and more generally the role of dissident intellectuals in Eastern bloc countries, was often cited as a model for developments in China. While I sympathize with the desire for the establishment of fundamental liberties and human rights in China, the imposition of a Western model for the development of civil society and the role of the public sphere is strongly reminiscent of postwar efforts to apply uncritically a Western model of modernization on what were then, and still often are, termed "developing" countries.

This rush to apply a Western model is related to a long-standing dichotomy in Chinese studies. Consider the curious relationship of parallelism and antithesis between traditionalist sinological readings of late-imperial China as a despotic cultural system and contemporary China watchers who see a modern, nationalistic nation-state controlled by a totalitarian Leninist party unwilling or unable to permit unofficial modes of popular expression. The traditional view of China pictured an empire based on cosmic correspondences governed by means of a principle of homology, whereby every level of state and society down to the individual merely repeated in exalted or debased form a core set of rituals of dominance and subservience. This view leaves no room for creative response, resistance, or co-optation at lower levels of society.

The modern view of China's transcendence of this condition is equally exaggerated. By deceptively diverting honest nationalist feelings, China transformed overnight into a totalitarian, modern nation-state made up of citizens who by definition were different from peasants. The government controlled official culture, and the only unofficial culture that mattered was an urban-based, dissident one. The dissidents were regarded as champions of democracy and harbingers of civil society, and all would have gone on as in a familiar Polish fairy tale if it had not been for the vicious "tyranny" of the old dinosaurs who clung ferociously to power as paranoia settled over their dimming minds. What is amiss with this view is that it ignores the lives of the vast majority of Chinese living in rural areas.

Before turning to alternative approaches to Chinese culture that include rural life, I would like to raise four issues regarding the civil society/public sphere model as it has been used in the West: (1) Habermas' underlying notion of power; (2) the possibility of expanding the notion of a unitary public sphere to include contested, alternative public spheres; (3) the withering away of civil society in the West over the nineteenth and twentieth centuries; and (4) whether the rise of increasingly complex, disjunctive transnational flows of ethnic groups, multiple mass media, technology, capital, and ideas (Appadurai 1990) make it impossible to continue to speak of self-contained civil societies and public spheres anywhere in the world.

Habermas' notion of the powers of the emergent public sphere is sharply limited. He notes that in medieval Europe "*publicare* meant to claim for the lord." Later, he backs away from the direct implementation of public opinion by stating that the public sphere "is a forum in which the private people, come together to form a public, readied themselves to *compel* public authority to legitimate itself before public opinion" (Habermas 1989: 6, 25-26). This is not compulsion but a preparation for it. What is compelled is merely an act of legitimation that calls for further dialogue, rather than a pressure for fundamental political or economic change. We are left with a static, reified notion of power as a reservoir of force in the hands of legitimacy.

The second issue concerns the putative unity of the public sphere. Jeff Weintraub has distinguished four competing definitions of the split between public and private that raise questions about the viability of this notion. The liberal-economistic model defines the public as state administration while the private is the market economy, whereas Habermas' republican virtue model uses the public to mean community and citizenship, as distinct from state sovereignty, on the one side and the economy on the other. The sociability model exemplified by Richard Sennet and Philippe Ariès emphasizes symbolic display and theatrical self-representation but has little if anything to do with collective decision-making or state power. Finally, feminist historians have developed a model opposing the privately domestic or familial economy to the public economy of wage earners. The contradictions between these ways of distinguishing public and private turn on the question of the nature of power. Negt and Kluge (1994) in their *Public Sphere and Experience* suggested in 1972 that public space(s) could be contested fields of power, thereby allowing one to conceive of multiple counter public spheres; yet even they back away in the face of the tension between the centralizing or totalizing of power (that moment when the bourgeoisie and its press seemed briefly to be able to speak for everyone) and the multiplicity that arises with identity politics. The problem may arise from the difficulty of applying the terms of this debate to recent fundamental transformations of capital, state, and society to which they may no longer apply. Many observers of the contemporary Western world have commented on the withering away of civil society (Negri 1991; Hardt and Negri 1994). Habermas himself suggests that the public sphere and civil society have declined, although he holds out hope for a renaissance of liberal values. Partha Chatterjee (1993) in *The Nation and its Fragments: Colonial and Postcolonial Histories* argues that, in the West, capitalist relations and capitalist forces have increasingly taken over the public sphere, which was originally conceived as a bridge between civil society and the state. As capital does so, state and society become linked in the form of the nation. At that point, the only community imaginable is the nation, which extends its disciplinary mechanisms throughout society in an effort to achieve cultural hegemony, homogenize social forms, and prevent the independent development of alternative communities.

In tracing the demise of civil society and the deepening impact of capital, Gilles Deleuze, Antonio Negri, and Michael Hardt have in their different ways distinguished three types of society that characterize phases in the process of capital's penetration: societies of sovereignty ("the rights state") with precapitalist relations of production and individual labor; disciplinary regimes ("the social state") in which labor is formally subsumed under capital but has to be continually recuperated, disciplined, and tamed within the productive processes to make it social; and societies of control ("the control state") in which labor has been fully subsumed and social capital appears to reproduce itself autonomously. The institutional backbone of civil society in the disciplinary state, comprised of church, school, family, factory, union, party, and other institutions has been regarded as providing democratic and pluralistic centers for the deployment of social forces on the state; alternatively, it has been analyzed in terms of sites for the authoritarian, hegemonic, and normalizing organization and recuperation of social forces by the state (the latter analysis being associated with Michel Foucault [1993]). The continued and deepening penetration of society by capital has resulted in the generalization of the factory model *beyond* the confines of classical capitalism into society at large.

In the resultant "postmodern" phase, when capital has triumphantly subsumed labor, and society as well, we have entered into a distinctly new social order that is no longer a disciplinary order but a society of control. The logic of capitalist relations spreads like a virus through the crumbling walls of the social enclosures of the family, the factory, the prisons, and the hospitals. The metaphor of structure and superstructure that was central to the conception of the mediating institutions of civil society no longer holds. The striation of disciplinary society, which was divided into various interconnected social realms, gives way to a smooth space of generalized control. The forms of resistance that tunneled mole-like within disciplinary civil society will find no footholds on the slippery surfaces of this new undulating model of rule (Deleuze 1995).

Contrary to neo-Gramscian conceptions of civil society as the space of liberation and the topos of the struggle for cultural hegemony, Negri (1991) and Deleuze (1995) suggest that this reformist socialist political vision is utopian. Civil society has vanished. The state no longer needs it as a site of mediation or recuperation of social antagonisms, and does not require it to legitimate its rule. The verticality that characterized state/society relations in an earlier age has been flattened out in a denial of dialectic, a simulacrum of the autonomous self-regulation and self-generation of the political. The control state separates itself from civil society, which it jettisons. Within the simultaneous articulation of interconnectedness and individuation that characterizes control society, there arises the phantasmagoria of a global public sphere that seems to hover before our eyes on the Internet, beckoning us into the Web.

This leads to the fourth and final critique of the applicability of Habermas' vision of civil society and the public sphere to contemporary China. A growing consensus seems to be emerging that the arenas of future political and cultural struggle are no longer at the level of the nation-state, but rather at very local, hybrid sites. At the same time these arenas are at the level of transnational flows of ethnic groups, images, technologies, finance, and desire (Appadurai 1990). This is to say that a unitary public sphere no longer resides within the parameters of an organic nation-state, if it ever did in the first place. The usefulness of the concept of an organic nation-state, with its well-defined public sphere and distinct civil society, may already have come and gone in the West, as well as in China, if it ever arrived at all. In its place we may have to develop new tools of analysis to chart the new transnational flows. At the local level as well, we may need to develop new modes of understanding the processes of local cultural self-organization as they intersect with transnational flows, generating what I would like to think of as "disruptive communities."

Disruptive Communities: Alternative Conceptions

Chatterjee suggests that *community* may be the disruptive term under the seamless surface of the interlocked discourse of reason and capital, and further that there is a great deal to be learned from the study of marginalized, subaltern communities, as well as of the contradiction between community and nation in postcolonial states. As mentioned, he argues that capitalist relations and forces have invested the public sphere in the West to the point that the only community imaginable is the nation itself, which extends its disciplinary mechanisms throughout society in an effort to expand its cultural hegemony. In his analysis of

Gandhi's political movement, Chatterjee suggests that nationalist thought in its anticolonial mode moves through a communitarian rejection of the pseudocommunity constructed by capital (Chatterjee 1986). He argues that this is a necessary moment in nationalist logic, but that with the successful establishment of the independent nationalist nation-state the drive towards development, whether socialist or capitalist, falls back into the narrative of the march of capital, which demands the homogenization of cultural forms and their subsumption under the aegis of a nation-state. Chatterjee's gesture towards subaltern, alternative communities is a move away from the constraining liberal discourse on civil society.

Anthropologists such as Marilyn Strathern (1992) have examined how alternative modes of exchange build up alternative modes of community and personhood. The narrative of the endless expansion of capital would appear to threaten to subsume all such alternative forms. The subject (in both senses of the term) of this narrative is the individual, narrowly defined as a rational decision-making agent. Nationalism appears as a particular moment in this all-consuming trajectory. The power of the local community to disrupt the nation and its narration(s) was, however, already suggested by Maurice Godelier (1978) in his cautious effort to revive a refurbished version of the Asiatic mode of production and to raise questions about historical necessity in a Marxist context. Godelier raised the possibility of a series of alternative rearrangements of the developmental phases of orthodox Marxist teleology. An analysis of multiplicity in community may enable us to think beyond determinate developmental schemes and find resources with which to respond to the rush of capital into the postmodern era.

Chakrabarty (1994) in his study of the sacrifice of goats by Calcutta factory workers has observed how this gesture creates an alternative temporality to that of abstract labor imposed by capitalist relations. He describes this alternative in terms of "worlding," a term taken from Spivak, which attends to the different kinds of spaces that can be opened up through ritual and the distinct models of temporality these rituals generate. These communal ritual practices recall Godelier's interest in new ways of understanding communal investments of labor and capital. What I will argue in this chapter is that the ritual activity in rural China over the past decade and a half has created alternative temporalities that interrupt the "normal" flow of capital into modernization and unidirectional "development." At the same time, this communal ritual activity has reconnected flows of external and internal labor and capital investment into unexpected fields (rural sectors, ritual excesses, community expression, and local autonomous organization).

In each period and region through Chinese history there have developed distinct ritual traditions in the context of distinct cultural arenas and apparatuses of power. These arenas and apparatuses have been developed for the induction of bodies into identities. Shaped by the determinant mechanisms of local culture, these identities accept certain parameters of repeatedly performed identification: the family, the lineage, the village, the culturally defined region, the economically oriented market region, the socially differentiated class membership, and the political administration. Many of these levels get established through rituals. Certain rituals mark and perform entry into specific groups over the life cycle. Others, such as exorcisms of the possessed, reinscribe identity within the accepted terms of the culture. Many celebrate the presumed divine sanction of these naturalized relations.

An analysis of the arenas and apparatuses of cultural production in China would require the elaboration of an alternative theory of force, which would be defined as pure relationality, infinite connectiblity—pure potential; that is, the excessive remainder of absolute immanence, the very movement of determination, of becoming. Force exists only in the moment of its application and resistance, and apparatuses such as institutions and ritual forms operate by capturing or interiorizing force by a complex separation of force from potential. The result is what we call power. The actions of the state foster the crystallization of power—regimentation, channelization, induction—through power phenomena such as walls and roads, functionalized things, and allegedly harmonious movements of bodies, utility, and organism (Dean and Massumi 1992).

The circulation of forces channeled on the bodies of the individuals within a local culture takes the form of culturally constructed codes. In aggregate ritual forms, these codes can be analyzed, for the coding of the body that acts through ritual is paralleled by the shaping of the parameters of the mind, in particular the categories of space and time within which the individual operates. Cultural codes embedded in ritual forms not only induce a range of affects from the body but achieve a parallel channeling of forms of cogitation on the mind. The material force of desire, the immanence of the potentiality of the body, always exceeds a particular cultural assemblage, which allows for particular avenues of flight from any given set of ritual forms, social institutions, and discourses. The task of cultural analysis is to map the flows of force, the formation of codes, and the channeling of affect and subjectivity in particular cultural contexts. The model of the individual implied here treats identity as a temporary calcification of potentiality, constantly struggling to reimpose itself on a seething flux of vectors of change, sensory trajectories, and affective investments.

Because the particular coalescence of flows that takes place in a given ritual (constituting its internal consistency) is unique, new ritual forms can present an entirely different set of relations in relation to the surrounding context. Similarly, rather than insisting on an essential nature of the individual or the a priori status of any particular process of the formation of individual identity, one could view participation in a ritual or particular ritual tradition as an abstract technology of the self.

At a theoretical level, these complex and contradictory processes can be described in terms of individuation and multiplicity. To draw an example from the philosophy of science, Gilbert Simendon (1990) has analyzed the process of individuation of living organisms, individuals, and social collectives. He argues that an individual is generated out of a complex metastable field of preindividual forces, potential forms, and possible coalescences of matter. The moment of individuation is determinative in physical processes as in the formation of a crystal, but even after attaining the consistency of energy, form, and matter that constitutes it, the crystal continues to interact with its milieu to maintain its consistency. In the case of living organisms, the realm of virtuosity Simendon refers to as the *preindividual* is carried along throughout the living being's lifetime of continuous individuation. Thus, attaining a particular identity is but a temporary aspect of a continuous interaction with milieu and a continuous process of individuation drawing on the virtual, or preindividual, realm. Many of the forces that move through a living being undergoing these processes may be described as transindividual. This is particularly the case with regard to establishing an individual identity vis-à-vis a social collective. Social collectives can themselves be said to take part in a process of individuation, actualizing virtual potentials.

The Three in One Movement in Xinghua, Fujian

To examine the formation of alternative communities and the opening up of contested public spaces in rural China, I will discuss the processes by which the Three in One religious movement spread through the Xinghua region of Fujian, China. The Three [Religions] in One was founded by Lin Zhao'en (1527-1592) in Putian, Fujian, on the southeast coast of China. New in comparison to Confucian, Daoist, and Buddhist ritual traditions, the Three in One began little more than a half century after Martin Luther's (1483–1546) Reformation and is now nearly five hundred years old.

Currently the Three in One is widespread in the Xinghua region, where it has over a thousand temples and half a million worshippers. The continued vitality of this distinct ritual tradition raises the issue of what should or could be the place of "tradition" in social movements and cultural studies. Imported Western theoretical tools for the analysis of cultural change tend to focus attention on the movement of investment capital into special economic zones and the often blatantly exploitative effects of unregulated capitalist production. In addition, the focus is on the consumption of imported, commodified cultural forms in those urbanized zones and in the media (Gold 1993). On this consumption side, the emphasis is often on creative appropriations of imported cultural forms that introduce a measure of self-definition and self-determination into an otherwise bleak picture (Chow 1991).

In both cases, the rural majority all but disappears from the picture. When the focus is on investment and production, the rural majority figures only negatively, as a reserve labor force drawn to the urban centers. On the consumption side, it does not figure at all, because it lacks the disposable income to appropriate imported cultural forms. One Western theoretical approach in which the rural population does figure prominently is ethnography. All too often, however, ethnography depicts rural culture as frozen in time, an archaic holdover completely unadapted to the modern, let alone postmodern, world. Thus, the rural world is either inert or disappears. One can attempt to maneuver around this shortcoming by combining cultural studies and ethnography in such a way that they critique and compensate for each other's weaknesses. After all, there is no viable option of simply going native and somehow miraculously stepping outside the Western systems of knowledge in which one was formed. But there is an option of combining Western theoretical approaches in a way that makes them interrogate each other, rooting that interrogation in a sustained participation and affective involvement in the cultural phenomenon under study. I have attempted to do this in my study of the Three in One in Xinghua (Dean forthcoming [a]).

By examining the Three in One in a way that includes preindividual potentiality, transindividual vectors of change, and a constantly changing milieu, we can perhaps avoid assigning it, or the individuals within it, a fixed identity or attempting to tease out a set typology. Such a procedure implies that institutional developments are inadequate as an explanatory framework in and of themselves, but also that the discourse or rhetorical realm opened up by the Three in One cannot be interpreted either as adequate in and of itself (transparently meaningful), or as a direct, if distorted, reflection of an underlying institutional or class nexus. Instead, we have to examine the gap between institutional formations/social milieus and rhetorical structures of discourse—the gap between things and words—in seeking to identify the forces at play in between, the forces of desire or the transformative creative force of actualization of the virtual at work in the complex process of individuation.

Over time, the Three in One developed more and more forms and potentials by building on new options arising in the context of late-imperial society. Each particular Three in One temple or community responded to these vectors of change through a process of forced selection and exclusion, thereby determining their relationship with both the tradition of the Three in One and the society in which they lived. Paradoxically, the drive to unification of the Three Religions, or the underlying desire to reunify Chinese culture through a movement to bring the pursuit of Confucian sagehood by Daoist alchemy and Buddhist meditation to Chinese society as a whole, led to the elaboration of a multiplicity of distinctly different forms of Three in One groups. These groups continue to transform and interact with new economic, political, and cultural forces sweeping through southeast China. The desire to unify has thus produced an ever-expanding multiplicity.

Participation in the rituals of the Three in One involves a particular relation to space and time. Liturgical handbooks or "flower patterns" (*huace*) for Three in One ritual provide bird's-eye-view diagrams of complex choreographic patterns enacted on the ground by the members of the ritual troupe. These patterns trace certain shapes or illustrate abstract patterns or particular figures such as the eight trigrams or the character for "longevity" (*shou*). Individual bodies thus act as moving elements in a flowing line that traces patterns in space.

Ritual space can be conceived in several ways. Most immediately, ritual involves a body or a group of bodies moving through prescribed gestures and patterns within a field configured with symbols charged with cultural meanings. Each body opens up space by actualizing one vector out of the virtual sum of all motion, which charges space with the forces moving through the bodies of the participants. The group dance of the Three in One ritualists opens up space in this way; so, too, does the establishment of an altar within a temple or in a private home, which reconfigures the relationship of spaces and forces within the architectural structure.[3] At another level, the spatial layout of the altars and gods within a temple is a permanent arrangement of ritual space that channels the flow of worshippers in and through the temple.

Ritual space is marked within the larger village by the performance of Three in One rituals in public spaces (or occasionally as processions through the village), and as well by Three in One temples, which form a complex spatial relationship with the other sites of charged power in the community. The temples are also involved in various nested hierarchies and spatial networks with other temples, and their circuits of shared ritual activity or interaction constitute another level of ritual space. These links between temples and across communities can take place either in an incense-division line, or in a circuit fashioned by the sharing of ritual resources. In the latter case, key annual rituals are performed over several days in different locales to allow an adequate number of ritualists to be drawn together for each ritual event. Joint participation at the consecration of a new or newly repaired temple is one way of reaffirming these spatial relations. Annual or semiannual incense-presentation processions by almost all local Three in One temples to the Ancestral Confucian Hall (*Zong Kong tang*) on East Mountain (*Dongshan*) in Putian, or to the gravesite of the sect founder Lin Zhao'en or other major figures in the Three in One tradition, provide another spatial network based on a central node.

These ritual spaces should not be regarded as stable fields or set places, but as the transformation of these places by the movements (vectors, velocities, variables of time) that traverse them. Space is a "practiced place" that is actualized by the multiple, conflicting movements deployed within it (de Certeau, 1984). Repeated rituals occupy space, causing space to unfold and charging it with force.

Transformations of the Xinghua Local Cultural/Ritual System

The Xinghua region of Fujian province consists of the two counties of Putian and Xianyou, which were founded over a thousand years ago. It is distinguished by the development of a complex irrigation system, control of which shifted over time from the central or provincial government to the local leadership ensconced in temple committees. Besides the government and the gentry, major players in the history of the area have included Buddhist monasteries, lineages, and popular temples. I have distinguished five phases in the historical development of the region (these phases are documented in Dean 1993 and forthcoming [a]). Each of these phases in Putian involves a different set of relationships between the elements of the local culture; between the central or local government and the locality; among Buddhist monastic estates, lineages, and popular cults; between communities living along the segments of the irrigation system; among rival or parallel ritual traditions; among the gentry, the government, and the commoners; and among the forces circulating through the regions, some captured, some translated, some intensified, others diverted. Each phase was marked by a new set of central ritual forms and apparatuses.

In phase 1 (sixth to eleventh centuries), government-sponsored rites were held at official shrines established to commemorate officials who had supervised the construction of irrigation systems. Buddhist and Daoist festivals were held around temples built in lineage settlements. Rituals were also held in Buddhist monasteries, which ran immense monastic estates that opened up the area for cultivation.

In phase 2 (eleventh to fifteenth centuries), lineages constructed their own noncanonical ancestral halls, local cults began to contest the prominence of official shrines, and differentiated processions began marking spiritual boundaries of different cults.

Phase 3 (sixteenth to eighteenth centuries) was marked by a nested hierarchy of rituals and processions involving larger and larger segments of the irrigation system. Popular cult temple systems transcended lineage structures and were marked in some areas by village-based rituals of collective spirit medium training. This was also the phase that saw the development and spread of the Three in One movement.

In phase 4 (nineteenth to early twentieth centuries), a patchwork of lineage feuds and secret religions and secret societies exploded into peasant rebellions. These entities were constituted by discrete ritual forms.

Finally, in phase 5 (early twentieth century onward), local cultural forms were politicized as the state intruded into village life and decision making. The central forms of culture were contested and local culture remitted. This fifth phase is currently ongoing, with powerful flows unleashed by the implosion of the state, the resurgence of "tradition" and the deterritorializing impact of multinational capitalism. The infrastructure of the irrigation systems, buttressed during the 1950s and 1960s, is now under attack. Deforestation, industrial pollution, an explosion in construction, and a breakdown of command structures are all putting impossible demands on the ecology of the area.

Yet, simultaneously, village-level, and increasingly regional, ritual systems are being restored. According to a survey I have started involving several hundred villages in the irrigated Putian plains, the average village has six temples, each housing an average of fifteen deities. Something like 45 days of ritual performances take place in each village every year. Some villages hold over 250 days of theater and ritual a year. Children in rural Putian have now reached adolescence in a world marked increasingly by temple festivals and ritual performance of cultural difference. Of course, these same years have seen the rapid expansion of multinational capitalism into southeast China. It is still too early to discern the boundaries or significance of the collision of flows at work in this period. We can only begin to map the process of the melting of some powerful institutions, the sedimentation of attitudes and identities induced through repeated rituals, and the lines of tension in play as the value and legality of these ritual forms are contested.

The five phases in the development of Putian's irrigation system can be seen as a process of individuation through the construction of changing rituals of identification. It can also be described as a process of local cultural self-definition. Rituals, arenas, and multiple levels of ritual interaction have been developed as apparatuses of individuation. They also engender a discursive practice in the textual production of the local gentry, forever reinterpreting classical practice in the light of local variations. In addition, Daoist priests, Buddhist monks, Three in One Masters, marionettists, playwrights, stone carvers, artists, actors, cooks, and mediums have all participated actively in this elaboration of local culture (Vermeer 1990a, 1990b). Through this process of elaboration, each phase takes on form and consistency from different kinds of highly charged festivals, which need to be analyzed on a case-by-case basis to examine the flow of affects and intensities circulating within them. For ritual form may be the leading element in the channeling of affect (intensity and sensation) sweeping through the community and the bodies of the participants and thereby elaborating local culture. The mingling of bodies with physical and supernatural forces proceeded by phases, however, linked not dialectically but through a process of self-organization. Self-organization leads to the channeling of flows, which over time leads to sedimentation in more or less supple structures, and in some cases to rigidification in long-lasting institutions such as political hierarchies and lineages. Yet even rigid structures flow, mutate, and become reincorporated into new self-organizing processes (DeLanda 1992).

The five phases that I have outlined suggest that different mechanisms of individuation are at work at different times, shaping particular bodies and subjectivities in distinctive ways in relation and reaction to the forces moving through the environmental and sociocultural fields. These forces are gathered into particularly intense relations in the course of the rituals that dominate specific phases. The transitions from one phase to another are moments of significant systemwide hesitation before dangerous bifurcations. They are not teleologically determined, dialectically impelled, or logically necessary. Lines of flight appear all the time, and bifurcations lead to distinctly different formations. Ritual apparatuses phase in and out, developing a growing pool of potential for the reinvention of ritual forms and the channeling of human and cosmic forces.

This model of the phasing in and out of ritual apparatuses in the course of the cultural development of the Putian plains does not fit with the static, homological model conventionally applied to the role of ritual in Chinese culture. According to that model, imperial ritual is the model of modeling, descending from the court to the fief to the family. Kinship ritual is thus presumed to be modeled on imperial court ritual. The government is presumed to work through institutional homologies through the ritual sacrifices at the altars of soil and grain of each district, the City God temples, and the shrines to officially recognized and canonized local deities. I suggest, however, that many other features of environment and evolving local cultural power relations determine the ways in which this system of homology can be incorporated and co-opted by local culture. This is more than saying that every homology of the center runs the risk at the peripheries of achieving too great a local independence and striving for a life beyond the limits of being merely a copy. Rather, this view challenges the claims of the imperial model (and its easy acceptance to demonstrate the passivity and abjectness of Chinese culture).

To challenge such a fundamental principle of both the Chinese discourse of ritual and the common Western model of Chinese ritual is to raise the possibility of a multivocal understanding of Chinese culture from below. Rather than seeing all local cultures at all times rising to a common level of unity in a vision of the inevitable centrality of the cosmic role of the Chinese emperor, perhaps we can imagine a vast variety of locally rooted and constantly changing conceptions of cosmos and individuality rising out of local and immediate contests of power and metamorphoses of bodies. This interpretation does not mean that the cosmos looks different according to where you are situated, as in functionalist readings of Chinese religion. Rather, it means that the cosmos itself is constructed and subject to change along with the individual, and that the changing set of perspectives on a changing cosmos can never be encompassed in a single system.

Phasing and Space

Let us look once again at the Three in One, this time in relation to a set of four intermingling yet analytically distinct spaces: the earth, territory, commodity and cultural networks, and collective experimentation (based, with alterations, on Levy 1994). These spaces can provisionally be conceived as geological levels, with one building on rather than overcoming the other, and all emerging from the virtual as concrete actualizations that maintain their distinct potentialities. Thought of in this way, each of these spaces can be roughly associated with the phases of Xinghua culture outlined above, although all nonetheless interpenetrate and coexist in each of the phases.

The early settlements and secluded Buddhist monastic estates of the first phase of Xinghua local culture represent an opening up of the space of the earth. This space is opened by myths and rites, and characterized as a relationship between the earth and the cosmos. Identity is primarily structured in relation to lineage and totem.

With the elaboration of state administration and the consolidation of settlements on kinship principles, we see the opening up of the second space, that of territory. Territorial space is characterized by writing and mapping, and is in intimate relationship with the state. Identity is primarily a function of territorial inscription, the establishment of boundaries. In this space, lineages compose genealogical records, establish ancestral halls, and organize rituals at the graves of their ancestors. A patrilineal ideology is elaborated in text, territory, and rite. Property becomes subject to a level of collective lineage control (including the establishment of lineage estates and a principle of priority in land claims), while rules are established for partible inheritance. Writing is also used in this space to transform the chants and ecstatic possession of the space of the earth into Buddhist or Daoist scripture, as cults emerge from isolated communities and claim wider powers. Cults begin to expand their temples, and some temples begin to divide incense. The state interacts with the territory through taxation and corvée and through the performance of graduated homological ritual displays or enactments of authority, which are achieved by constructing state temples, shrines, and altars.

The third space is the space of networks: networks of commodity exchanges and of cultural interactions. The relationship to capital becomes important for identity, which is primarily a function of one's place within processes of production and consumption. In the third phase of Xinghua local culture, the lineages expand beyond single settlements into extended, higher-order lineages. They respond to commodification by establishing tax shelters and joint-stock corporations. But an even greater transformation in this phase is the rise of temple networks. These took several forms, the most common of which were nested hierarchies of temples within geographically defined boundaries such as irrigation systems. A second form is an alliance of temples representing scattered single-surname and multisurname communities in opposition to extended lineages in the vicinity. Another form is the division of incense from a founding temple, such as the Ancestral Confucian Hall on East Mountain. These networks extended beyond territorial limits. The network that grew most rapidly in this period was that of regional markets, which linked the Xinghua region to coastal, overland, and international trade circuits.

The fourth space is the space of collective experimentation opened up by transversal and transnational flows. Although it is difficult to see anything besides chaos in the fourth and fifth phases of Xinghua local culture, one can conceive of the last hundred years as a period of intense reexamination brought on by internal pressures as well as external forces. This is also the space of the imagination: of technological experimentation, collective transformations, and hybridization. The renaissance of the Three in One and a multitude of other reinvented ritual traditions and reconstructed communities in the Republican period, as well as over the last decade and a half, represents a collective return to the powers of the earth and a reassertion of the relationship of the individual to the cosmos. This is not to say that these are primitivist or anachronistic movements. On the contrary, they constitute viable networks working out of newly revitalized communities and dealing creatively with the new transversal flows of transnational capital, ideologies, floating populations, and tourism.

The spaces of the earth, territory, commercial and cultural networks, and collective experimentation are traversed by the spheres of economics, politics, and knowledge. Each has its specific form, but the spaces can also fold in on one another. Thus, the transformation of the state folds back on these spaces, as the transversal flow of a new conception of the modern nation-state forces a reimagining of the nature of territory and the nature of identity at all levels. Economic forces fold back on the different levels as well, with capital searching out natural resources at the level of the earth, speculating in real estate at the level of territory, and partitioning collective experimentation into individual work and careers.

One concrete example of the reopening of these spaces over the past fifteen years is the ritual system of the Jiangkou plains of northern Putian county (Dean and Zheng 1993). In the late 1970s, isolated individual villages in this area began reclaiming their local temples and reviving or reinventing rituals that opened a space of the earth, of individual and cosmic identification, at the level of the immediate physical surroundings of the village. As these underground ritual events began to take place sporadically around the area, coalitions of villages held processions to reestablish territorial alliances. As more territories came to life in this manner, the network of the area was gradually restored, culminating in 1993 in the five-day procession of the Belvedere of the Eastern Peak, which involved over seventy villages and tens of thousands of participants. This procession was financed in part by capital donated by overseas Chinese from Indonesia, Malaysia, Taiwan, and the Philippines. These groups successfully urged the expansion of the procession beyond its "traditional" limits to include areas of the adjoining county of Fuqing, from which many of them had emigrated. Through collective experimentation with traditional forms, new spaces were opened up for a reconstructed and redefined community.

The Three in One has also opened up the four spaces of the earth, territory, network, and collective experimentation. Certain Three in

One temples became centers of village life. Other filiations, such as local lines of division of incense or circuits of ritual collaboration between Three in One shrines in particular regions, have opened up territorial spaces. The interrelationships among the various branches of the Three in One have led to the opening up of complex transregional networks, for the revival of the Three in One in the 1970s and early 1980s has involved both local and overseas Chinese in collective experimentations in which the Three in One tradition has been reinvented and reshaped.

Looking at the Three in One over time relative to the phases of Xinghua local culture, we can see that the movement arose long after a complex local culture had developed. The Three in One originated as a collective experiment: an opening up of the fourth kind of space described above. Beginning at the margins of local society, the movement expanded into village life, established regional filiations, and developed regional and transregional networks. From a marginal group, the movement gradually transformed into a central feature of Xinghua local culture. This transformation required the appropriation and reinvention of a multitude of local cultural forces, for in order for the Three in One to achieve a position of leadership in local society, it had to merge with local institutions and link with local classes. In some villages, this took place through a merging of the Three in One with localized lineages. Thus, in Lindou village in Xianyou, the head of the single lineage of the village is also the hereditary Master of the Three in One altar. The tendency of the Three in One to merge with the local lineage-based leadership class is most evident in the less commercialized, less culturally sophisticated villages of the Xianyou area. In the complex society of the Putian-Hanjiang corridor, a vast array of nested temple systems, commercial circuits, centers of Confucian study, and tightly knit higher-order lineages have made it difficult for the Three in One to rise to a leading role or to achieve a broad popular base.

The inclusion of more women in the Three in One in the Republican period is another instance of the employment of new cultural strategies to expand the power and influence of the Three in One. The involvement of overseas Chinese is yet another instance of collective experimentation opening up new spaces for the expansion of the Three in One. Each step is a matter of invention. Its communal ritual and inner alchemical practices were invented collectively first by the founder and early disciples of the Three in One, then again by the many different groups in separate locations throughout the Xinghua area who fused the Three in One with local cults and practices. What is significant in the lives of its adherents is how they are gathered into flows of ritual events and intensities, whether as children attending a festival, as worshippers preparing food offerings or burning incense and consulting divination poems, as mediums relaying the words of the gods, as initiates practicing meditation, or as ritualists combining inner alchemy, liturgical practice, and scriptural study. The ritual events of the Three in One actualize some of the virtual planes of Xinghua local culture, traversing the four spaces to reconnect the individual with the cosmos.

On the Public Sphere and Civil Society

The opening up of space through ritual performance and the investment by local religious movements of different levels of space in a particular region point to a model of "multiple public spheres" other than what the Habermasian model would allow. It might be objected that this model of the opening up and occupation of public spaces and spheres is only viable at the scale of regional systems, and possibly not applicable even at the level of the economic macroregions of China. Hence it fails to meet the criteria of the Western public sphere. To discuss China in this way would mean that it is no longer possible to talk about Chinese society as a whole or Chinese culture as a single unified entity.[4]

Laclau and Mouffe (1985) reach similar conclusions about the impossibility of a unitary concept of the social in any radical critique of contemporary social change. It is possible to talk about Chinese imperial or Communist Party ideological and ritual models of space that attempt hierarchically to encompass local difference (Hevia 1995; Zito forthcoming) or to massify local cultural forms (Apter and Saich 1994), but we should bear in mind that these imperial ritual forms were being articulated in ever-greater complexity and intensity over a period in which the reach of imperial power was increasingly limited (Littrup 1994). As tax reforms in the late Ming and Qing commuted corvée labor and various local fees into a cash standard, and fiscal needs at the imperial center absorbed more and more of these funds, which could not expand because they were based on a static land assessment, county governments were compelled to relinquish elements of local governance, including the performance of some imperial rituals at the local level. Similarly, the imperial civil service examinations could no longer meet the needs of an expanding literate population. Under these conditions, local appropriations of elements of imperial ritual strategies were widespread, which happened as the Three in One spread through Fujian.

Given the increasing gap between imperial ideology and ritual modeling and local ritual traditions, it is more important to develop models of the rise of regional and local cultural formations within different parts of China than to search for parallels with Western models of public sphere and civil society. An analysis of the way in which space is opened up in communal ritual and regional ritual systems may in turn shed light on the nature of the multiple public spheres of the Western world. Understanding the collapse of these systems in the wake of the homogenization of space by the nation-state and by capital (in different ways that now are transcending the nation-state) may enable us to see the notion of civil society as a nostalgic myth that Westerners live by and still seek to impose on others. The richness of Chinese local cultures is thus not a sign of the imminent collapse of the Chinese state, but an indication of flexibility and potentiality within regions of China for local movements to avoid the rigidity of state desire without becoming entirely absorbed by the spread of transnational capital.[5] At the same time, however, while local formations of desire escape the totalizing pressure of transnational capital and the individualizing, homogenizing pressures of the nation-state, we should not deceive ourselves into thinking that local Chinese communities will renounce their patrilocal nature, with its attendant patriarchal domination of women. The potential for human abuse is enormous under these conditions. It is precisely in its ability to achieve and activate a sphere of domination separate from the totalizing and individualizing powers of the state that the community manifests its powers of resistance. Part of the task of analysis is to uncover the assemblages of desire operating at the communal level simultaneously to resist the state and inscribe the all too human.

Epilogue

China and the Future of Civil Society

Timothy Brook and B. Michael Frolic

At the conclusion of this volume we would like briefly to ponder on what we feel this collective study has achieved. Our initial call for papers reflecting on China in relation to the concept of civil society produced a variety of responses. These ranged from Roger Des Forges' dynamic proposal that some form of civil society has long existed in China, to Kenneth Dean's equally aggressive argument that the application of any civil society model to China is problematic, if not utterly misguided. Within these extremes, the authors in this volume have worked with and against various notions of civil society to present challenging new insights based on substantial empirical research, bringing forward such concepts as "auto-organization," "state-led civil society," "social representation," and "disruptive communities" to challenge and broaden how we think about China.

We feel obliged to acknowledge that there is a measure of uncertainty to our collective project, despite the conceptual and empirical gains of the individual chapters. We make this acknowledgment as a way of suggesting that the project of understanding civil society in China is far from finished, and the issues it raises far from resolved. We could not agree—and see no particular benefit at this stage in the development of China-related social science in agreeing—as to whether civil society (or something like it) is emerging in China, whether it can emerge, whether in fact it has been there all along, or even whether we should be asking a completely different set of questions to assess what is going on in China today. We all recognize that China is experiencing change, and accept that that change might or might not be expressed in terms of the development of civil society, but we do not concur on how quickly that change will happen, or in what direction.

To the extent that we accept the value of working with the civil society model, we see it as representing a process rather than a fixed set of structures or relations. It is a process wherein people acquire the habits and values of individual autonomy within an extensive network of authority relations, and of citizenship within the context of public action, including the obligation to voice dissent against unjust actions of the state. But the change of values and institutions that the emergence of civil society implies is neither fully nor purely corrosive to social integration. While the practice of civil society does furnish a pathway for the separation of state and society, it also provides integuments enabling state and society to be reintegrated subsequently through the formation of new forms and patterns of public behavior. In the Chinese context, that reintegration may not immediately take what we might consider democratic forms, but it should tend to favor solutions to questions of power that conspire toward the shaping of a more open political system.

The recognition that civil society has a reintegrative function stands as a corollary to our sense that the model of "civil society against the state" popular in Western ideologies of confrontation and dissent does not apply smoothly to China. In almost every chapter of this volume, the state is seen to play an incremental and associative role, acting at times as a benevolent, if usually self-serving, partner of social entities seeking to make claims against the state rather than as their opponent. Even in the West, for that matter, civil society as a practice and as a set of institutions has often been advanced historically through evolutionary processes that acknowledge a partnership between state and society. Civil society can of course be the arena in which conflict between them is initiated, but it can also provide a buffer to mediate that conflict.

In acknowledging that a particular model of civil society has gained prominence in the recent Western discourse on political transitions, we confront the thorny issue of China's exceptionality. China may be regarded as unique by virtue of its massive size, its claim to a long continuous history as a culture, or its continuing commitment to Leninist principles of organization and ideology. Whether the differences are rooted in any of these or other factors, civil society doesn't easily fit the Chinese case. Chinese and Western practices of civil society diverge. Some of the contributors (Frolic, Zhang, Nesbitt-Larking, and Chan) attribute the marks of divergence, and therefore a measure of Chinese exceptionality, to the simple fact that China is still actively Communist in a Leninist sense. The differences between China and the West are seen very much to be differences of the present. Most of us accordingly prefer not to trace divergences in civil society practice to the final realm of culture and values. Some of us (Brook, Des Forges, Hayhoe, and Zhong), in fact, are more likely to regard practices of social organization and habits of public conduct in Chinese society before the twentieth century as positively conducive to the formation of elements of civil society in that China that have much in common with the West, rather than as inhibitors.

It is important not to be more than tentative in declaring what point we have now reached in the unfolding of the civil society discussion. We took up the concept of civil society, with all the complexities that arise from its application and with all its limitations as an ideal type, to see whether it might serve as a device capable of explaining China's political development in a more dynamic way. The success of the volume is to be measured in terms of what this method has thrown up as each contributor pursues his or her research topic, rather than in any final conclusions to which all future observations on civil society in China must be attached. To express the basis for this evaluation in a somewhat extreme fashion, civil society is a method rather than a truth. As a method it has accomplished a great deal in our enquiry. It has enabled us to focus on arenas other than peak politics or local community studies, while maintaining potential links to both. It has pushed us to attend to aspects of society and history that the established methodological shadows have obscured. And it has meant that while working in different disciplines on different particularities we have been able to pursue a dialogue in common.

Is there then a future for the study of civil society in China? The question is presumptuous, given the lack of consensus within the field of China studies—as among the contributors to this volume—as to whether it even has a presence. It also rests on a plethora of assumptions that need constantly to be re-examined. It assumes a coherence to the idea of civil society; it also assumes that there can be a productive relationship between this idea, Western in origin, and the social and political realities we perceive in China. The question of the future of civil society in China is really therefore two questions. First of all, will the concept be of any value for the ongoing process of constructing a social theory for China? That is, will it have a place in our analysis, or is it, as Kenneth Dean declares on the final page of his chapter, "a nostalgic myth that Westerners live by and still seek to impose on others"? And secondly, is what is currently in formation at least in urban China, which looks something like civil society, a reliable indicator of what is to come? In other words, will the various attributes of civil society that strike us as familiar be traceable in familiar ways in the future?

We raise these incautious questions not so much to bring the individual inquiries in this book to a collective conclusion—given the diversity of approaches taken, that would be presumptuous indeed—as to a reflective pause. We are well aware that asking about the future propagates a false sense of knowing in advance what may happen. This can lead to looking for structures that are not there and anticipating outcomes that can never come to pass, thereby recycling old Orientalist notions about China's "inferiority" and "failure." Even though the scholars writing in this volume sensibly avoid speculating about the future, each recalls in different ways the surprising events of 1989. In the wake of that disaster, civil society provides a hopeful, even if possibly misplaced, language by which to formulate concern about China's future. Michel Bonnin and Yves Chevrier (1991: 50) have urged in this regard that civil society not be dismissed simply as a foreign yardstick against which to show that the altered state-society relations in China since 1989 fall short of what "should" have happened. To set expectations for the concept too high would be to "deprive ourselves of a powerful tool for understanding the social dynamics" of both the political system in general and the particular visible elements that seem to be altering its shape. As this volume has amply demonstrated, there is much evidence that Chinese in recent decades have acted among themselves, in the workplace, and even sporadically in the public realm in ways that are altering the terms of their social and political lives. Trade union mediation, human rights activism, and the founding of private universities are not wholly or only explicable in terms of civil society. On the other hand, civil society provides a provisional analytical logic through which we can begin to associate the notions of social representation, auto-organization, and autonomy that these initiatives appear to represent.

The interest in the China field in invoking the concept of civil society has not purely been induced by 1989. It derives as well from the state of Western social theory at the end of the twentieth century. We struggle in the face of competing urges, which Jürgen Habermas and Michel Foucault at each extreme may be taken to represent. Habermas seeks to intervene on behalf of what has been termed "the unfinished project of Enlightenment" (Honneth et al. 1992), whereas Foucault rejects the attempt outright. On Habermas' side stand those who would persevere in the developmentalist strategies of the postwar world-economy and see the upsurge of civil society as confirmation that the gradual proliferation of capitalism must bring in its wake beneficial social transformation; civil society from this perspective is recognized as variously agent or outcome of that transformation. On the other side are those who critique developmentalism from the standpoint of cultural or political critique. Postmodernism, for example, assesses the Enlightenment project is an impossible and dangerous illusion: to agitate for the realization of civil society serves only to press a Western, gendered agenda for hegemony over consumers in the capitalist core, over producers and elites in the Third World, and over the environment everywhere. From a world-system perspective, it can be argued, to more or less the same end, that the global economy and the politics of nation-states "make projects based on the concept of civil society irrelevant, corresponding identities unstable, [and] interpretations one-sided" (Cohen and Arato 1992: 121). In the midst of conflicting assessments of the Enlightenment project as alive, defunct, or irrelevant, the prospects for civil society's future as a concept and as a practical model appear compromised. This seems to place any theory of society that embraces civil society in doubt.

Thinking about civil society in relation to China only intensifies the sense that social theory is in crisis. Ideals of state-society relations in China do not appear to conform to the privileging of society over the state that is generally at work in Western social science. What are we to conclude from this dissonance? Is it that China is simply an anomaly and therefore of no consequence to theory? Or is it, at the other extreme, that the evolution of the concept of civil society in Europe is purely a local history that cannot be generalized into theory? Or should we pursue, in Chinese fashion, a middle course and regard the historical and cultural embeddedness of the concept of civil society as a significant finding that will enable social theory to move away from its Western moorings and develop in a more global direction?

Given the evidence marshalled in this volume, this middle way is certainly persuasive. And yet we should be cautious about making concessions to what are deemed to be the realities of Chinese state-society relations that erase the critical purpose of the concept, which historically has been to recognize social power as a potential counterweight to state power. In the case of China, the concept of civil society may be useful to the extent that it enables us not only to recognize that state-society relations are complex, but that that complexity involves resistance and misalignment between state and social interests as often as it attests to the triumph of social harmony and the satisfaction of individual demands. For even though the state may enjoy clear hegemony in the orchestration of public life and take preponderance in the private calculations of individual Chinese, it does not dictate these relationships. The critical citizenship, social representation, and autonomy attested in several of the chapters—however conditioned and circumscribed they may be by state initiatives—should remind us that the state does not always set the terms for society, nor does society always fold its interests into the state. Ironically, perhaps, it is Dean's chapter that celebrates unambiguously a vision of China as composed of "a vast variety of locally rooted and constantly changing conceptions of cosmos and individuality rising out of local and immediate contests of power," not as a single, totalizing entity dominated by the state.

Where then does China's future lie? Do trade unions and entrepreneurs' associations signal that civil society, or something like it, is on the rise in China? Or does their presence merely confirm the triumph of state over society? Can we expect a growing integration among people in society, or an expanding network of social institutions, that might strengthen the power of society to distinguish the social from the state, thereby "guaranteeing intimacy and personal autonomy, on the one hand, and communication and association, on the other" (Cohen and Arato 1992: 138)? Or are these possibilities nothing but the illusions of observers who do not grasp the extent to which they are already embedded in control systems beyond their influence? Should we look for "even relatively small and finite steps in political and economic democratization" with the expectation that these may lead eventually to "a multiplicity of more autonomous roles, solidary and egalitarian relations, and forms of participation" in Chinese public life (ibid: 139)? Or does this modest expectation defeat the purpose of analysis by prescheduling changes into a misleading teleology? Finally, will a more internally integrated society be able to resist the commoditization of social relations through which the capitalist economy usurps and dominates the public sphere? Or will it help smooth the way for capitalism to establish its regime?

Perhaps the only conclusion to be drawn at this juncture is the simple one that our interpretations of social change, no matter whether they remain China-centered or range widely into other traditions, must always keep pace with the dynamic unfolding of state-society relations, not just in China but elsewhere as globalization remakes the world. It is to these changes that social theory must respond. Whether that means expanding, refining, or ultimately rejecting the concept of civil society will depend on the robustness of the sorts of analyses presented in this volume in the light not just of theory but of what proves to be politically possible in China.

Notes

Introduction: The Ambiguous Challenge of Civil Society

1. Bryna Goodman (1996: 165–65) has argued against invoking civil society on the grounds that this concept projects "a binary view of state and society" that does not apply to Republican China, where state and social organizations interpenetrated. The argument for interpenetration is well taken, but using it to deny the value of applying civil society to China rests on an interpretation of civil society in the West as completely autonomous from the state. This interpretation is problematic. States in the West regulate and register popular bodies far more thoroughly than the Guomindang regime was ever able to do. Only in the rarest instances did public associations in the West "oppose the state in any direct or abstract fashion" (177), the standard against which Goodman measures the development of civil society. By this standard, however, every culture would fail the test.

2. The review essay by Huang Yang (1997) in *Dushu* (Readers' magazine), the leading popular journal on cutting-edge scholarly issues, is evidence of the issue's continuing importance.

Chapter 1: Auto-Organization in Chinese Society

1. An earlier version of this chapter appeared in 1996, in the *Eastern Asia Policy Papers* series published by the Joint Centre for Asia Pacific Studies, Toronto.

2. The remarkable expansion of state capacities for surveillance and revenue taking in the twentieth century has reduced the extent to which society in the West may be thought of as effectively separable from the state, as Habermas (1989) has argued in the context of the decline of the public sphere.

3. One element of Diamond's definition that I exclude is the presence of an institutionalized legal order. Its formation and role require more thorough consideration than is possible in this study. On the lack of juridical basis for activism in the Republican era, see Strand 1994: 326.

4. The well-field system is analyzed in Zhao (1989): see especially 70–75. Zhao directs his discussion toward the problem of the legal status of persons and land within communes (78–79), thereby implicitly tying his analysis to a critique of the People's Communes as the most recent manifestation of the "Asiatic" conviction that society is best ordered under state direction.

5. Business, entered into on provision of a "share" or "stake" (*gu*) in the form of labor, capital, or access to a closed market, is another principle of association and quite as important as the others for inducing distinct organizational forms. However, it lies outside the scope of this chapter. I am grateful to Takeshi Hamashita for suggesting this principle and the forms it promotes.

6. Guilds, native-place associations, and trade associations in nineteenth-century Shanghai are surveyed in Zhang Zhongli 1990: 509–35, and Johnson 1995: 124–44.

7. On the ambiguity of the claims to autonomy that may be made for academies, see the chapter by Hayhoe and Zhong in this volume. Shanghai's one academy of note was Shenjiang Academy (Johnson 1995: 91).

8. A group of seven eunuchs headed by Liu Jin who took power in 1505–10 "at the time was called the faction (*dang*) of seven" (Chen 1985: 70). Similarly, the eunuchs led by Wei Zhongxian who took control of the court in the 1620s were called "the Wei faction (*dang*)" (Ye 1986: 3).

9. For Shunzhi's edict of 1652, see Wakeman 1985: 941; regarding Yongzheng's edict of 1724, see Huang 1974: 90–92.

10. Henriot (1996: 164) notes that professional associations in Shanghai are the subject of a 1993 Columbia University dissertation by Xu Xiaoqun, entitled "State and Society in Republican China: The Rise of Shanghai Professional Associations, 1912–1937."

11. Distinguishing by type is a precarious, because artificial, method. The categories are imposed from outside, the boundaries between types' fluid, and the names of organizations often not in direct correspondence, and sometimes in direct variance, with their substance. For example, when the Special Branch investigated the Shanghai Fish Peddlers' Mutual Help Association for nonregistration in August 1938, it found that the association had been formed by a former Guomindang official, cashiered two years earlier for financial misconduct, for extorting protection money from the Cold Storage Owners' Association (SMP file D-8679). That same month, the SMP tracked down another unregistered organization called the Chinese and Foreign Grocery Merchants' Lien Yih (Friendship) Society, only to find that it was, in the words of their report, "a bazaar" or "an old style society established for the purpose of discussing market prices and conditions in the trade" rather than a public body (D-8692).

12. The five women's organizations were the Chung Hwa Women's Temperance Association, the Federation of Shanghai Women's Bodies, the Shanghai Women's Culture Acceleration Association, the Shanghai Women's Movement Acceleration Association, and the Young Women's Club. All targeted middle-class women for membership.

13. By Municipal Notification No. 4878 (21 October 1937), the SMP maintained a parallel registration system for news organizations and publishers, which of course also functioned as entities representing interests in the political sphere (SMP file D-8149).

14. "Yanzhe you Zhongguo tese de shehuizhuyi daolu qianjin" (Forward along the road of socialism with Chinese characteristics) (1987), reprinted in Chen, Pang, and Zhu, eds., 1992: 220–21. On Chinese understandings of "masses," see Strand 1994: 312.

15. The independent Shanghai radio station Voice of Democracy and Freedom, which operated briefly in the spring of 1989, might be numbered alongside these organizations as an entity based on common cause (Amnesty International 1996: 86). Although I have excluded media organizations from this survey, they should be understood as constituting a significant auto-organizational forum in twentieth-century China. In this regard, the interventions in public opinion by the *World Economic Herald* newspaper, and its suppression, were important factors shaping the Democracy Movement in Shanghai (see Wright 1991).

Chapter 2: State-Led Civil Society

1. An earlier version of this chapter appeared in 1996 in the *Eastern Asia Policy Papers* series published by the Joint Centre for Asia Pacific Studies, Toronto. I wish to thank the political science graduate students at York University who attended my seminar on postcommunist transitions for stimulating my thinking on civil society.

2. Chinese are still searching for the right terminology to describe tendencies and initiatives that in the West have been identified broadly as civil society. It has been referred to variously as "townspeople's society" (*shimin shehui*) and "public or citizens' society" (*gongmin shehui*) the distinctions between which Des Forges explores in the following chapter. In the contemporary Chinese context, this terminology sounds foreign and lacks credibility (Ma 1994: 180–93). In the limited Chinese literature on civil society, these terms are used hesitantly, often without much coherence or historical depth.

3. This point is discussed by the contributors to the April 1993 issue of the journal *Modern China,* in which various authors debate whether China had a civil society in the past, focusing on Habermas' concept of the public sphere. See also Strand 1990.

4. Mary Rankin identified a nascent civil society in this part of China in the nineteenth century. In her view, a "minimalist and noninterventionist" Qing government permitted a significant degree of autonomy to local elites in the management of commercial activities (Rankin 1986, 1993). Following Rankin, one could speculate that the current growth of social organizations may have emerged from the "social capital" of prior experience with local autonomy. On social capital, see Putnam 1993.

5. Departing from the "normal" Western pattern, a case can be made that, if the "political realm" is underdeveloped but a strong authoritarian state exists, the separation of state and society can occur without the emergence of an independent political realm. In this case, civil society and the realm of politics, rather than being separated, will be merged. Functional separation will occur later when political parties and legitimate oppositions exist and can debate their agendas in public.

6. For more on Chinese intellectuals and civil society, see Hua 1994.

7. Nevitt's study of private business associations in Tianjin supports the concept of state-led civil society and the possibility that a strong Chinese state can promote its emergence, at least at the local level: "It seems that in the Chinese context a civil society may not develop separate from and in opposition to the state but rather in the niches and spaces that the state leaves open, and that it will grow in response to opportunities deliberately engineered or accidentally created by the state" (1996: 43).

Chapter 3: States, Societies, and Civil Societies in Chinese History

1. See also Wang 1991 and Gan 1993. I am grateful to Luo Xu for bringing these two essays to my attention, as well as the articles in Zhou Xuegang 1992.

2. Metzger 1994: 1 traces the Western idea of civil society back to Roman times. See also Shils 1991.

3. See also Brook's chapter in this volume. Although civil society and public sphere are treated separately, I shall simplify my account by referring only to civil society, which accompanies and serves to institutionalize the public sphere.

4. I am grateful to Claude Welch for bringing this article to my attention.

5. The conflict between civil society and the state is emphasized in Habermas 1989: 52, 60, and passim.

6. Aspects of this kind of civil society had also appeared in the Greek city-states, but nineteenth-century Europeans were less interested in historical precedent than in novelty; so, too, are many twentieth-century Europeans, for example, Habermas 1989: 3–5. For unresolved Western tensions between the views that civil society has deep roots in the past and that it is a recent invention, see Shils 1991.

7. This was recognized by Chinese thinkers of the nineteenth century as well as by Western historians such as Spengler and Toynbee writing in the twentieth century (Cohen 1974: 92; Drake 1975: 131; Meskill 1965: 20–24; Pusey 1983: 416–417).

8. In the past, the ideology of this form of civil society was often called democratic socialism or socialist democracy (Lukes 1973). Currently, it goes under the labels of economic democracy and communitarianism.

9. But see Shils (1991: 20), who argues that "the ideal of the common good is a practicable ideal, even though there is likely at any given moment to be disagreement about its substance, and even though it can never be completely realized."

10. The association between *Han ren* and "Chinese" was not just by default, although there was clearly an important distinction between the two concepts that has not always been observed by Chinese or Westerners. Compare Lipman and Harrell 1990: 4. We can maintain this distinction by reserving the English term "Chinese" for the Chinese term *zhongguo ren* ("people of the central state[s]").

11. Of course, the Tang was a relatively recent age compared with that of the Qing's other favorite model, the Zhou.

12. See Chin and Freeman 1990; Waley 1969: 23, 47, 59, 103; Nivison 1966: 35–36, 75, 232–233; and Li 1966.

13. This idea, first developed by the Japanese historian Naitō Konan, has inspired many subsequent accounts, for example, Shiba 1970; and McNeill 1982.

14. As I have noted elsewhere (Des Forges 1993: 35–36), this view is one-sided and ignores certain positive aspects of these orders, but it remains dominant among Chinese even today.

15. While the Western name for China alludes to the centralized bureaucracy of the Qin, the Chinese name alludes to the cultural centrality claimed by all pre-Qin, Qin, and post-Qin states. Chinese expatriate scholars increasingly acknowledge that the key to Chinese identity in the twentieth century is the quest for cultural and political centrality more than for economic and military power (Chen 1994; Ci 1994).

16. In 1988, students organizing for human rights compared themselves with those who had plotted to kill Qin Shihuang; like them, they thought, they could not afford to turn back once they had set out on their mission (Shen 1990: 139).

17. Sun was Han-centric, believing that minority nationalities had to acculturate to the majority Han if China was to be strong, but he also admired the Zhou dynasty, the civilization of which he considered to be comparable to that of twentieth-century Europe and America (Yü 1989: 92–93). The Chinese term for Republic (*gonghe guo*) went back to a Zhou reign that was dominated by several nobles rather than a single son of heaven (Hsü 1988: 144–46).

18. For Mao's interest in other periods, see Hsü 1988: 68, 122–23.

19. For uses of the past during the Ming-Qing transition, see Des Forges 1994 and forthcoming. To what extent they continue to be part of the popular consciousness is a question worthy of research.

20. For the argument that the mobile workers (or floating people) created by the reforms are part of a Chinese civil society that is both autonomous from and supportive of the state, see Solinger 1992.

21. The association of the Spring and Autumn period with militarism in the 1930s is made in Link 1981: 14.

22. For a similar distinction between forms of civil society that nurture democracy and those that do not, see Diamond 1994.

23. For an extended and, to my mind, convincing defense of *guanxi xue* as a distinctively Chinese form of civil society, see Yang 1994.

24. Another translation, *xin quanwei zhuyi,* makes neoauthoritarianism more akin to totalitarianism. Ding Xueliang asserts, however, that this is a mistranslation (Zhou 1992: 39, 107).

25. Young Chinese advocates of civil society readily cite contemporary Western political theorists such as Barrington Moore, Robert Dahl, Daniel Bell, Guillermo O'Donnell, Philippe Schmitter, Samuel Huntington, and Zbigniew Brzezinski. They also invoke American China specialists such as Franz Schurmann, Chalmers Johnson, William Skinner, Tang Tsou, Andrew Nathan, Andrew Walder, and Thomas Gold on the nature of Chinese society and its prospects (see Zhou 1992; Des Forges 1993).

26. For a different view that sees China as vulnerable on human rights issues and willing to change, see Nathan 1994.

27. Ma's translation of *zuqun shehui* as "collective society" is misleading, reinforcing the pervasive tendency among Chinese intellectuals to posit only two kinds of society, collectivist and individualist.

28. David Ownby reminded us at the symposium where this chapter was first presented, on the other hand, that sects and associations are often driven to illegal activities precisely because their existence is banned by the state.

29. Current trends in Chinese education as discussed by Hayhoe and Zhong in this volume do not augur well for the realization of this vision.

30. For problems of democracy in the contemporary United States, see also Chomsky 1991, Greider 1992, Elshtain 1995, and Lasch 1995. The *New York Times* reported on 17 April 1995 that the top 20 percent of the population of the U.S. now owns over 80 percent of the wealth in their respective spheres, while the bottom 20 percent in each case owns less than 6 percent (King and Elliott 1994).

31. On China's status with regard to international human rights agreements, see Brook 1993b, and Nathan 1994: 628.

32. "Human Rights in China," *Beijing Review*, 4–10 November 1991: 8 (cited in Peerenboom 1993: 46). Ed. note: Peerenboom's interpretion of rights in China has been severely critiqued by Svensson 1996.

Chapter 4: University Autonomy and Civil Society

1. A recent example of the new type of corporate decision-making that is now possible was the selection of the president of Tongji University in Shanghai by a vote within the institution, rather than an appointment made by the State Education Commission. The choice was a woman engineer in her late forties (Song 1995). The recent emergence of about eight hundred private institutions of higher education, sixteen having the right of granting state-approved diplomas (Tang 1995), means that this kind of corporate decision-making will increase in the future.

2. Emperors founded schools, enacted degrees regarding school rules, presided over the imperial examinations at the highest level (*dianshi*), inspected and lectured at the Imperial Academy, and passed judgment on policy recommendations regarding education.

3. Robert Hymes (1989: 442–43) argues that academies were formed not so much in opposition to the state, but simply "to give institutional expression and structure to the local community as something apart from the central state and its organs." He sees them becoming prominent as a result of the failure of a weak state to take action. "Neo-Confucian reformers in the Southern Song built their new nonstate institutions in the space left by the failure: the space, to return to de Bary's formulation, 'between state power and family interests.' "

4. Most of the modern institutions of higher learning that came into being at the end of the Qing and the beginning of the Republican period had charters, although their legal status varied depending on the type of institution. The American missionary colleges had charters, but these were registered in the American states from which their founders came. It was only after the Nationalist government passed legislation to regulate private institutions of higher learning that these documents gained legal status in China. The private institutions founded by Chinese philanthropists, such as Nankai University, China Engineering University (Zhongguo Gongxue), and Fudan University, also had charters. Although these charters had quasi-legal status, the well-being of an institution depended to a large degree on the connections that its leaders were able to forge with government officials.

5. Zhu Jiusi (1992: 2–3), who went to Yan'an from Wuhan University as a young intellectual in 1937 and later devoted his career to making Huazhong University of Science and Technology one of China's top institutions, regretted that the universities of the Republican period had lost their original identity when the Soviet model was imposed.

6. Two examples are Lu Ping, president of Beijing University in the 1970s and head of the Party's Hong Kong and Macao Offices in the late 1980s and 1990s, and Sun Zhu, head of the Foreign Languages Department at Fudan University in the early 1980s and later deputy director of the Shanghai Municipality Foreign Affairs Department.

7. One merger currently under discussion involves Chongqing University (a major polytechnical university), the Chongqing Architecture University, and the Southwest University of Political Science and Law. All are on contiguous campuses, having been parts of a single comprehensive university in the Nationalist period. The complexity of merging three institutions under different jurisdictions may jeopardize this move.

8. Interviews by Ruth Hayhoe at the Chincse Culture Academy in March 1990; the secretary of the academy is Liang Yida, a grandson of Liang Qichao.

Chapter 5: From State Corporatism to Social Representation: Local Trade Unions in the Reform Years

1. I am grateful to Timothy Brook for encouraging me to write this chapter. I have been inspired by his extraordinary diligence and conscientiousness as a scholar. My thanks go also to B. Michael Frolic, who has been a source of inspiration for my study of China, to Victor Falkenheim, from whose seminars on China I have greatly benefited, and to Arthur Silver, who has shown much interest in my work.

2. The Guomindang was equally unable to subjugate trade unions or substantially change their popular character due to constraints such as factional struggles within the regime and foreign and communist competition. This point is examined in further detail in my doctoral dissertation, "Rivalry and Alliance: Chinese Trade Unions and State Power in the Twentieth Century."

3. Interviews by the author in Qingdao in July 1993.

4. On neoauthoritarianism, see Ma 1990.

5. Most of the labor scholars who have been outspoken in advocating the reform of the trade union work in the Chinese Workers' Movement College (*Zhongguo Gongyun Xueyuan*), the Ministry of Labor, or research institutes affiliated with trade unions at city, provincial, and national levels. See Guo Zhefeng 1989; Tian and Xu 1988; An, Huang, and Cui 1990; and *Gongren ribao*, 5–26 January, 27 April 1994.

6. Sun Bingyue was deputy Party secretary of Qingdao and later president of the Qingdao General Trade Union. The other three articles cited from *Qingdao ribao* were by Yang Xingfu, president of the General Trade Union of Shandong Province; Zang Hewang, president of the trade union at the Qingdao Second Plastics Plant; and Zhang Zuodong, president of the Qingdao General Trade Union from 1985 to 1990.

Chapter 6: Chinese Youth and Civil Society

1. We thank Professor B. Michael Frolic, participants at the China and Civil Society Symposium, and the anonymous reviewers for their valuable criticisms of our work in progress. This chapter is dedicated to Min Qi.

2. Lei Feng, also known as "the rustless screw," was promoted as an exemplary youth who was absolutely loyal to the Party and the state and selflessly dedicated to his work tasks. His cult has been textualized through a "found" series of full and detailed posthumous diaries detailing each of Lei Feng's acts of heroism. Recently, it has been suggested that Lei's image needs updating to conform with Deng's dictum "to get rich is glorious." But the notion of converting Lei into a snappily dressed entrepreneur with a girlfriend was not acceptable. Largely sponsored by the military, Lei was instead portrayed as someone interested in firm discipline and in serious study of science and technology in the service of the party-state. See Dreyer 1990: 264.

3. Bai Hua's screenplay, *Unrequited Love,* about a patriotic intellectual's poorly repaid devotion to his country asks, "You love the motherland, but does the motherland love you?" In a 1985 article, journalist Liu Binyan argued that loyalty to one's country, society, and even the Communist Party does not require allegiance to the leaders and their policies. The regime's reaction to these mild ideas was hostile; both were severely criticized and held to be "unpatriotic." Bai was the major target of a nationwide campaign against "bourgeois liberalization" launched in 1981. See Goldman et al. 1993: 132ff.

4. Youth are not alone in their propensity to discriminate among objects of political support. Other influential sectors of society, such as academics, have shown similar tendencies in recent years. See *Lien ho pao,* 14 April 1994.

5. According to Nathan and Shi (1993: 119), the Chinese State Statistical Bureau was conducting survey research on behalf of Ronald Inglehart at the time they were writing their article. To the best of our knowledge, these data are not yet available. In the late 1980s, rock star Cui Jian's "I Have Nothing" expressed the idea that youth lacked everything from material goods to political freedom. In a popular song of 1993 called "My 1997," singer Ai Jing seems to be yearning for everything that capitalist Hong Kong can offer. See Jones 1994.

6. Easton (1965) characterizes the objects of support as follows: The *political community* refers to "that aspect of a political system that consists of its members seen as a group of persons bound together by a political division of labor. The existence of a political system must include a plurality of political relationships through which the individual members are linked to each other and through which the political objectives of the system are pursued, however limited they may be" (177). The *regime* is composed of "sets of constraints on political interaction in all systems" that "may be broken down into three components: values (goals and principles), norms, and structure of authority. The values serve as broad limits with regard to what can be taken for granted in the guidance of day-to-day policy without violating deep feelings of important sections of the community. The norms specify the kinds of procedures that are expected and acceptable in the processing and implementation of demands. The structures of authority designate the formal and informal patterns in which power is distributed and organized with

regard to the authoritative making and implementing of decisions—the roles and their relationship through which authority is distributed and exercised" (193). *Authorities* "include members of a system who conform to the following criteria. They must engage in the daily affairs of a political system; they must be recognized by most members of the system as having the responsibility for these matters; and their actions must be accepted as binding most of the time by most of the members as long as they act within the limits of their roles. Specifically, we refer to such occupants of authority roles as elders, paramount chiefs, executives, legislators, judges, administrators, councilors, monarchs, and the like" (212).

7. Nathan and Shi (1993: 97) point out that Min Qi's data "severely undersampled women, older citizens, rural residents, and other key sectors of the population," but they exaggerate the problem. Of those sampled, women accounted for 38 percent, and residents of villages, small towns, and remote areas an acceptable 47 percent.

8. Given an old tradition of politeness in interpersonal relations and intricate folkways designed to make and save face for the other, Chinese tend to oblige and comply with the perceived feelings of others (Walder 1987: 74, 83; Pye 1988: 31; Rosen 1989b: 194, 199, 1990a: 266–67, 1990b: 285–86). These factors may have affected the manner in which people responded to the questionnaire.

9. Since the number of cases in each variable in each of Tables 6.13 to 6.7 varies somewhat, these data have not been included. The range in the number of cases for each age cohort is as follows: younger than 26, 452–557; age 26–35, 343–488; age 36–45, 227–361; age 46–55, 193–237; age 56–65, 67–81; age 66 and older, 9–16.

Chapter 7: Ritual and Space

1. See, for example, the sixty volumes of ethnographic reports on fifteen provinces of China being edited by C.K. Wang. In an analysis of the reassemblage of fragments of "traditional" ritual elements in religious activity in Guangdong in the 1980s, Helen Siu (1990) has pointed out the reinvented and contingent quality of this "revival." Ann Anagnost (1994) has shown that these reinvented traditions based on older cultural practices are continually challenging the symbolic order of the state in an effort to reappropriate specific sites. My fieldwork in Fujian has traced the increasing complexity and intensity of this ritual activity over the past fifteen years in southeast China (Dean, 1993, forthcoming [b]; Dean and Zheng 1993, 1995).

2. For an analysis of an urban setting where the system of ward temples has been partially revived, see Mingming Wang (1992, 1995) on Quanzhou, Fujian. By contrast, most large-scale religious activity (except the activity of officially recognized Buddhist monasteries) within the provincial capital of Fuzhou was still sternly prohibited into the mid-1990s (personal communication, Michael Szonyi).

3. In some villages in Fujian, even recently built private homes maintain an inner courtyard that can turn into a public space when the ritual procession enters. This folding of the public into the private is a key element of ritual space in rural China.

4. Michel Foucault also pointed out the problems involved in thinking always and only in terms of the unified social whole: "You wonder if a global society could function on the basis of such divergent and diverse experiences, without a general discourse. I think on the contrary that it is precisely the idea of a 'social ensemble' that resorts to utopia. This idea has taken root in the Occidental world, in the quite particular historical lineage that resulted in capitalism. To speak of a 'social ensemble' outside of the only form that we know it is to dream on the basis of yesterday's elements. We blithely believe that to demand of experiences, actions, strategies, and projects that they take into account the 'social ensemble' is to demand the minimum of them. The minimum needed for existence. I think on the contrary that it is to demand the maximum of them; that it is even to impose upon them a single impossible condition, because the 'social ensemble' functions exactly in such a way that, and with the aim that, they can't take place or succeed or be perpetuated. The social ensemble is that which should not be taken into account, unless it is with the object of destroying it. One can only hope then that there will no longer be anything that resembles a social ensemble" (Foucault 1993: 8).

5. This model of contested spaces occupied by rhythmic repetitions of ritual can be extended to the realm of discursive practice. Different discursive positions contended against the hegemonic status of imperial ritual forms, imposing their own hegemony on local cultural formations. The epigraphic records of the Xinghua area are replete with debates on the "true meaning" of the classical rites of ancestral worship, which were in fact being radically transformed in the process of the expansion of the corporate lineages in the area (Dean and Zheng 1995). My point is that the opening up of public spaces involves not only communal ritual events and institutional transformations but the elaboration of hegemonic discursive formations. These processes continue today in new discursive and communal practices. I have discussed elsewhere the phenomenon of "conferences of the gods," official conferences devoted to the principal cults of the Fujian area, supported for different reasons by the state, local intellectuals, overseas Chinese sponsors, and local temple committees (Dean forthcoming [a]). In these new venues, university-level intellectuals and local scholars (should one say "literati"?) generate new discourses on the legitimacy and force of the expanding popular cults of the area.

Bibliography

ACFTU (All-China Federation of Trade Unions). 1985. *Zhongguo zhongyang guanyu gongren yundong wenjian xuanbian* (Selected documents of the CCP Central Committee on the workers' movement). Beijing: Dang'an Chubanshe.

———. 1988. "Gonghui gaige de jiben shexiang" (The basic design for trade union reform). Reprinted in *Zhongguo gonghui zhongyao wenjian xuanbian* (Selected important documents on Chinese trade unions): 99–110. Beijing: Jixie Gongye Chubanshe, 1990.

———. 1989. *Jianguo yilai zhonggong zhongyang guanyu gongren yundong wenjian xuanbian* (Selected documents of the CCP Central Committee on workers' movements since the founding of the People's Republic of China). Beijing: Gongren Chubanshe.

Adshead, S.A.M. 1988. *China in World History.* London: MacMillan.

Almond, Gabriel, and Verba, Sidney. 1965. *The Civic Culture.* Boston: Little Brown.

Amnesty International. 1996. *China: Repression in the 1990s—A Directory of Victims.* London: Amnesty International Publications.

An Miao; Huang Shaoguo; and Cui Yi. 1990. *Gongren jieji xianzhuang yu zhigong daibiao dahui zhidu yanjiu* (The current situation of the working class and the system of workers' congress). Shenyang: Liaoning Renmin Chubanshe.

Anagnost, Ann S. 1994. "The Politics of Ritual Displacement." In *Asian Visions of Authority: Religion and the Modern States of East and Southeast Asia,* ed. Charles F. Keyes, Laurel Kendall, and Helen Hardacre. Honolulu: University of Hawaii Press.

Appadurai, Arjun. 1990. "Disjuncture and Difference in the Global Cultural Economy." *Public Culture* 2 (Spring).

Apter, David, and Saich, Tony. 1994. *Revolutionary Discourse in Mao's Republic.* Cambridge: Harvard University Press.

Australian-Asian Perceptions Project. 1993. *Perceiving Citizenship,* Working Paper No.1. Sydney: Academy of the Social Sciences in China and the Asia-Australia Institute, University of New South Wales.

Bai Zhou. 1993. "Guanyu dangqian gaodeng xuexiao shizi duiwu xianzhuang de diaocha baogao" (Report on a survey concerning the contemporary situation of the faculty contingent in higher institutions). *Zhongguo gaodeng jiaoyu* (Chinese higher education) 12 (December): 21-22.

Barmé, Geremie R. 1995. "To Screw Foreigners Is Patriotic: China's Avant-garde Nationalism." *The China Journal* 34: 209–34.

Barnard, H.C. 1969. *Education and the French Revolution.* Cambridge: Cambridge University Press.

Barnett, Robert. 1941. *Economic Shanghai: Hostage to Politics, 1937–1941.* New York: Institute of Pacific Relations.

Bei Xiaoyi. 1995. " '211' gongcheng ying bimian de piancha ji duiche (Problems in the 2/1/1 engineering project and the solutions). *Shanghai gaodeng jiaoyu yanjiu* (Shanghai higher education research) 5: 33-36. Reprinted in *Gaodeng jiaoyu* (Higher education) 1995: 12, 32-35.

Beiner, Ronald. 1995. "Why Citizenship Constitutes a Theoretical Problem in the Last Decade of the Twentieth Century." In *Theorizing Citizenship,* ed. Ronald Beiner: 1–28. Albany: State University of New York Press.

Bell, Catherine. 1992. *Ritual Theory, Ritual Practice.* Oxford: Oxford University Press.

Benda, Vaclav. 1991. "The Parallel 'Polis.' " In *Civic Freedom in Central Europe: Voices from Czechoslovakia,* ed. H. Gordon Skilling and Paul Wilson: 35–41. London: MacMillan.

Bergère, Marie-Claire. 1992. "The Shanghai Bankers' Association, 1915–1927: Modernization and the Institutionalization of Local Solidarities." In *Shanghai Sojourners,* ed. Frederic Wakeman Jr. and Wen-hsin Yeh: 15–34. Berkeley: Institute of East Asian Studies, University of California.

Black, George, and Munro, Robin. 1993. *Black Hands of Beijing: Lives of Defiance in China's Democracy Movement.* New York: John Wiley and Sons.

Bonnin, Michel, and Chevrier, Yves. 1991. "The Intellectual and the State: Social Dynamics of Intellectual Autonomy during the Post-Mao Era." *China Quarterly* 127 (September): 569–93.

Brandauer, Frederick P., and Huang, Chun-chieh, eds. *Imperial Rulership and Cultural Change in Traditional China.* Seattle: University of Washington Press.

Brook, Timothy. 1990. "Family Continuity and Cultural Hegemony: The Gentry of Ningbo, 1368–1911." In *Chinese Local Elites and Patterns of Dominance,* ed. Joseph Esherick and Mary Rankin: 27–50. Berkeley: University of California Press.

———. 1992. *Quelling the People: The Military Suppression of the Beijing Democracy Movement.* New York: Oxford University Press.

———. 1993a. *Praying for Power: Buddhism and the Formation of Gentry Society in Late-Ming China.* Cambridge: Council on East Asian Studies, Harvard University.

———. 1993b. "Differing Agendas: China and the Human Rights Treaties." *China Rights Forum* (Winter): 16–19.

———. 1996. "Auto-Organization Within Chinese Society: A Historical View." Eastern Asia Policy Papers no. 15, University of Toronto—York University Joint Centre for Asia Pacific Studies.

Brook, Timothy, and Luong, Hy V., eds. 1997. *Culture and Economy: The Shaping of Capitalism in Eastern Asia.* Ann Arbor: The University of Michigan Press.

Buber, Martin. 1992. *On Intersubjectivity and Cultural Creativity.* Chicago: Chicago University Press.

Calhoun, Craig. 1994. *Neither Gods nor Emperors: Students and the Struggle for Democracy in China.* Berkeley: University of California Press.

CCP (Chinese Communist Party). 1989. "Zhonggong zhongyang guanyu jiaqiang he gaishan dang dui gonghui, gongqingtuan, fulian gongzuo lingdao de tongzhi" (A circular of the CCP Central Committee on strengthening and improving the Party's leadership over the work of trade unions, youth leagues, and women' federations). Reprinted in *Zhongguo gonghui zhongyao wenjian xuanbian* (Selected important documents on Chinese trade unions): 165–79. Beijing: Jixie Gongye Chubanshe, 1990.

Chakrabarty, Dipesh. 1994. "Marx after Marxism: History, Subalternity, and Difference." *positions* 2 (Fall): 446-63.

Chamberlain, Heath B. 1993. "On the Search for Civil Society in China." *Modern China* 19 (April), 199–215.

———. 1994. "Coming to Terms with Civil Society." *Australian Journal of Chinese Affairs* 31 (January): 113–17.

Chan, Alfred L., and Nesbitt-Larking, Paul. 1995. "Critical Citizenship and Civil Society in Contemporary China." *Canadian Journal of Political Science* 28: 293–310.

Chan, Anita. 1993. "Revolution or Corporatism? Workers and Trade Unions in Post-Mao China." *Australian Journal of Chinese Affairs* 29 (January): 31–61.

Chan, Hok-lam. 1984. *Legitimation in Imperial China, Discussions under the Jurchen-Chin Dynasty (1115–1234).* Seattle: University of Washington Press.

Chan, Wing-tsit. 1989. "Chu Hsi and the Academies." In *Neo-Confucian Education: The Formative Stage,* ed. Wm. Theodore de Bary and John W. Chaffee: 389-413. Berkeley: University of California Press.

Chatterjee, Partha. 1986. *Nationalist Thought and the Colonial World: A Derivative Discourse?* London: Zed Books.

———. 1993. *The Nation and Its Fragments: Colonial and Postcolonial Histories.* Princeton: Princeton Univerity Press.

Cheek, Timothy. 1992. "From Priest to Professionals: Intellectuals and the State under the CCP." In *Popular Protest and Political Culture,* ed. Jeffrey N. Wasserstrom and Elizabeth J. Perry: 124–41. Boulder: Westview Press.

Chen Hongmo. 1985. *Jishi jiwen* (Further notes on things I have heard about governing the realm). Reprint. Beijing: Zhonghua Shuju.

Chen, Jian. 1994. *China's Road to the Korean War: The Making of the Sino-American Confrontation.* New York: Columbia University Press.

Chen, Jo-shui. 1992. *Liu Tsung-yüan and Intellectual Change in T'ang China, 773–819.* Cambridge: Cambridge University Press.

Chen Nailin and Gu Guanhua. 1993. "Lun shehuizhuyi shichang jingji tizhi xia de gaodeng jiaoyu hongguan yunxing jizhi" (A discussion of the macro mechanisms for the activity of higher education under the economic system of market socialism). *Jiaoyu yanjiu* (Education research), August: 22-26.

Chen Ruisheng, Pang Yuanzheng, and Zhu Manliang, eds. 1992. *Zhongguo gaige quanshu: zhengzhi tizhi gaige juan* (Complete book on the reform in China: the reform of the political system). Dalian: Dalian Chubanshe.

Chin, Ann-ping, and Freeman, Mansfield, trans. 1990. *Tai Chen on Mencius: Explorations in Words and Meaning: A Translation of the Meng Tzu tzu-i shu-cheng with a Critical introduction.* New Haven: Yale University Press.

Chomsky, Noam. 1991. *Deterring Democracy.* New York: Verso.

Chow, Rey. 1991, "Listening Otherwise, Music Miniaturized: A Different Type of Question about Revolution." *Discourse* 13 (Winter).

Ch'ü, T'ung-tsu. 1972. *Han Social Structure,* ed. Jack Dull. Seattle: University of Washington Press.

Ci, Jiwei. 1994. *Dialectic of the Chinese Revolution: From Utopianism to Hedonism.* Stanford: Stanford University Press.

Cohen, Jean, and Arato, Andrew. 1992. "Politics and the Reconstruction of the Concept of Civil Society." In Honneth et al. 1992: 121–42.

Cohen, Myron. 1991. "Being Chinese: The Peripheralization of Traditional Identity." *Daedalus* 120, 2: 113-34.

Cohen, Paul. 1974. *Between Tradition and Modernity: Wang T'ao and Reform in Late Ch'ing China.* Cambridge: Harvard University Press.

Creel, Herlee G. 1970. *The Origins of Statecraft in China.* Chicago: University of Chicago Press.

Dai Shujun and Hayhoe, Ruth. 1991. "Vocational Universities in China." *Chinese Education* 24 (Spring and Summer): 2.

Dardess, John W. 1983. *Confucianism and Autocracy: Professional Elites in the Founding of the Ming Dynasty.* Berkeley: University of California Press.

de Bary, Wm. Theodore. 1970. "Individualism and Humanitarianism in Late Ming Thought." In *Self and Society in Ming Thought,* ed. Wm. Theodore de Bary: 145–225. New York: Columbia University Press.

———. 1983. *The Liberal Tradition in China.* New York: Columbia University Press.

———. 1991. *The Trouble with Confucianism.* Cambridge: Harvard University Press.

Dean, Kenneth. 1993. *Taoist Ritual and Popular Cults of Southeast China.* Princeton: Princeton University Press.

———. Forthcoming (a). *Lord of the Three in One: The Spread of a Cult in Southeast China.* Princeton: Princeton University Press.

———. Forthcoming (b). "Despotic Empire/Nation-State: Local Responses to Chinese Nationalism in an Age of Global Capitalism."*Trajectories in Cultural Studies,* ed. Chen Kuan-hsing. London: Routledge.

Dean, Kenneth, and Massumi, Brian. 1992. *First and Last Emperors: The Absolute State and the Body of the Despot.* New York: Autonomedia.

Dean, Kenneth, and Zheng Zhenman. 1993. "Group Initiation and Exorcistic Dance in the Xinghua Region." In *Zhongguo Nuoxi, Nuo wenhua guoji yantaohui lunwenli* (Proceedings of the international conference on Nuo theater and Nuo culture in China), ed. Wang Qiugui, 2: 105-95.

———. 1996. *Epigraphical Materials on the History of Religion in Fujian.* Vol. 1: The Xinghua Region. Fuzhou: Fujian Renmin Chubanshe.

de Certeau, Michel. 1984. *The Practice of Everyday Life,* trans. Steven Rendall. Berkeley: University of California Press.

DeLanda, Manual. 1992. "Nonorganic Life." In *Zone 6: Incorporations*: 129-67.

Deleuze, Gils. 1995. "Postscript on Control Societies." In *Negotiations,* trans. Martin Johnson: 177–82. New York: Columbia Univeristy Press.

Deleuze, Gils, and Guattari, Felix. 1989. *A Thousand Plateaus,* trans. Brian Massumi. St. Paul: University of Minnesota Press.

Des Forges, Roger V. 1993. "Democracy in Chinese History." In Des Forges et al. 1993: 21–52.

———. 1994. "Shilun Ming-Qing shanti zhi ji Henan dongbei bu zhishi qunti di zhengzhi dongxiang" (Political trends among scholarly groups in northeast Henan during the Ming-Qing transition). *Zhongguo shi yanjiu* (Studies on Chinese history) 1: 152–63.

———. Forthcoming. *The Center Holds: Northeast Henan in the Ming-Qing Transition.*

Des Forges, Roger; Luo, Ning; and Wu, Yanbo, eds. 1993. *Chinese Democracy and the Crisis of 1989: Chinese and American Perspectives.* Albany: State University of New York Press.

Diamond, Larry. 1994. "Toward Democratic Consolidation." Introduction to the issue entitled "Rethinking Civil Society." *Journal of Democracy* 5 (July): 4–17.

Ding, Gang. 1991. "Ziranzhuyi jiaoyu yu ru-dao fubu" (Natural education and reciprocation between Confucianism and Daoism). In *Zhongguo jiaoyushi yanjiu* (Studies in the history of Chinese education), ed. Chen Xuexun: 291-398. Shanghai: Huadong Shifan Daxue Chubanshe.

———. 1996. "The Shuyuan and the Development of Chinese Universities in the Early 20th Century." In *East-West Dialogue in Knowledge and Higher Education,* ed. Ruth Hayhoe and Julia Pan: 218–44. Armonk, N.Y.: M.E. Sharpe.

Dong Qichang. 1630. *Rongtai ji* (Collected works from Rong Terrace).

Drake, Frederick W. 1975. *China Charts the World: Hsü Chi-yü and His Geography of 1848.* Cambridge: Center for East Asian Studies, Harvard University.

Dreyer, June T. 1990. "The Military in China." *Current History* (September): 261–64.

Duan Yue. 1995. "The Ten Ethical Problems That Bewilder the Chinese Youth." *Zhongguo qingnian* (Chinese youth) 5: 10–11.

Duiker, William. 1977. *Ts'ai Yüan-p'ei: Educator of Modern China.* University Park: The Pennsylvania State University Press.

Eastman, Lloyd. 1974. *The Abortive Revolution: China under Nationalist Rule, 1927–1937.* Cambridge: Harvard University Press.

Easton, David. 1965. *A Systems Analysis of Political Life.* New York: Wiley.

Ebrey, Patricia, and Gregory, Peter N., eds. 1993. *Religion and Society in T'ang and Sung China.* Honolulu: University of Hawaii Press.

Elshtain, Jean Bethke. 1995. *Democracy on Trial.* New York: Basic Books.

Esherick, Joseph. 1976. *Reform and Revolution in China: the 1911 Revolution in Hunan and Hubei.* Berkeley: University of California Press.

———, and Rankin, Mary. eds., 1990. *Chinese Local Elites and Patterns of Dominance.* Berkeley: University of California Press.

Esherick, Joseph, and Wasserstrom, Jeffrey N. 1990. "Acting Out Democracy: Political Theater in Modern China." *Journal of Asian Studies* 49 (November): 835–65.

Fang, Lizhi. 1991. *Bringing Down the Great Wall: Writings on Science, Culture, and Democracy in China.* New York: Knopf.

Farmer, Edward. 1976. *Early Ming Government: The Evolution of Dual Capitals.* Cambridge: East Asian Research Center, Harvard University.

Farmer, Edward, and Des Forges, Roger. 1994. "Report on the Fifth International Conference on Ming History, Xi'an, August 1993." *Ming Studies* 33: 56–76.

Farquhar, Judith, and Hevia, James. 1993. "Culture and Postwar American Historiography of China." *positions* 1 (Fall): 486-525.

Fewsmith, Joseph. 1985. *Party, State, and Local Elites in Republican China: Merchant Organizations and Politics in Shanghai, 1890–1930.* Honolulu: University of Hawaii Press.

Fisher, Tom. 1993. " 'The Play's the Thing': Wu Han and Hai Rui Revisited." In *Using the Past to Serve the Present: Historiography and Politics in Contemporary China,* ed. Jonathan Unger: 9–45. Armonk, N.Y.: M.E. Sharpe.

Foucault, Michel. 1993. "Michel Foucault: propos recellis par M.-A.Burnier et Phillipe Graine." *C'est demain la veille.* Trans. T. LaMarre. Paris: Editions du Seuil.

Franke, Herbert. 1982. "Wang Yun (1227–1304): A Transmitter of Chinese Values." In *Yuan Thought: Chinese Thought and Religion under the Mongols,* ed. Hok-lam Chan and W. Theodore de Bary: 152–93. New York: Columbia University Press.

Friedman, Edward. 1974. *Backward Toward Revolution: The Chinese Revolutionary Party.* Berkeley: University of California Press.

Frolic, B. Michael. 1996. "The Emergence of Civil Society in China." Eastern Asia Policy Papers, no. 14, University of Toronto—York University Joint Centre for Asia Pacific Studies.

Fu Shutang. 1987. "Sifang jichang shengdanhui de douzheng" (The struggle of the Christian Society in Sifang Rolling Stock Plant). In *Qingdao dangshi ziliao* (Materials on the CCP's history at Qingdao), ed. Zang Miao et al.: 110–14. Qingdao (internally circulated).

Fu, Zhengyuan. 1991. "Continuities of Chinese Political Tradition." *Studies in Comparative Communism* 3: 259–79.

Fukuyama, Francis. 1995. *Trust, the Social Virtues and the Creation of Prosperity.* New York: The Free Press.

Fuma Susumu. 1995. "Infant Protection Societies in the Late Qing." Trans. Peter Perdue. *Sino-Japanese Studies* 7 (April): 42–64.

Gan Yang. 1993. "Minjian shehui gainian pipan" (A critique of the concept of popular society). In *Beiju di liliang: cong minzhu yundong zouxiang minzhu zhengzhi, 1989–* (The power of tragedy: From the Democracy Movement to democratic politics, 1989–), ed. Lin Daoqun and Wu Zanmei: 141–53. Hong Kong: Oxford University Press.

Garrett, Shirley. 1974. "The Chambers of Commerce and the YMCA." In *The Chinese City Between Two Worlds,* ed. Mark Elvin and G. William Skinner: 213–38. Stanford: Stanford University Press.

Gasster, Michael. 1969. *Chinese Intellectuals and the Revolution of 1911: The Birth of Modern Chinese Radicalism.* Seattle: University of Washington Press.

Gellner, Ernest. 1994. *Conditions of Liberty: Civil Society and Its Rivals.* London: Hamish Hamilton.

Geng Hailing. 1995. "Daxue de zhengzhi xuexi" (College political classes) *Zhongguo qingnian* (Chinese youth) 1: 51–53.

Gil, Jose. 1989. *Metamorphoses du corps*. Paris: La difference.

Godelier, Maurice. 1978. "The Concept of the 'Asiatic Mode of Production' and Marxist Models of Social Evolution." In *Relations of Production,* ed. D. Seddon. London.

Gold, Thomas. 1991. "Youth and the State." *China Quarterly* 127: 654–72.

———. 1993. "Go with Your Feelings: Hong Kong and Taiwan Popular Culture in Greater China." *China Quarterly* 136.

Goldman, Merle; Link, Perry; and Su Wei. 1993. "China's Intellectuals in the Deng Era: Loss of Identity with the State." In *China's Quest for National Identity,* ed. Lowell Dittmer and Samuel Kim: 125–153. Ithaca: Cornell University Press.

Goldman, Merle. 1994. *Sowing the Seeds of Democracy in China: Political Reform in the Deng Xiaoping Era*. Cambridge: Harvard University Press.

Goodman, Bryna. 1992. "New Culture, Old Habits: Native-Place Organization and the May Fourth Movement." In *Shanghai Sojourners,* ed. Frederic Wakeman Jr. and Wen-hsin Yeh: 76–107. Berkeley: Institute of East Asian Studies, University of California.

———. 1995. *Native Place, City, and Nation: Regional Networks and Identities in Shanghai, 1853–1937*. Berkeley: University of California Press.

———. 1996. "Creating Civic Ground: Public Maneuverings and the State in the Nanjing Decade." In *Remapping China: Fissures in Historical Terrain,* ed. Gail Hershatter et al.: 164–77. Stanford: Stanford University Press.

Goodrich, L. Carrington, and Fang, Chaoying eds. 1976. *Dictionary of Ming Biography, 1368–1644*. 2 vols. New York: Columbia University Press.

Graham, A.C. 1985. "The Right to Selfishness: Yangism, Later Mohism, Chuang Tzu." In *Individualism and Holism: Studies in Confucian and Taoist Values,* ed. Donald Munro: 73–84. Ann Arbor: Center for Chinese Studies, University of Michigan.

Greider, William. 1992. *Who Will Tell the People? The Betrayal of American Democracy*. New York: Simon and Schuster.

Gu Mingyuan, ed. 1992. *Zhongguo jiaoyu daxi: lidai jiaoyu lunzhu xuanping* (The Chinese education series: selected works on education in history). Wuhan: Hubei Jiaoyu Chubanshe.

Guisso, Richard W.L. 1979. "The Reigns of the Empress Wu, Chung-tsung and Jui-tsung (684–712)." In *The Cambridge History of China: Sui and T'ang China,* ed. Denis Twitchett: 290–344. Cambridge: Cambridge University Press.

Guo Jing. 1995. "Guanyu gaodeng xuexiao lianhe banxue de jidian sikao" (Some thoughts on higher institutions linking up to run education). *Zhongguo gaodeng jiaoyu* (Chinese higher education) 6 (June): 24-25.

Guo Zhefeng, ed. 1989. *Gonghui gongzuo "redian" tantao* (Discussion on some "hot issues" of trade union work). Shanghai: Tongji Daxue Chubanshe.

Habermas, Jürgen. 1989. *The Structural Transformation of the Public Sphere: An Inquiry into a Category of Bourgeois Society*. Trans. Thomas Berger. Cambridge: MIT Press.

Haeger, John. 1975. *Crisis and Prosperity in Sung China*. Tucson: University of Arizona Press.

Hall, David L., and Ames, Roger T. 1987. *Thinking Through Confucius.* Albany: State University of New York Press.

Hall, John A., ed. 1995. *Civil Society: Theory, History, Comparison.* Cambridge, England: Polity Press.

Halpern, Nina. 1991. "Economic Reform, Social Mobilization, and Democratization in Post-Mao China." In *Reform and Reaction in Post-Mao China: The Road to Tiananmen,* ed. Richard Baum: 38–59. New York: Routledge.

Hamrin, Carol, and Cheek, Timothy, eds. 1986. *China's Establishment Intellectuals.* Armonk, N.Y.: M.E. Sharpe.

Hardt, Michael, and Negri, Antonio. 1993. *Labor of Dionysus: A Critique of the State-Form.* Minneapolis: Univeristy of Minnesota Press.

Havel, Vaclav. 1991. "The Power and the Powerless." In *Open Letter,* ed. Paul Wilson: 125–214. London: Faber and Faber.

———. 1995. "The Responsibility of Intellectuals." *The New York Review of Books* 42: 11, 36–37.

Hayhoe, Ruth. 1984. "German, French, Soviet and American University Models and the Evaluation of Chinese Higher Education Policy since 1911." Ph.D. diss., University of London.

———. 1993a. "China's Universities since Tiananmen: A Critical Assessment." *China Quarterly* 134 (June): 291–309.

———. 1993b. "Student Enrolment and Job Assignment Issues." *China News Analysis* 1481 (March).

———. 1995. "An Asian Multiversity? Comparative Reflections on the Transition to Mass Higher Education in East Asia." *Comparative Education Review* 39 (August): 299-321.

———. 1996. *China's Universities 1895-1995: A Century of Cultural Conflict.* New York: Garland Publishing.

Hayhoe, Ruth, and Wu Huiping. 1995. "The Introduction of Fee-Paying in Public Institutions and the Development of Private Higher Education in China." *China News Analysis* 1534 (May).

———. 1996. "Faculty Issues in Chinese Higher Education." *China News Analysis* 1553 (February).

Henderson, John. 1984. *The Development and Decline of Chinese Cosmology.* New York: Columbia University Press.

Henriot, Christian. 1993. *Shanghai 1927–1937: Municipal Power, Locality, and Modernization,* trans. Noël Castelino. Berkeley: University of California Press.

———. 1996. "Cities and Urban Society in China in the Nineteenth and Twentieth Centuries: A Review Essay in Western Literature." *Jindai Zhongguo shi yanjiu tongxun* (Newsletter for modern Chinese history) 21 (March), 151–75.

Hevia, James L. 1995. *Cherishing Men From Afar: Qing Guest Ritual and the Macartney Embassy of 1793.* Durham: Duke University Press.

Honneth, Axel; McCarthy, Thomas; Offe, Claus; Wellmer, Albrecht, eds. 1992. *Cultural-Political Interventions in the Unfinished Project of Enlightenment.* Trans. Barbara Fultner. Cambridge: The MIT Press.

Hooper, Beverley. 1991. "Chinese Youth: The Nineties Generation." *Current History* (September), 264–69.

Howell, Jude. 1994. "Striking a New Balance: New Social Organisations in Post-Mao China." *Capital and Class* 54: 89–111.

Hsiao, Kung-ch'üan. 1960. *Rural China: Imperial Control in the Nineteenth Century.* Seattle: University of Washington Press.

———. 1975. *A Modern China and a New World: K'ang Yu-wei, Reformer and Utopian, 1858–1927.* Seattle: University of Washington Press.

Hsü, Cho-yun. 1965. *Ancient China in Transition: An Analysis of Social Mobility, 722–222* B.C. Stanford: Stanford University Press.

———. 1980. *Han Agriculture: The Formation of Early Chinese Agrarian Economy* (106 B.C.–A.D. 220), ed. Jack Dull. Seattle: University of Washinton Press.

Hsü, Cho-yun, and Linduff, Katheryn. 1988. *Western Chou Civilization.* New Haven: Yale University Press.

Hua, Shiping. 1994. "One Servant, Two Masters: The Dilemma of Chinese Establishment Intellectuals." *Modern China* 20: 1 (January): 93–121.

Huang, Pei. 1974. *Autocracy at Work: A Study of the Yung-cheng Period, 1723–1735.* Bloomington: Indiana University Press.

Huang, Philip. 1991. "The Paradigmatic Crisis in Chinese Studies: Paradoxes in Social and Economic History." *Modern China* 17: 3, 299–341.

———. 1993. " 'Public Sphere'/'Civil Society' in China? The Third Realm Between State and Society." *Modern China* 19: 2 (April): 216–40.

Huang, Ray. 1981. *1587: A Year of No Significance, the Ming Dynasty in Decline.* New Haven: Yale University Press.

Huang Yang. 1997. "Zhuisu 'shimin shehui' de lishi yuanyuan" (Tracing back to the historical origins of 'civil society'). *Dushu* (Reader's magazine) 5: 133–40.

Hucker, Charles. 1978. *The Ming Dynasty: Its Origins and Evolving Institutions.* Ann Arbor: Center for Chinese Studies, University of Michigan.

Hymes, Robert. 1989. "Lu Chiu-yüan, Academies and the Problem of the Local Community." In *Neo-Confucian Education: The Formative Stage,* ed. Wm. Theodore de Bary and John W. Chaffee: 432-56. Berkeley: University of California Press.

Ignatieff, Michael. 1995. "On Civil Society: Why Eastern Europe's Revolutions Could Succeed." *Foreign Affairs* (March/April): 128–36.

Inglehart, Ronald. 1990. *Culture Shift in Advanced Industrial Society.* Princeton: Princeton University Press.

Israel, John. 1966. *Student Nationalism in China 1927-1937.* Stanford: Stanford University Press.

Johnson, Linda Cooke. 1995. *Shanghai: From Market Town to Treaty Port, 1074–1858.* Stanford: Stanford University Press.

Johnston, Todd. 1991. "Wages, Benefits and the Promotion Process for Chinese University Faculty." *China Quarterly* 125 (March): 137-55.

Jones, Andrew F. 1994. "The Politics of Popular Music in Post-Tiananmen China." In *Popular Protest and Political Culture in China,* ed. Jeffrey N. Wasserstrom and Elizabeth J. Perry: 155–62. 2nd ed. Boulder: Westview Press.

Jones, Susan Mann. 1974. "The Ningpo *Pang* and Financial Power at Shanghai." In *The Chinese City Between Two Worlds,* ed. Mark Elvin and G. William Skinner: 73–96. Stanford: Stanford University Press.

Kahn, Harold. 1971. *Monarchy in the Emperor's Eyes.* Cambridge: Harvard University Press.

Keane, John. 1988. *Democracy and Civil Society.* London: Verso.

———, ed. 1988. *Civil Society and the State, 1750–1850.* London: Verso.

Kelly, David, and He Baogang. 1992. "Emergent Civil Society and the Intellectuals in China." In *The Developments of Civil Society in Communist Systems,* ed. Robert Miller: 24–39. Sydney: Allen and Unwin.

Kent, Ann. 1991. "Waiting for Rights: China's Human Rights and China's Constitutions, 1949–1989." *Human Rights Quarterly* 13 (May): 170–201.

King, Maurice, and Elliott, Charles. 1994. "Cairo: Damp Squib or Roman Candle?" *The Lancet* 344: 528.

Kiss, Elizabeth. 1992. "Democracy Without Parties? 'Civil Society' in East-Central Europe." *Dissent* (Spring): 226–31.

Kuhn, Philip A. 1994. "Civil Society and Constitutional Development." In *La société civile face à l'État,* ed. LéonVandermeersch: 301–307. Paris: École française d'Extrême-Orient.

Kwong, Julia. 1994. "Ideological Crisis among China's Youths: Values and Official Ideology." *British Journal of Sociology* 45: 247–64.

Kymlicka, Will, and Norman, Wayne. 1995. "Return of the Citizen: A Survey of Recent Work on Citizenship Theory." In *Theorizing Citizenship,* ed. Ronald Beiner: 283–322. Albany: State University of New York Press.

Laclau, Ernesto, and Mouffe, Chantal. 1985. *Hegemony and Socialist Strategy: Towards a Radical Democratic Politics.* London: Verso.

Lai Ruoyu. 1957. "Guanyu dangqian gonghui gongzuo de ruogan wenti" (Certain issues about current trade union work). Reprinted in ACFTU 1989: 556–603.

LaMarre, Thomas. 1993. "Sexuality and Transgression in the Modern Japanese Novel (Nation and Literature after Foucault)." Paper presented at the Beyond Foucault conference, Toronto.

Langlois, John D. Jr., ed. 1981. *China under Mongol Rule.* Princeton: Princeton University Press.

———. 1982. "Law, Statecraft, and the Spring and Autumn Annals in Yuan Political Thought." In *Yuan Thought: Chinese Thought and Religion under the Mongols,* ed. Hok-lam Chan and W. Theodore de Bary: 89–152. New York: Columbia University Press.

Lao, Yen-shuan. 1981. "Southern Chinese Scholars and Educational Institutions in Early Yuan: Some Preliminary Remarks." In *China Under Mongol Rule,* ed. John D. Langlois: 107–33. Princeton: Princeton University Press.

Lasch, Christopher. 1995. *The Revolt of the Elites and the Betrayal of Democracy.* New York: Norton.

Lee, Leo Ou-fan. 1985a. "Romantic Individualism in Modern Chinese Literature: Some General Explorations." In *Individualism and Holism: Studies in Confucian and Taoist Values,* ed. Donald Munro: 239–56. Ann Arbor: Center for Chinese Studies, University of Michigan.

———. 1985b. "The Solitary Traveler: Images of the Self in Modern Chinese Literature." In *Expressions of Self in Chinese Literature,* ed. Robert E. Hegel and Richard C. Hessney: 282–307. New York: Columbia University Press.

Lee, Thomas H. C. 1994. "Academies: Official Sponsorship and Suppression." In *Imperial Rulership and Cultural Change in Traditional Change,* ed. Frederick Brandauer and Chun-chieh Huang: 117–43. Seattle: University of Washington Press.

Levy, Pierre. 1994. *L'intelligence collective: pour une anthropologie du cyberspace.* Paris: Éditions la Découverte.

Lewis, Mark Edward. 1990. *Sanctioned Violence in Early China.* Albany: State University of New York Press.

Li Fuchun. 1951. "Zai gonghui wenti shang de fenqi" (Divergence of views on the issue of trade union work). Reprinted in ACFTU 1989: 96–116.

Li, Ju-chen. 1966. *Flowers in the Mirror,* trans. Lin Tai-yi. Berkeley: Unversity of California Press.

Li, Xueqin. 1985. *Eastern Zhou and Qin Civilizations,* trans. K.C. Chang. New Haven: Yale University Press.

Li, Yu-ning. 1975. *The First Emperor of China.* White Plains: International Arts and Sciences Press.

Li, Zhisui. 1994. *The Private Life of Chairman Mao.* New York: Random House.

Lieberthal, Kenneth, and Lampton, David, ed. 1992. *Bureaucracy, Politics, and Decision-Making in China.* Berkeley: University of California Press.

Link, Perry. 1981. *Mandarin Ducks and Butterflies: Popular Fiction in Early Twentieth-Century Chinese Cities.* Berkeley: University of California Press.

Lipman, Jonathan N., and Harrell, Stevan, eds. 1990. *Violence in China: Essays in Culture and Counterculture.* Albany: State University of New York Press.

Littrup, Leif. 1994. "The Un-oppressive State and Comparative History: Some Observations on Ming-Qing Local Society." In *La société civile face à l'État dans les traditions chinoise, japonaise, coréenne et vietnamienne,* ed. Léon Vandermeersch: 301–9. Paris: École française d'Extrême-Orient.

Liu, Alan P.L. 1996. *Mass Politics in the People's Republic of China: State and Society in Contemporary China.* Boulder: Westview Press.

Liu Haifeng. 1994. "Zhongguo gaodeng xuexiao de xiaoshi zhuisu wenti (The problem of founding dates in the institutional histories of Chinese higher education). *Jiaoyu yanjiu* (Education research) 5: 63-75.

Liu, James T.C. 1959. *Reform in Sung China, Wang An-shih (1021–1086) and his New Policies.* Cambridge: Harvard University Press.

———. 1967. *Ou-yang Hsiu, An Eleventh Century Neo-Confucianist.* Stanford: Stanford University Press.

———. 1988. *China Turning Inward: Intellectual-Political Changes in the Early Twelfth Century.* Cambridge: Council on East Asian Studies, Harvard University.

Liu Jinghui, and Zeng Mingzi. 1994. "Sanzi qiye laogong baohu yousilu" (The worrying labor protection conditions in foreign-related enterprises). *Liaowang* (Outlook) 5 (January): 26–29; 6 (February): 15–17.

Liu Lantao. 1958. "Zai quanguo zonggonghui dangzu disan ci kuoda huiyi shang de fayan" (Speech at the third expanded meeting of the ACFTU's party group). Reprinted in ACFTU 1989: 654–77.

Lo, Jung-pang. 1969. "Policy Formation and Decision Making on Issues Respecting Peace and War." In *Chinese Government in Ming Times: Seven Studies,* ed. Charles Hucker: 41–72. New York; Columbia University Press.

Lu Jianhua. 1995. "Concerns of China's Young Generation." *Zhongguo qingnian* (Chinese youth) 4: 9–13.

Lukes, Steven. 1973. *Individualism.* Oxford: Basil Blackwell.

Luo Gan. 1987. "Gonghui bixu daibiao zhigong jianghua weihu zhigong liyi"

(Trade unions must speak for workers and defend their interests). *Gongren ribao* (Workers' daily), 28 October.

Ma, Shu Yun. 1990. "The Rise and Fall of Neo-Authoritarianism in China." *China Information* 5 (Winter): 1–18.

———. 1994. "The Chinese Discourse on Civil Society." *China Quarterly* 137 (March): 180–93.

Macpherson, C.B. 1962. *The Political Theory of Possessive Individualism.* Oxford: Oxford University Press.

Madsen, Richard. 1993. "The Public Sphere, Civil Society and Moral Community: A Research Agenda for Contemporary China Studies." *Modern China* 19: 2 (April): 183–98.

Mao Lirui and Shen Guanjun. 1988. *Zhongguo jiaoyu tongshi* (The history of Chinese education). Jinan: Shangdong Jiaoyu Chubanshe.

March, Andrew L. 1974. *The Idea of China: Myth and Theory in Geographical Thought.* New York: Praeger.

McCormick, Barrett L.; Su Shaozhi; and Xiao Xiaoming. 1992."The 1989 Democracy Movement: A Review of the Prospects for Civil Society in China." *Pacific Affairs* 65 (Summer): 182–202.

McMullen, David. 1973. "Historical and Literary Theory in the Mid-Eighth Century." In *Perspectives on the T'ang,* ed. Arthur F. Wright and Denis Twitchett: 307–344. New Haven: Yale University Press.

McNeill, William. 1982. *The Pursuit of Power: Technology, Armed Force, and Society since A. D. 1000.* Chicago: The University of Chicago Press.

Meskill, John, ed. 1965. *The Pattern of Chinese History: Cycles, Development, or Stagnation?* Lexington: Heath.

———. 1982. *Academies in Ming China: An Historical Essay.* Tucson: University of Arizona Press.

Metzger, Thomas A. 1994. "Modern Chinese Utopianism and the Western Concept of the Civil Society." *Asian Perspective* 18: 1 (Spring/Summer), 1–6.

Miller, Robert. 1992. "Civil Society in Communist Systems: An Introduction." In *The Developments of Civil Society,* ed. Robert Miller: 1–10. Sydney: Allen and Unwin.

Min Qi. 1989. *Zhongguo zhengzhi wenhua: minzhu zhengzhi nanchande shehui xinli yinsu* (China's political culture: the social psychological obstacle to democratic politics). Kunming: Yunnan Renmin Chubanshe.

Min, Tu-ki. 1989. *National Polity and Local Power: The Transformation of Late Imperial China,* ed. Timothy Brook and Philip Kuhn. Cambridge: Council on East Asian Studies, Harvard University.

Mote, Frederick W., and Twitchett, Denis eds. 1988. *The Cambridge History of China,* Vol. 7: *The Ming Dynasty, 1368–1644, Part 1.* Cambridge: Cambridge University Press.

Mu, Fusheng. 1962. *The Wilting of the Hundred Flowers.* Westport, Conn.: Greenwood Press.

Munro, Donald, ed. 1985. *Individualism and Holism: Studies in Confucian and Taoist Values.* Ann Arbor: Center for Chinese Studies, University of Michigan.

Muzaffar, Chandra. 1995. "Who Benefits? Capitalism, Rights and Development." *China Rights Forum* (Spring): 8–11, 30.

Nathan, Andrew. 1988. *Chinese Democracy.* New York: Knopf.

———. 1990a. *China's Crisis.* New York: Columbia University Press.

———. 1990b. "The Place of Values in Cross-Cultural Studies: The Example of Democracy in China." In *Ideas Across Cultures,* ed. Paul Cohen and Merle Goldman: 293–314. Cambridge: Council on East Asian Studies, Harvard University.

———. 1994. "Human Rights in Chinese Foreign Policy." *The China Quarterly* 137: 622–43.

Nathan, Andrew, and Shi, Tianjian. 1993. "Cultural Requisites for Democracy in China: Findings from a Survey." In *China in Transformation,* ed. Tu Weiming: 95–123. Cambridge: Harvard University Press.

National Committee on U.S.-China Relations. 1994. *Rise of Nongovernmental Organizations in China: Implications for Americans.* Washington.

Negishi Tadashi. 1951. *Shanghai no girudo* (Guilds of Shanghai). Tokyo: Nihon Hyōronsha.

Negri, Antonio. 1991. "Journeys Through Civil Society." In *The Politics of Subversion: Manifesto for the Twenty-First Century:* 169-76. Cambridge: Polity Press.

Negt, Oskar, and Kluge, Alexander. 1994. *Public Sphere and Experience: Toward an Organizational Analysis of Proletariat and Middle-Class Public Opinion.* Minneapolis: University of Minnesota Press. Reprint. First published 1972.

Nevitt, Christopher Earle. 1996. "Private Business Associations in China: Evidence of Civil Society or Local State Power?" *China Journal* 36 (July): 25–43.

Nivison, David. 1966. *The Life and Thought of Chang Hsüeh-ch'eng.* Stanford: Stanford University Press.

O'Brien, Kevin. 1994. "Implementing Political Reform in China's Villages." *Australian Journal of Chinese Affairs* 32 (July): 33–60.

Oksenberg, Michel; Sullivan, Lawrence R.; and Lambert, Marc, eds. 1990. *Beijing Spring, 1989: Confrontation and Conflict: The Basic Documents.* Armonk, N.Y.: M.E. Sharpe.

Oxnam, Robert. 1970. *Ruling from Horseback: Manchu Politics in the Oboi Regency, 1661–1669.* Chicago: University of Chicago Press.

Pearson, Margaret M. 1994. "The Janus Face of Business Associations in China: Socialist Corporatism in Foreign Enterprises." *The Australian Journal of Chinese Affairs* 31 (January): 25–46.

Peerenboom, R. P. 1993. "What's Wrong with Chinese Rights? Toward a Theory of Rights with Chinese Characteristics." *Harvard Human Rights Journal* 6: 29–57.

Pepper, Suzanne. 1978. *Civil War in China: The Political Struggle 1945-1949.* Berkeley: University of California Press.

Perry, Elizabeth J. 1992. "Casting a Chinese 'Democracy' Movement: The Roles of Students, Workers, and Entrepreneurs." In *Popular Protest and Political Culture in Modern China,* ed. Jeffrey N. Wasserstrom and Elizabeth J. Perry: 146–60. Boulder: Westview Press.

Peterson, Charles. 1975. "First Sung Reactions to the Mongol Invasion of the North, 1211–17." In *Crisis and Prosperity in Sung China,* ed. John Haeger. Tucson: University of Arizona Press.

———. 1979. "Court and Province in Mid- and Late-T'ang." In *The Cambridge*

History of China, Vol. 4, ed. Denis Twitchett: 464–560. Cambridge: Cambridge University Press.

Pusey, James R. 1983. *China and Charles Darwin.* Cambridge: Harvard University Press.

Putnam, Robert. 1993. *Making Democracy Work: Civic Traditions in Modern Italy.* Princeton: Princeton University Press.

Pye, Lucian W. 1985. *Asian Power and Politics.* Cambridge: The Belknap Press.

———. 1988. *The Mandarin and the Cadre: China's Political Cultures.* Ann Arbor: Center for Chinese Studies, University of Michigan.

———. 1990. "Tiananmen and Chinese Political Culture." *Asian Survey* 30: 331–47.

———. 1993. "How China's Nationalism Was Shanghaied." *Australian Journal of Chinese Affairs* 29: 107–33.

Qian Zhipei et al. 1989. "Dui gonghui yu zhengfu guanxi de tantao" (Inquiring into the relations between trade unions and government). In *Gonghui gongzuo "redian" tantao* (Discussions on some "hot issues" of trade union work), ed. Guo Zhefeng: 33–41. Shanghai: Tongji Daxue Chubanshe.

Rankin, Mary Backus. 1986. *Elite Activism and Political Transformation in China: Zhejiang Province, 1865–1911.* Stanford: Stanford University Press.

———. 1993. "Some Observations on a Chinese Public Sphere." *Modern China* 19: 158–82.

———. 1994. "The Local Managerial Public Sphere: Refashioning State-Societal Relations in Late Imperial China." In *La société civile face à l'État,* ed. Léon Vandermeersch: 173–201. Paris: École française d'Extrême-Orient.

Rosen, Stanley.1989a. "Political Education and Student Response: Some Background Factors Behind the 1989 Beijing Demonstrations." *Issues and Studies* 25 (October): 12–39.

———. 1989b. "Value Change Among Post-Mao Youth: The Evidence from Survey Data." In *Unofficial China: Popular Culture and Thought in the People's Republic,* ed. Perry Link, Richard Madsen, and Paul Pickowicz: 193–216. Boulder: Westview Press.

———. 1990a. "The Impact of Reform on the Attitudes and Behavior of Chinese Youth: Some Evidence from Survey Research." In *Political Implications of Economic Reform in Communist Systems,* ed. Donna L. Bahry and Joel C. Moses: 264–94. New York: New York University Press.

———. 1990b. "The Impact of Reform Policies on Youth Attitudes." In *Chinese Society on the Eve of Tiananmen,* ed. Deborah Davis and Ezra Vogel: 283–305. Cambridge: Council on East Asian Studies, Harvard University.

———. 1992. "Students and the State in China: The Crisis in Ideology and Organization." In *State and Society in China: The Consequences of Reform,* ed. Arthur Lewis Rosenbaum: 167–191. Boulder: Westview Press.

Rosenbaum, Arthur Lewis. 1992. "Introduction." In *State and Society in China: The Consequences of Reform,* ed. Arthur Lewis Rosenbaum: 1–30. Boulder: Westview Press.

Rossabi, Morris, ed. 1983. *China among Equals: The Middle Kingdom and its Neighbors, 10th–14th Centuries.* Berkeley: University of California Press.

Rowe, William T. 1984. *Hankow: Commerce and Society in a Chinese City, 1796–1889.* Stanford: Stanford University Press.

———. 1985. "Approaches to Modern Chinese History." In *Reliving the Past: The Worlds of Social History,* ed. O. Zinz: 236-96. Chapel Hill: University of North Carolina Press.

———. 1989. *Hankow: Conflict and Community in a Chinese City, 1796–1895* Stanford: Stanford University Press.

———. 1993. "The Problem of 'Civil Society' in Late Imperial China." *Modern China* 19 (April): 139-57.

Sa Mengwu. 1966–1968. *Zhongguo zhengzhi shehui shi* (A political and social history of China). Taibei: Minshe ju.

Saich, Tony, and van de Ven, Hans, eds. 1995. *New Perspectives on the Chinese Communist Revolution.* Armonk, N.Y.: M.E. Sharpe.

Said, Edward. 1979. *Orientalism.* New York: Vintage Books.

Sakai, Naoki. 1989. "Modernity and Its Critique: The Problem of Universalism and Particularism." In *Postmodernism and Japan,* ed. Masao Miyooshi and H.D. Harootunian. Durham: Duke University Press.

Sangren, P. Steven. 1984. "Traditional Chinese Corporations: Beyond Kinship." *Journal of Asian Studies* 43: 3, 391-415.

———. 1986. *History and Magical Power in a Chinese Town.* Stanford: Stanford University Press.

Schipper, Kristofer M. 1990. "The Cult of Baosheng Dadi and Its Spread to Taiwan: A Case of Fenxiang." In *Development and Decline of Fukien Province in the 17th and 18th Centuries,* ed. Edouard Vermeer. Leiden: E.J. Brill.

Schneider, Lawrence. 1971. *Ku Chieh-kang and China's New History.* Berkeley: University of California Press.

———. 1980. *A Madman of Ch'u: The Chinese Myth of Loyalty and Dissent.* Berkeley: University of California Press.

Schoppa, Keith R. 1982. *Chinese Elites and Political Change: Zhejiang Province in the Early Twentieth Century.* Cambridge: Harvard University Press.

Schram, Stuart. 1974. *Chairman Mao Talks to the People: Talks and Letters, 1956–1971.* New York: Pantheon Press.

Schwarcz, Vera. 1987. *The Chinese Enlightenment: Intellectuals and the Legacy of the May 4th Movement of 1919.* Berkeley: University of California Press.

Schwartz, Benjamin. 1985. *The World of Thought in Ancient China.* Cambridge: The Belknap Press.

Shanghai Bowuguan Tushu Ziliaoshi (Historical Materials Section of the Shanghai Museum), ed. 1980. *Shanghai beike ziliao xuanji* (Selected epigraphic materials from Shanghai). Shanghai: Shanghai Renmin Chubanshe.

Shen Tong (with Marianne Yen). 1990. *Almost a Revolution.* Boston: Houghton Mifflin.

Sheng Mingfu et al. 1994. "Shekou gongye qu gonghui qishilu" (Inspirations from the trade unions of the Shekou Industrial District). *Gongren ribao* (Workers' daily), 30 November, 1 December, 5–8 December.

Shiba, Yoshinobu. 1970. *Commerce and Society in Sung China,* trans. Mark Elvin. Ann Arbor: University of Michigan Cènter for Chinese Studies.

Shils, Edward. 1975. *Center and Periphery: Essays in Macrosociology.* Chicago: University of Chicago Press.

———. 1991. "The Virtue of Civil Society." *Government and Opposition* 26: 1, 3–20.

Shue, Vivienne 1988. *The Reach of the State: Sketches of the Chinese Body Politic.* Stanford: Stanford University Press.

Sima Qian. 1993. *Records of the Grand Historian: Qin,* trans. Burton Watson. Hong Kong: Chinese University of Hong Kong and Columbia University Press.

Simendon, Gilbert. 1990. *L'individuation pyschique et collectif.* Paris.

———. 1992. "The Genesis of the Individual." *Zone 6: Incorporations:* 297-319.

Simeon, Richard, and Elkins, David. 1974. "Regional Political Cultures in Canada." *Canadian Journal of Political Science* 7: 397–437.

Siu, Helen. 1990. "Recycling Ritual." In *Unofficial China: Popular Culture and Thought in the Peoples' Republic,* ed. P. Link, R. Madsen, and P. Pickowicz: 121–37. Boulder: Westview Press.

SMP (Shanghai Municipal Police). Files of the Special Branch, 1894–1949. RG 263, Military Archives Division, National Archives, Washington, D.C.

Solinger, Dorthy J. 1992. "Urban Enterprises and the State: The Merger of State and Society." In *State and Society in China: The Consequences of Reform,* ed. Arthur Lewis Rosenbaum: 121–41.Boulder: Westview Press.

Song Shaomeng. 1995. "Tongji daxue minzhu tuiju xiaozhang" (Tongji University selected the president through a democratic process). *Guangming ribao* (Guangming daily), 15 Feburary. Reprinted in *Gaodeng jiaoyu* (Higher education) 1995: 3, 45.

Spence, Jonathan. 1974. *Emperor of China: Self-Portrait of K'ang-hsi.* New York: Knopf.

Strand, David. 1989. *Rickshaw Beijing: City People and Politics in the 1920s* Berkeley: University of California Press.

———. 1990. "Protest in Beijing: Civil Society and Public Sphere in China." *Problems of Communism* 40 (May/June): 1–19.

———. 1993. "Civil Society and Public Sphere in Modern Chinese History." In *Chinese Democracy and the Crisis of 1989,* ed. Roger V. Des Forges et al.: 53-86. Albany: State University of New York Press.

———. 1994. "Changing Dimensions of Social and Public Life in Early Twentieth Century Chinese Cities." In *La société civile face à l'État,* ed. Léon Vandermeersch: 309–30. Paris: École française d'Extrême-Orient.

Strathern, Marilyn. 1992. "Qualified Value: The Perspective of Gift Exchange." In *Barter, Exchange and Value: An Anthropological Approach,* ed. C. Humphrey and S. Hugh-Jones: 169–91. Cambridge: Cambridge University Press.

Sullivan, Lawrence. 1990. "The Emergence of Civil Society in China, Spring 1989." In *The Chinese People's Movement: Perspectives on Spring 1989,* ed. Tony Saich: 129–44. Armonk, N.Y.: M.E. Sharpe.

———. 1996. "Upheaval on the Yangzi: Population Relocation and the Controversy over the Three Gorges Dam." *China Rights Forum* (Summer): 14–17.

Sun Bingyue. 1988. "Gonghui yinggai zai shenhua qiye gaige zhong fahui jiji zuoyong" (Trade unions should play an active role in deepening enterprise reform). *Qingdao ribao* (Qingdao daily), 29 August.

———. 1992. *Shetuan zhi* (Gazetteer of social organizations). Qingdao. Internally circulated.

Sun Daren. 1979. "Lun 'Wen Jing zhi zhi' di jige wenti" (Some questions concerning the "good rule of Wen and Jing"). In *Zhongguo nongmin zhanzheng shi yanjiu jikan* (Collected essays on the history of Chinese peasant wars): 77–84. Shanghai: Shanghai Renmin Chubanshe.

Svensson, Marina. 1996. *The Chinese Conception of Human Rights: The Debate on Human Rights in China, 1898–1949*. Lund: Lund University.

Tang Shonghua. 1995. "Woguo gaodeng xuexiao guanli tizhi de weilai moshi chutan" (On future modes of higher education governance in our country). *Jiaoyu yanjiu* (Education research) 9: 19-24. Reprinted in *Gaodeng jiaoyu* (Higher education) 1995: 11, 88-93.

Tang Zhen. 1984. *Qian shu zhu* (Writings while out of sight, annotated). Chengdu: Sichuan Renmin Chubanshe.

Taylor, Michael. 1987. *The Possibility of Cooperation*. Cambridge: Cambridge University Press.

Terrill, Ross. 1980. *Mao: A Biography*. New York: Harper and Row.

———. 1984. *The White Boned Demon: A Biography of Madame Mao Zedong*. New York: William Morrow and Co.

Thompson, Roger. 1995. *China's Local Councils in the Age of Constitutional Reform, 1898–1911*. Cambridge: Council on East Asian Studies, Harvard University.

Thomson, James C. Jr. 1969. *While China Faced West: American Reformers in Nationalist China, 1928–1937*. Cambridge: Harvard University Press.

Thurston, Ann. 1995. "Village Elections: The Seeds of Democracy in China?" *China Focus* (1 April): 3–4.

Tian Ming and Xu Jianchuan. 1988. *Gonghui gaige wencong* (Essays on trade union reforms). Beijing: Jingji Guanli Chubanshe.

Tillman, Hoyt. 1982. *Utilitarian Confucianism: Ch'en Liang's Challenge to Chu Hsi*. Cambridge: Council on East Asian Studies, Harvard University.

———. 1992. *Confucian Discourse and Chu Hsi's Ascendancy*. Honolulu: University of Hawaii Press.

Tu, Wei-ming. 1982. *Neo-Confucian Thought in Action: Wang Yang-ming's Youth (1472–1509)*. Berkeley: University of California Press.

———. 1989. "Towards an Understanding of Liu Yin's Confucian Eremitism." In *Yuan Thought and Religion Under the Mongols*, ed. W. Theodore de Bary and Hok-lam Chan: 233–77. New York: Columbia University Press.

———. 1985. *Confucian Thought: Selfhood as Creative Transformation*. Albany: State University of New York Press.

———. 1992. "Intellectual Effervescence in China." *Daedalus* 121: 2, 251–292.

———. 1993. "Introduction: Cultural Perspectives." *Daedalus* 122: 2, vii-xxiii.

———. 1993a. *Way, Learning and Politics: Essays on the Confucian Intellectual*. Albany: State University of New York Press.

Turner, Bryan. 1993. "Preface." In *Citizenship and Social Theory*, ed. Bryan Turner: vii-xii. London: Sage.

Unger, Jonathan, and Chan, Anita. 1995. "China, Corporatism, and the East Asian Model." *The Australian Journal of Chinese Affairs* 33 (Janauary): 29–53.

Vandermeersch, Léon, ed. 1994. *La société civile face à l'État dans les traditions chinoise, japonaise, coréenne et vietnamienne*. Paris: École française d'Extrême-Orient.

Vermeer, Eduard B. 1990a. "Introduction." In *Development and Decline of Fukien Province in the 17th and 18th Centuries*, ed. Eduard Vermeer: 5–34. Leiden: E.J. Brill.

———. 1990b. "The Decline of Hsing-hua Prefecture in the Early Ch'ing." In *Development and Decline of Fukien Province in the 17th and 18th Centuries,* ed. Eduard Vermeer: 101–62. Leiden: E.J. Brill.

Wakeman, Frederic, Jr. 1985. *The Great Enterprise: The Manchu Reconstruction of Imperial Order in Seventeenth-Century China.* Berkeley: University of California Press.

———. 1993. "The Civil Society and Public Sphere Debate: Western Reflections on Chinese Political Culture." *Modern China* 19 (April): 108-38.

Walder, Andrew G. 1987. "Communist Social Structure and Workers' Politics in China." In *Citizens and Groups in Contemporary China,* ed. Victor C. Falkenheim: 45–89. Ann Arbor: Center for Chinese Studies, University of Michigan.

———. 1993. "The Decline of Communist Power: Elements of a Theory of Institutional Change." *Theory and Society* 23: 311–15.

———, ed. 1995. *The Waning of the Communist State: Economic Origins of Political Change in China and Hungary.* Berkeley: University of California Press.

Waley, Arthur. 1969. *Yuan Mei, Eighteeenth Century Chinese Poet.* Stanford: Stanford University Press.

Walton, Linda. 1989. "The Institutional Context of Neo-Confucianism: Scholars, Schools and Shu-yüan in Sung-Yüan China." In *Neo-Confucian Education: The Formative Stage,* ed. Wm. Theodore de Bary and John W. Chaffee: 457-92. Berkeley: University of California Press.

Walzer, Michael, ed. 1995. *Toward a Global Civil Society.* Oxford: Berg Hahn Books.

Wang, C.K., ed. 1995–. *Minsu quyi congshu* (Collected studies on Chinese ritual and drama). Taibei: Shihezheng Minsu Wenhua Jijinhui. 60 vols.

Wang, Mingming. 1992. "Flowers of the State, Grasses of the People: Yearly Rites and Aesthetics of Power in Quanzhou in the Southeast Coastal Macro-region of China." Ph.D. diss., University of London.

———. 1995. "Place, Administration, and Territorial Cults in Late Imperial China: A Case Study from South Fujian." *Late Imperial China* 16 (June): 33–78.

Wang Yongxi, et al. 1992. *Zhongguo gonghui shi* (A history of Chinese trade unions). Beijing: Zhonggong Dangshi Chubanshe.

Wang Zhenhuan. 1991. "Chuxianzhong de shimin shehui ji qi xianzhi" (The emerging civil society and its limitations). *Ershiyi shiji* (The twenty-first century) 5: 57–67.

Wang Zhongshu. 1982. *Han Civilization,* trans. K.C. Chang et al. New Haven: Yale University Press.

Wank, David. 1995. "Private Business, Bureaucracy, and Political Alliance in a Chinese City." *Australian Journal of Chinese Affairs* 33 (January): 55–74.

Warner, Shelley. 1991. "Shanghai's Response to the Deluge." In *The Pro-Democracy Protests in China: Reports from the Provinces,* ed. Jonathan Unger: 215–31. Armonk, N.Y.: M.E. Sharpe.

Wasserstrom, Jeffrey N. 1991. *Student Protests in Twentieth-Century China: The View from Shanghai.* Stanford: Stanford University Press.

———. 1992. "The Evolution of the Shanghai Student Protest Repertoire; or, Where Do Correct Tactics Come From?" In Wakeman and Yeh: 108–44.

———. 1994. "History, Myth, and the Tales of Tiananmen." In *Popular Protest and Political Culture in Modern China,* ed. Jeffrey N. Wasserstrom and Elizabeth J. Perry: 273–308. Boulder: Westview Press.

Wasserstrom, Jeffrey. 1992. –The Evolution of the Shanghai Student Protest Repertoire; or, Where Do Correct Tactics Come From?" In Wakeman and Yeh 1992: 108–44.

Wasserstrom, Jeffrey, N., and Liu Xinyong. 1995. "Student Associations and Mass Movements." In *Urban Spaces in Contemporary China,* ed. Deborah S. Davis et al.: 362–93. Washington and Cambridge: Woodrow Wilson Center Press and Cambridge University Press.

Wechsler, Howard Jr. 1974. *Mirror to the Son of Heaven: Wei Cheng at the Court of T'ang T'ai-tsung.* New Haven: Yale University Press.

White, Gordon. 1993. "Prospects for Civil Society in China: A Case Study of Xiaoshan City." *The Australian Journal of Chinese Affairs* 29 (January): 63–87.

———. 1996. "The Dynamics of Civil Society in Post-Mao China." In *The State and the Individual in China,* ed. Brian Hook: 196–221. Oxford: Oxford University Press.

Whyte, Martin. 1992. "Urban China: A Civil Society in the Making?" In *State and Society in China: The Consequences of Reform,* ed. Arthur Lewis Rosenbaum: 77–102. Boulder: Westview Press.

Wilkerson, James. 1994. "The 'Ritual Master' and His 'Temple Corporation' Rituals." *Proceedings of the International Conference on Popular Beliefs and Chinese Culture.* Taipei: Center for Chinese Studies.

Williams, Raymond. 1983. *Keywords: A Vocabulary of Culture and Society.* Rev. ed. London: Fontana.

Wilson, Dick. 1979. *The People's Emperor: Mao.* New York: Doubleday.

Wittfogel, Karl. 1957. *Oriental Despotism: A Comparative Study of Total Power.* New Haven: Yale University Press.

Wong, R. Bin. 1993. "Great Expectations: The 'Public Sphere' and the Search for Modern Times in Chinese History." *Studies in Chinese History* 3: 7–50.

Wood, Ellen Meiksins. 1990. "The Uses and Abuses of 'Civil Society.' " In *The Retreat of the Intellectuals: Socialist Register, l990,* ed. Ralph Miliband and Leo Panitch: 60–84. London: Merlin Press.

Woodside, Alexander. 1997. "The Struggle to Rethink the Vietnamese State in the Era of Market Economics." In *Culture and Economy: The Shaping of Capitalism in Eastern Asia,* ed. Timothy Brook and Hy V. Luong. Ann Arbor: The University of Michigan.

Wright, Kate. 1991. "The Political Undoing of Shanghai's *World Economic Herald.*" In *The Pro-Democracy Protests in China: Reports from the Provinces,* ed. Jonathan Unger: 204–14. Armonk, N.Y.: M.E. Sharpe.

Wright, Mary C. 1957. *The Last Stand of Chinese Conservatism: The T'ung-chih Restoration, 1862–74.* Stanford: Stanford University Press.

Wu Han. 1948. *Zhu Yuanzhang zhuan* (Biography of Zhu Yuanzhang). Hong Kong: Quanji Wenxueshe.

Wu Qingyun. 1995. *Female Rule in Chinese and English Literary Utopias.* Syracuse: Syracuse University Press.

Wu Zhong. 1995. "Survey Reveals People 'More Capitalist-Oriented'." Foreign Broadcast Information Service Daily Report—China (19 January): 25–26.

Xiong Mingan. 1983. *Zhongguo gaodeng jiaoyushi* (The history of Chinese higher education). Chongqing: Chongqing Chubanshe.

Xu Bing et al. 1988. "Weifang shi gonghui lianhehui diaocha" (An investigation of trade union federations in Weifang). In *Gonghui gaige wencong* (Essays on trade union reforms), ed. Tian Ming and Xu Jianchuan: 388–96. Beijing: Jingji Guanli Chubanshe.

Xu Dunheng, Xiang Liting and Liu Dawei. 1993. "Guanyu juban minban gaodeng jiaoyu ruogan wenti" (Concerning certain problems in running people-managed higher institutions). *Zhongguo gaodeng jiaoyu* (Chinese higher education) 10 (October).

Xue Renyang. 1939. *Zhongguo jiaoyu xingzheng zhidu shiyue* (A brief history of Chinese educational administration). Shanghai: Zhonghua Shuju.

Yang, Mayfair Mei-hui. 1989. "Between State and Society: The Construction of Corporateness in a Chinese Socialist Factory." *Australian Journal of Chinese Affairs* 22: 31–60.

———. 1994. *Gifts, Favors, and Banquets: The Art of Social Relationships in China.* Ithaca: Cornell University Press.

Yao, Qihe. 1996. "A Difficult Choice: Breaking Away from Soviet Educational Patterns." In *East-West Dialogue in Knowledge and Higher Education,* ed. Ruth Hayhoe and Julia Pan: 245–255. Armonk, N.Y.: M.E. Sharpe.

Ye Shaoyuan. 1986. *Qi-Zhen jiwen lu* (Record of things I heard during the Tianqi and Chongzhen reigns). Reprint. Taibei: Taiwan Yinhang Jingji Yanjiusuo.

Yin, Qiping, and White, Gordon. 1994. "The Marketization of Chinese Higher Education: A Critical Assessment." *Comparative Educative* 30: 3, 217-37.

Yu Dawei. 1970. *Tan Chen Yinque* (On Chen Yinque). Taibei: Quanji Wenxue Chubanshe.

Yu Qinghe. 1987. *Zhongguo zhigong duiwu zhuangkuang diaocha 1986* (An investigation of the situation of Chinese workers). Beijing: Gongren Chubanshe.

Yü, Ying-shih. 1967. *Trade and Expansion in Han China.* Berkeley: University of California Press.

———. 1985. "Individualism and the Neo-Taoist Movement in Wei-Chin China." In *Individualism and Holism: Studies in Confucian and Taoist Values,* ed. Donald Munro: 121–156. Ann Arbor: Center for Chinese Studies, University of Michigan.

———. 1989. "Sun Yat-sen's Doctrine and Traditional Chinese Culture." In *Sun Yat-sen's Doctrine in the Modern World,* ed. Chu-yuan Cheng: 80–98. Boulder: Westview Press.

———. 1991a. "Clio's New Cultural Turn and the Rediscovery of Tradition in Asia." Hong Kong: University of Hong Kong International Association of Historians of Asia.

———. 1991b . "Dai chong tou, shoushi jiu shanhe" (Let's start again and recover the old mountains and rivers). *Ershiyi shiji* (The twenty-first century) 2: 5.

———. 1993. "The Radicalization of China in the Twentieth Century." *Daedalus* 122, 2: 125–50.

Zakaria, Fareed. 1995. "Bigger than the Family, Smaller than the State" (Review of Francis Fukuyama, *Trust: The Social Virtues and the Creation of Prosperity,* Free Press, 1995). *New York Times Book Review,* 13 August.

Zha Jianying. 1995. *China Pop: How Soap Opera, Tabloids and Bestsellers Are Transforming a Culture.* New York: The New Press.

Zhang, Yunqiu. 1977. "Rivalry and Alliance: Chinese Trade Unions and State Power in the Twentieth Century." Ph.D. diss., University of Toronto.

Zhang Zhanxin and Wang Xiangdong. 1988. "Laoquan, chanquan, he jingyingquan" (Labor power, ownership and management). In *Gonghui gaige wencong* (Essays on trade union reforms), ed. Tian Ming and Xu Jianchuan: 288–303. Beijing: Jingji Guanli Chubanshe.

Zhang Zhongli, ed. 1991. *Jindai Shanghai chengshi yanjiu* (Studies in the history of modern Shanghai). Shanghai: Shanghai Renmin Chubanshe.

Zhao Lisheng. 1989. "The Well-Field System in Relation to the Asiatic Mode of Production." In *The Asiatic Mode of Production in China,* ed. Timothy Brook: 65–84. Armonk, N.Y.: M.E. Sharpe. First published in Chinese in 1982.

Zhao Yi. 1972. *Ershier shi zhaji* (Notes on the twenty-two histories). Reprint. Taibei: Guangwen.

"Zhonghua renmin gongheguo jiaoyufa" (Education law of the People's Republic of China). 1995. *Zhongguo gaodeng jiaoyu* (Chinese higher education) 5 (May): 5-8.

Zhou Nanzhao et al. 1995. *A Study on NGO-Sponsored and Private Higher Education in China.* Beijing: China National Institute of Educational Research and Unesco Office of the Representative to China.

Zhou Xuegang, ed. 1992. *Dangdai Zhongguo de guojia yu shehui guanxi* (Relations between state and society in present-day China). Taibei: Kuiguan Tushu. Includes essays by Chen Kuide (53–78), Ding Xueliang (29–52), Gao Xiaoyuan (271–90), Lü Xiaobo (193–222), Shi Zhengfu (125–48), Su Shaozhi, Mai Kangmian and Xiao Xiaoming (79–106), Wang Feng (239–58), Xie Wen (107–24), Yin Ding (259–70), and Zhao Suisheng (171–92).

Zhu, Jianhua; Zhao, Xinshu; and Li, Hairong. 1990. "Public Political Consciousness in China: An Empirical Profile." *Asian Survey* 30: 992–1006.

Zhu Jiusi. 1992. "Lishi de huigui" (Historical reflections). *Gaodeng jiaoyu yanjiu* (Studies in higher education) 4: 1-13.

Zhu Youxian, ed. 1986. *Zhongguo jindai xuezhi shiliao* (Materials on Chinese educational systems in the modern period). Shanghai: Huadong Shifan Daxue Chubanshe.

Zhuang Hunming. 1979. "Kangzhan shiqi Zhonggguo gaodeng jiaoyu zhi yanjiu" (Research on Chinese higher education in the period of the anti-Japanese War). Ph.D. diss., Sili Zhongguo Wenhua Xueyuan Lishi Yanjiusuo, Taibei.

Zito, Angela. Forthcoming. *Of Body and Brush: Grand Sacrifice as Text/Performance in 18th Century China.* Chicago: University of Chicago Press.

Index